When
the cheering
stopped

GENE SMITH

When the cheering stopped

---

the last years of Woodrow Wilson

*With an Introduction
by Allan Nevins*

Time Reading Program Special Edition
Time-Life Books Inc., Alexandria, Virginia

Time-Life Books Inc.
is a wholly owned subsidiary of
TIME INCORPORATED

TIME Reading Program: *Editor,* Max Gissen

Library of Congress CIP data following page 295.

For information about any Time-Life book, please write:
Reader Information, Time-Life Books,
541 North Fairbanks Court, Chicago, Illinois 60611

To S.R.S. and J.S.S.

Contents

GENE SMITH

Editors' Preface

Any list of the 10 most effective American Presidents must include the 27th, the scholarly teacher, university president, New Jersey state Governor and historian, Thomas Woodrow Wilson. His Administration, which started in 1913, sponsored a series of reforms and innovations—the Federal Reserve System, the Federal Trade Commission, a powerful antitrust act, lower tariffs, the income tax, direct election of United States senators and votes for women—that he collectively called The New Freedom. In 1917, after winning a second term on the slogan "He Kept Us Out of War," he sent the country into "The War to End Wars"—just in time to swing the balance of battle to the side of the staggering Western Allies. Afterward, at the Peace Conference, his was the strong voice for the Covenant of the League of Nations, which, he hoped, would redeem the pledge of a world without wars.

It did not work, of course. In fact, after all the wars and mass killings that have since occurred, it is difficult to evoke the mood of that pearl-gray, influenza-drenched winter and the warm and golden spring of 1919, when the whole world clung to Woodrow Wilson. He moved through the cities of Europe under signs proclaiming him the champion of peace and the apostle of justice, and he heard cheering such as few men ever hear, reflecting the relief of Europeans that four and a quarter years of horror were done and their hope that this confident American would somehow arrange a permanent peace. (Years later a man of much experience with cheering crowds would say that he had never heard the like of the welcome Paris gave Wilson in 1919. That man, then a captain of artillery, was the 32nd President of the United States, Harry S. Truman.)

President Wilson had still another cause for exultation in those first months of 1919. Standing by his side and witnessing the adulation pouring down upon him was his wife of just three years, Edith Bolling Wilson. She was a lovely lady of flashing dimples whom he had met and fallen in love with after the death of his first wife in 1914. An amused Secret Service man had watched the 59-year-old President on the morning after his wedding night leap into the air on the honeymoon train, click his heels and burst into a popular song of the day, "Oh you beautiful doll, you great big beautiful doll."

The new Mrs. Wilson was a charming companion. The President cherished her more each day, and she was devoted to him. She was widely traveled, and she was turned out by the best dressmakers of Paris (her first husband had left her a profitable jewelry shop); she made a fine and decorative First Lady. But she had very little interest in her second husband's business of politics and statecraft, and she had completed only two years of formal schooling in her life. And this was a pity, because for 17 long and crisis-ridden months she would be the nearest thing to a President that the United States would have.

This is the high drama that Gene Smith recounts in *When the Cheering Stopped*. It is a tale straight out of Greek tragedy: the fascinating account of what happened when, at the President's moment of greatest triumph, the fates fell upon him with implacable fury, destroyed him physically and crushed his great plans for American participation in the League of Nations. The tragedy transcended the man and the country and became global: perhaps the League would have failed anyhow—but without the United States, failure was certain.

Smith's book plows reaches of almost virgin territory. Save for a little group of frightened people in Washington, few Americans knew what was happening in the White House during late 1919, 1920 and the early months of 1921. All was obscured by bland official announcements and outright lies. And afterward, while Edith Bolling Wilson lived out a life that lasted into 1961, most writers approached the subject gingerly, for she was no woman to tangle with lightly: where her husband's interests were concerned she bruised everyone from his foe Senator Henry Cabot Lodge (that "stinking snake") to his friendly Assistant Secretary of the Navy Franklin D. Roosevelt (that "common thief"). But shortly after Mrs. Wilson's death, editor J. Lawrence Hughes of the William Morrow publishing company asked Smith, a journalist with a strong sense of history's drama, to explore the mysterious years. For the next 30 months Smith buried himself in the Wilson papers. For four months he lived in a Washington boardinghouse and spent his days in the Library of Congress reading the old letters and diaries. His research was exhaustive; in the new introduction he wrote to this special edition, Allan Nevins, one of the most eminent American historians, praises Smith highly for the diligence, honesty and perceptiveness with which he dug into these "murky" years. Indeed, the bibliography and notes citing and discussing Smith's sources, which are at the end of the book, are nearly as fascinating as the book itself, for Smith has opened up a subject that the historians will no longer be able to duck in deference to the memory of an idealistic President or the morbid sensitivity of family and friends.

The tragedy began, Smith believes, in Paris in early April when the President, worn out by endless wrangles with his spoils-hungry European partners, David Lloyd George of Great Britain, Georges Clemenceau of France and Vittorio Orlando of Italy, fell ill. The symptoms were high fever, a racking cough and an upset stomach; his doctor, Rear Admiral Cary Grayson, who had been physician to both President Theodore Roosevelt and President William Howard Taft, diagnosed influenza. But Smith, basing his argument on the personality changes that came over the President, believes Wilson suffered a brain thrombosis.

The earlier Wilson had been a cheery, chipper fellow who masked his erudition under many an endearing foible. He was a constant problem to the Library of Congress because he kept detective stories too long. He enjoyed going to vaudeville shows; at home he loved to do soft-shoe dance routines and imitations of the town drunk or a haughty Englishman. He enjoyed singing and never tired of the World War I favorites "Over There," "There's a Long, Long Trail a-Winding" and "K-K-K-Katie."

Now everything changed. Suddenly he was convinced that all the French servants in the house he had rented in Paris were spies or, if not that, that they were stealing the furniture. He ordered inventories to be made. Formerly he had urged his aides, when not wanted at the Peace Conference, to relax and take automobile rides into the country; now he ordered that the cars were to be used only for official business. And now he began to hector his own experts in the very fields of their expertise. Eventually he accepted the rapacious Versailles Treaty, which was a far cry from the generous peace he wanted, in return for the League Covenant. The League, he hoped, would adjust the inequities later.

The second stage of the tragedy came when the President and the League proposal were confronted by a hostile Republican Senate. His opponents, headed by Senator Lodge, were determined either to reject the League Covenant or to limit American participation by passing it subject to a series of reservations. To stir support for the Covenant as written, Wilson set out on a 27-day coast-to-coast speaking tour. Day by day, as ever-larger and more enthusiastic crowds turned out to hear him, he seemed to be gaining in his fight. But day by day he visibly tired, until, after a speech at Pueblo, Colorado, on his way home from the Pacific Coast, he collapsed in nervous exhaustion. Dr. Grayson and the President's secretary, Joseph P. Tumulty, begged him to cancel the rest of his tour, but he stubbornly refused until the First Lady added her entreaties. Then, weeping, he agreed. It was, Edith Wilson said later, the hardest thing she had ever had to do in her life.

When they reached Washington's Union Station the President walked casually by a curious crowd of perhaps a thousand people who saw nothing wrong. Smith describes the rest:

> When they came out into the plaza in front of the station he got into an open car and headed for the White House. Because it was Sunday morning the streets were practically empty. But as they rode the President reached up and took off his hat and bowed as if he were returning the greetings of a vast throng. Enough people saw what he had done to send flying through Washington the information that the President is physically all right but salutes empty sidewalks. He has lost his mind.

He had not. But a few days later, in the morning of October 2, he suffered a stroke while in his bathroom that left his left side paralyzed. For five long months he remained ill, most of the time lying in Abraham Lincoln's great bed on the second floor of the White

House, sometimes weeping for his lost strength, more often gazing vacantly off into space, unable to carry out the functions of his office, unaware for the most part that there were any functions to carry out. Strikes and ugly race riots swept the country, but the White House stood mute. Diplomatic crises arose in Central America and Mexico, but there was no guidance from the President. The British Ambassador, former Foreign Secretary Lord Grey of Fallodon, sent over especially to help in the League of Nations fight, was not received at the White House. Wartime Food Administrator Herbert Hoover, unable to get anyone to accept his resignation, closed up his wartime office and left. Letters from Cabinet officers demanding immediate action were ignored. Naval Academy midshipmen who had caught "immoral diseases" during a cruise remained on the rolls for want of the Presidential endorsement on the documents expelling them.

Some of the Cabinet members (notably Secretary of Agriculture David F. Houston, Secretary of the Navy Josephus Daniels and Secretary of State Robert Lansing) knew exactly how helpless Wilson was. Lansing in particular thought the Constitutional provisions requiring the Vice President to take over the duties of a disabled President should come into force. But he was balked on two sides. On the one hand Grayson and Tumulty promised to fight tooth and nail against any effort to declare the President disabled. "He has been too kind, too loyal and too wonderful to me to receive such treatment at my hands," cried Tumulty. On the other hand, Vice President Thomas Marshall, a rural wit who made the main part of his income on the lecture trails, was horrified at the prospect that he might become President and left town.

The country floundered on. The President was in almost complete isolation from all save his doctor and his wife. The Cabinet met once a week in an effort to hold things together—until February 1920, when a letter came from the sickroom firing Secretary of State Lansing for calling the meetings. Letters to the President from members of the Cabinet were answered in a large school-girlish handwriting that meandered down the left-hand margin of the original letter, then across the bottom and up the right-hand margin to close the circuit across the top. They could seldom be understood. Later the First Lady received Cabinet officers in a sitting room off the President's bedroom. When they explained what they wanted she went in to see the President and came out to pass on his answer. Two Cabinet officers were appointed in chats with Mrs. Wilson and never saw the President at all.

Wilson's advisors at the Paris Peace Conference urged him to accept some of Lodge's reservations for the sake of getting some kind of league, but word came from the sickroom that the reservations were dishonorable, and so the Covenant went down to defeat in two successive sessions.

But he began to get a little better. He watched a movie most mornings, napped at noon and went for an automobile ride in the afternoons. He even attended to some government business, carefully screened so that it would not excite him, and he began coming downstairs for dinner in evening clothes. He treasured a secret hope that the 1920 Democratic Convention might urge him to run for a third term—and was bitterly disappointed when it did not. Then he turned the White House over to the new President, Warren Harding, and went off to live in the house on S Street that became a shrine to him and his ideals in the few years he had to live there. And there, slowly, the bitterness drained away. Reports Smith:

> One day Margaret [one of his daughters] came to sit with
> him in peaceful silence and he slowly began to talk in what
> she thought was contemplation of the past. It was the great
> soul that spoke, Margaret thought, not the tired body. He said,
> "I think it was best after all that the United States did not join
> the League of Nations." She was startled. "Why, Father dar-
> ling?" He said, "Because our entrance into the League at the
> time I returned from Europe might have been only a personal
> victory. Now, when the American people join the League it
> will be because they are convinced it is the only right time for
> them to do it." He was smiling a little. He said, "Perhaps God
> knew better than I did after all."
>
> —THE EDITORS

⟦R|P⟧ *Introduction*

The drama of Woodrow Wilson's last days comprises one of the most poignant stories of modern history, and Gene Smith has written it with a verve that holds our interest and a feeling that commands our sympathy. His book is appealingly human, for his portrait of Wilson brings out all the virtues and the limitations of that very complicated leader. Yet the drama he relates transcends the ordinary historical tale of aspiration, struggle and failure. It will be a dull reader who does not feel that it lifts him to the high plane of the Grecian story of Agamemnon and Clytemnestra, with its uncontrollable collision of spiritual and material forces. The Fates, and sometimes the Furies, take control of the action. And how profoundly significant a narrative Mr. Smith has given us! America, in these pages, stands at the parting of the ways. Had the republic avoided a timid isolationism, it might have remained in harmony with the visions of its founders; it might have vindicated Lincoln's assertion that America was "the last, best hope of mankind." Possibly, perhaps even probably, world history might have avoided some of the appalling catastrophes that selfish nationalism made unescapable.

It was President Wilson's justifiable belief and hope that by battling for U.S. participation in the League of Nations he was opening the gates to a safer future for all peoples. Would the nations pass through? His last day of high hope was February 14, 1919, when he presented the League Covenant to the Peace Conference in Paris. "It is at one and the same time a practical document and a humane document," he said. "It is practical, and yet it is intended to purify, to rectify, to elevate." From that time his path led downward to the hour of tragedy on September 25 when he was felled at Pueblo, Colorado—after he had made a series of fighting speeches on behalf of the League—and to his ensuing defeat in the Senate. It is a grim story.

Most Americans know how close to Wilson's heart the idea of a League of Nations had become by the time Germany laid down her arms after World War I. They know that when the armistice was imminent, he made a passionate speech in New York calling for a peace of justice and for a league which would be "the most essential part of the peace settlement itself." How he went to Paris with this demand and, rallying the finest elements of European as well as American sentiment behind him, did make the League the "keystone" (as he termed it) of the treaty is a familiar story. This is the background of Mr. Smith's engrossing book. British Prime Minister David Lloyd George later challenged the common belief that Wilson had forced the League upon reluctant European leaders. He asserted that his government and that of French Premier Georges Clemenceau were not only ready to accept a league but had made as much progress as Wilson in working out the details of its organization. Nevertheless, Wilson's confidant, Colonel Edward House, was unquestionably correct in reporting at the time that Lloyd George and Clemenceau regarded the League of Nations as "an after-consideration."

Why was it that, after Woodrow Wilson had thus riveted the

League into the Treaty of Versailles, it was defeated in his own land, the country where workers for a League to Enforce Peace had lifted so inspiring a banner? The President made serious errors, some of which Mr. Smith notes. It was a mistake not to place an influential Republican leader of the stature of Senator Elihu Root or former President William Howard Taft on the delegation to Paris. It was a still greater mistake not to insist that a stronger light of publicity be thrown upon the work of the men drafting the Treaty of Versailles. The secrecy shrouding the activities of the Big Four—Premier Vittorio Orlando of Italy, Lloyd George, Clemenceau and Wilson— was carried to a disastrous extreme. Deprived of the support of world opinion, Wilson agreed to concessions in the text of the treaty that many of his advisers considered damaging and unnecessary.

But unhappy as these errors were, they do not account for Wilson's ultimate defeat. Little doubt can exist that when he came home from Paris a majority of Americans desired ratification of the League. Hence, though the issue was uncertain, it was by no means a desperate struggle into which Woodrow Wilson plunged when he began his valiant Western journey. Its rigors were exhausting. Between September 3 and 25, he spoke with unflagging heart in more than two-score addresses.

Then came the disabling stroke—and, as John W. Davis said, the sword was struck out of his hand on the battlefield. The drama of combat ended. The drama of the sickroom, to which Mr. Smith does such justice as imperfect evidence permits, began.

And while Wilson lay helpless—just how helpless nobody yet knows—the contest in the Senate over ratification of the League treaty moved on to defeat. Just why? The story is complex, for the elements of opposition were many. One obstacle lay in a resurgence of isolationism, a resurrection of doctrines falsely attributed to Washington and Jefferson. This was natural as the wave of wartime emotion subsided, as two million homesick and disillusioned soldiers returned from France and as plain Americans began counting the costs of war. America was strong and self-sufficient, she had long prospered in comparative isolation, and she might do so again. Journalists like William Randolph Hearst made a demagogic use of this argument. Another obstacle lay in the heated emotions of foreign-born groups. Many German-Americans were embittered by the harsh penalties laid on the fatherland; many

Italian-Americans and Irish-Americans disliked provisions of the Versailles Treaty which they felt discriminated against their homelands.

It is now plain, however, that the central reason for the defeat of the League lay in considerations of party politics. Many Republican leaders, especially in the Senate, had become fanatical haters of Wilson. Never concealing his contempt for "pigmy-minded" opponents in the Upper House, he had sometimes marched over them roughshod. Reactionary politicians, supported by conservative businessmen, deeply feared a resumption of the Wilsonian New Freedom, which had put so many progressive measures on the statute books in 1913-1917. Republicans were quick to see in 1918-1919 that if Wilson and his party not only won the war but achieved a great result in the peace settlement, the Democrats might be entrenched in power for many years. "What we seek," Wilson said on Independence Day of 1918, "is the reign of law, based upon the consent of the governed and sustained by the organized opinion of mankind." To undermine and shatter that concept became the burning ambition of a tireless Republican group—with some Democratic allies. They would make the most of ignorance of the treaty, discontent with war burdens, confusion about the League Covenant, national animosities, jealousy for the Senate's powers and dislike of Wilson's personality.

In this book we see how gallantly Wilson faced his foes and how fate itself seemed to intervene against him. The shrewd program of the opposition proved successful beyond its architects' hopes. Theodore Roosevelt, just before the Congressional elections of 1918, issued two stinging attacks on Wilson's leadership, urging the Senate in effect to take the peace negotiations from his hands. Thus challenged, Wilson appealed to the voters to sustain him as their "unembarrassed spokesman at home and abroad" by giving him a Democratic majority in both Houses. This was a tactless blunder. By narrow majorities, the voters sent a Republican margin to the Senate.

Republican leaders promptly packed the Foreign Relations Committee with critics of the League, giving it a core of 10 irreconcilables, or "strong reservationists," in a total membership of 17. Already Senator Henry Cabot Lodge of Massachusetts, the chairman of the committee, had suggested the plan of campaign to be followed. It would be an error, he wrote, to make a frontal attack on the League as an evil organization, for the American people believed it had beneficent possibilities. The proper course was to "show up the impossibility of any of the methods proposed." He rapidly developed this strategy of attack-by-dilution. He and Senator William E. Borah of Idaho agreed that "there was only one thing to do, and that was to proceed in the discussion of the treaty by way of amendment and reservation."

Lodge saw to it that the Foreign Relations Committee not only adopted a half hundred reservations but opened a series of hearings to which it invited everyone who held a grievance. The tide of opinion swung, and the Senate voted down the League.

The lesson of this story is clear: that narrow partisanship, and poisonous national suspicions and animosities, can defeat the will of a majority of intelligent Americans and do injury to the best interests of the nation and the world. That possibility was memorably illustrated in 1918-1920. Only one parallel of equal importance can be found in our history. This was the flouting of the desire of most Northerners, in the years 1865-1866, for a moderate, conciliatory and generous treatment of the conquered South, in accordance with the policy of President Lincoln. In that instance also, a group of narrow-minded Republican leaders, intent upon partisan advantage, used the machinery of Congress to impose upon the country a program which contravened the majority will, and thus did heavy injury to the welfare of the nation.

The personal tragedy of Woodrow Wilson, as here traced, is profoundly saddening; but far more grievous and more deeply distressing was the national and international tragedy bound up with it.

—ALLAN NEVINS

When
the cheering
stopped

PART ONE

The President

If we do not know courage

1   She who in her youth had been Miss Elly Lou
Axson of Rome, Georgia, but who more latterly was First Lady of
America, lay dying. In March she had slipped and fallen heavily,
and during the spring she ceased to come downstairs for meals. In
late July her doctor took up residence in the room next to hers, and
as August began it was obvious that she could not live very much
longer. And in fact the case was hopeless from the start, for she
was suffering from Bright's disease and complications, the complications being tuberculosis of both kidneys.

Her husband, the President, either did not understand or could
not to himself admit that she must die. All through July and into
the first days of August he wrote friends that there was no real
cause for alarm. But when her meals were served to her in the sickroom, it frightened him that she would not eat, and he would take
a plate of food and sink to his knees beside her bed. "You will soon
get well, darling, if you'll try hard to eat something," he would
say. "Now please take this bite, dear." Often he got up at three in
the morning to be with her when she could not sleep, and that he
was there seemed to give her a degree of peace, for she was restless
in those brief intervals when he left her. "Is your father looking
well? Is your father looking well?" she kept asking her daughters
when her husband was out of the room.

To one of the daughters, Eleanor—Little Nell or Nellie to the family—her sickness seemed like the coming-true of a terrible premonition. The day before her father's 1913 inauguration Nellie helped her mother dress for a teatime call on the outgoing President and his wife, Mr. and Mrs. William Howard Taft. Arranging her mother's hair and adjusting her prettiest hat, the girl, excited and young, chattered away. But her mother was utterly silent. At the end, Nellie kissed her and told her how lovely she looked. And the mother put both hands over her face and burst into tears. Nellie found spirits of ammonia for her and after a while her mother said she was all right. But Nellie had seen an awful, sudden despair in her mother's face, something she had never seen there before, and it terrified her. When her parents had gone off to the Tafts', she began to walk around the room, saying over and over, "It will kill them; it will kill them both." She was crying, and soon she was screaming, and after a time she was crawling under the bed and pounding the floor with her hands and crying over and over again, "It will kill them! It will kill them both!"

But when the next day the sun came out just as her father, taking his oath of office, lifted his wife's small Bible to his lips, Nellie forgot her fears and took the light as an omen that all would go well. During the inauguration speech, it touched the girl to see her mother leave her seat to stand just beneath her father, looking up at him like a small child, a look of rapture on her face.

There was no Inaugural Ball—the President and First Lady did not want one—but there was a party in the White House, with the many relatives of the family, nearly all from the South, roaming through the rooms and singing around a piano. Cousin Florence Hoyt, a cripple, arrived at the railroad station and, unable to find a cab, hailed an old Negro selling frankfurters from a wagon pulled by a skinny scarecrow of a horse. She asked him to take her to the White House, main entrance, please, and he doubtfully agreed, suggesting, however, that they go in the back way. Cousin Florence would have none of that, though; nestling among the hot dogs, she told the man to make for the front door. Liveried attendants there lifted her out and, relatives shouting with laughter at her carriage, she was taken in to offer her congratulations. In the kitchen even an old servant of the President's late father was celebrating with the Negroes of the White House staff; to him the President—

Cousin Woodrow and Uncle Woodrow to the majority of the guests—was still the Mister Tommy of boyhood days.

As Cousin Florence was being welcomed, someone came to say that Aunt Annie Howe, the President's sister, had fallen on a marble staircase and cut her forehead. A servant was sent for a doctor and returned with Lieutenant Cary Travers Grayson of the U. S. Navy, the White House physician under President Taft and Taft's predecessor, Theodore Roosevelt. Grayson at once sewed up the slight wound and quickly put Aunt Annie right, and the President said to him that it had all been so promptly and efficiently done that Lieutenant Grayson must have been prepared for Aunt Annie's fall even before it happened. The party went on: there was a stand-up buffet lunch, a parade, and in the evening wonderful fireworks.

In the days that followed, the Wilson daughters, Margaret, Jessica and Nellie, the first two blue-eyed blondes, the last a brunette with blue-gray eyes very like her father's—"a noticeable man, with large gray eyes," his wife called him, quoting Wordsworth—enjoyed themselves enormously. They were all single and in their twenties and Washington was marvelously stocked with young officers and aides to take them dancing and to the horse shows and parties. They frolicked around their new home, jumping out of dark corners to scare the servants, and they went on the White House tours incognito, loudly criticizing the President's daughters to the out-of-town tourists. Their father, looking better than he had ever looked before (or would ever look again), did not find his duties onerous. He spent no more than four or five hours a day on his work, and saying he still kept to a schoolboy schedule, he did not work on Saturdays or Sundays. Nights when the girls were home the family gathered by a piano, and the President and Margaret, an aspiring singer, performed duets together. Or the President did the imitations which had for years convulsed his daughters: The Drunken Man, during which performance he staggered about with a cow-like look in his eyes and an incoherent mumble coming from his slack lips; The Heavy Englishman, with an insufferably superior accent and an invisible monocle; The Villain, done with a scowl and a dragging foot; The Fourth of July Orator, gesturing not with his hands but with his feet, and Theodore Roosevelt, waving his fist and shouting, "We stand at Armageddon and battle for the

Lord!" There were limerick recitations also, including the much-loved one with which, as head of Princeton University, he had surprised a dinner party:

"There was a young monk of Siberia,
Whose existence grew drearier and drearier,
Till he burst from his cell with a hell of a yell,
And eloped with the Mother Superior."

Sometimes in the Oval Room on the second floor, which the First Lady filled with their old furniture from Princeton, he romped with Nellie and Margaret around the table in so fast and furious a fashion that his wife cried out, "Woodrow, what is the matter with you?" Jessie would generally only watch, not participate, when the fun grew too boisterous, for she was, according to her father, classified along with her mother as one of the Proper Members of the family, as opposed to himself and Nellie, who were the Vulgar Members. Margaret, he said, was in between: she was Proper part of the time and Vulgar all the rest.

In the afternoons when the weather was good he and one or more of his womenfolk went riding in one of the White House Pierce-Arrows, big open cars with right-hand drive and the President's Seal on the door. He mapped out a series of routes, and the chauffeur was not allowed to deviate from them: The Number One Ride, The Southern Maryland Ride, The Potomac. Going on these rides, the First Lady saw things that shocked her. She was born in a small town and grew up there and after her marriage lived in a series of small college towns, and the crowded big-city back streets and alleys of Washington were a revelation to her. She walked through the slums and talked a great deal to the Negro servants about their homes, and it became her passion to do something for the people who lived in the houses that appalled her. She urged the President to get a bill passed that would clean up the slums, and he sent one on to Congress. That she was involved in such a project amused diplomatic and political Washington, and people smiled at the mention of her name. Her clothing also caused derisive comment, for she was far from fashionable. When she let it be known that she did not intend to spend more than one thousand dollars a year for clothes, she was marked down as an eccentric. Actually, for the former Miss Elly Lou Axson and former Mrs. Professor Wilson and former Mrs. President of Princeton, one thousand dollars for clothing was a fantastic sum. In the middle years of her marriage she was accustomed to spending less than fifty a year on her attire, and it was said in Princeton that every fall, year after year, Mrs. Wilson looked sweeter and sweeter in her brown fall dress. She had never in her life owned furs until after her husband was elected President of the United States; then she let him give her sables. She was tiny and gentle and had golden hair and spoke in the softest of Southern tones and painted landscapes in a studio she created in the White House attic. When, anonymously, several of her paintings were sold through a gallery, she donated the money to educational funds for Southern mountaineer people and for crippled children.

She loved flowers and plants and remodeled the gardens on the south lawn of the White House. She planted boxwood, rosebushes and rose trees, tall cypresses and clipped hedges, and placed among them a statue of a small Pan, which the servants said must be symbolic of the boy she had wanted to continue her husband's name. For that husband she had the very greatest of solicitude and worried constantly over his health, which had never been strong. A doctor once told her that as long as a man's neck was full and firm there was little need to worry about him, and often the First Lady massaged that of the President, calling to her daughters to come and see that there were no hollows there. Thinking of her husband's health, she sent for Lieutenant Grayson, who had patched up Aunt Annie with such efficiency, and asked him if he would not look after the President. Grayson took on the job. He found that the President had suffered for years from neuritis and respiratory troubles and that a retinal hemorrhage in his left eye had damaged his sight badly. Grayson's patient had been operated on for phlebitis—"I was flea-bitten," he explained—and was also subject to headaches, but his greatest trouble came from digestive upsets that caused nausea, heartburn and gastritis, all of which he treated himself with his own stomach pump and a series of powders. It was a matter of "turmoil in Central America," he said, of "disturbances in the equatorial regions." Grayson took away the pump and the powders and put the President on a rigid diet based on raw eggs and orange juice. The President did not mind the juice, but he balked at the raw eggs. "I feel as if I were swallowing a newborn baby," he groaned. Grayson forced him to stick to it, however, and also instituted regular golf sessions in Virginia and Maryland, getting up himself in the very early morning hours to make sure the President played the entire course. Himself a very mediocre golfer, Grayson was a fit partner for a player who, hampered by his poor sight, rarely broke 100, although his approach and putting shots were not bad. And the outings led to a new Presidential imitation: Grayson Approaching a Golf Ball. Soon the digestive problems were all but completely cleared up and Grayson, working with the President's valet, arranged for the President to be regularly served only well-chosen foods that would also appeal to him: oatmeal, chicken, steak, Virginia country ham, a bit of port after dinner.

But as the President's health improved, that of the First Lady declined. Jessica and Nellie had both gotten married, but as the family's second summer in the White House began, both came back to be with their mother. Then came August, the August of 1914, and she was dying. Holding her hand, the President worked by her bedside, and his secretary, Joseph Patrick Tumulty of Jersey City, New Jersey, gave it out that there by her bed he wrote his note offering to mediate the disputes of the Europeans falling into the disaster called the Great War. By his instructions the First Lady was not told of the war—"Don't say anything to your mother about it"—but when she asked about her bill to help the slum dwellers they were able to tell her it had passed Congress and would soon be implemented.°

In the end the President knew that she was dying, for she told him so herself, saying also that it was her wish that he marry again. On the morning of August 6, even with the impact of her words upon him, he was able to write a friend that he was hoping still. But in the late morning or early afternoon of that day a Princeton classmate of his 1879 class, now a Philadelphia doctor, plainly said to him that she could not live more than a few hours. All through that hot afternoon not forty-eight hours after the first German troops crossed the frontier and met Belgian defenders, the President and the girls sat with Ellen in her room filled with flowered chintz and gay cushions and light-colored lampshades. Two nurses

---

° It was later declared unconstitutional. Many of the slums are still as they were when Ellen Wilson last saw them.

and Grayson were there also. In another room the husbands of the two married girls waited with Joe Tumulty, who, not very much older than the daughters, had loved Ellen Wilson like a mother ever since the days in the New Jersey Governor's mansion. They were all together in the other room and Grayson was alone for a few moments with her when she roused herself from a semi-stupor and took the doctor's hand to draw him to her. "Please take good care of Woodrow, Doctor," she whispered, uttering the last words of her life. A few minutes later Grayson told the family it would be well if they came back into her room. Twilight outside was about to begin; the day was still very warm. They walked to her bed and the girls knelt beside it. The President took her hand and was still holding it when, a little later, just before evening, she died. He was very controlled and looked over the bed at Grayson and said, "Is it all over?" Grayson nodded and the President quickly straightened up to fold her hands over her breast. She was fifty years old and they had been married twenty-nine years. He used to say, recalling the time they first met, when he was a little boy and she a baby, that he had loved her since she was in her cradle.

He walked to the window and looked south over the gardens she had planted and toward the Washington Monument and the Potomac and Virginia. Grayson was busying himself with the dead woman when he first heard the sobs. "Oh my God, what am I going to do? What am I going to do?" the President said over and over.

Outside, on the bell knob beside the main doorway, a heavy band of black crape soon appeared.

He did not want her to lie in a casket, so they placed her on a sofa in her room and he bent over to put a white silk shawl around her shoulders. For the rest of her time in the White House she was there, never alone at night, the President and one or more of the girls always sitting by her, talking quietly or reading or simply sitting still.

"God has stricken me almost beyond what I can bear," he wrote a friend, and the Assistant Secretary of the Navy, Franklin D. Roosevelt, said to the Secretary that he feared the President was about to have a breakdown. But in fact he did not again completely give vent to his feelings after his first sobs had stopped. At times it seemed as if he were about to, but he would pull himself together, saying, "I must not give way."

Monday the tenth, in the morning, was the time for her funeral service, she at last in a casket resting on the shining floor of the East Room with its marble fireplaces and concert piano in gold leaf. Afterward the President and the girls withdrew to a room nearby and sat alone looking out toward the south. At two in the afternoon the funeral train left Washington for Georgia and the hillside cemetery in Rome where lay her mother and father, who in life had been, like the President's father, a Presbyterian minister.

Riding down in the nearly empty special train, the President rarely left his wife but sat by the casket, only occasionally napping on a lounge in the car's compartment. By Tuesday morning they were deep in the South, and although only the tolling of the engine bell signaled their approach, at the railroad platforms of the small towns and even at the way stations silent people stood with their hats off. Going through the hills and valleys of north Georgia, they saw old men standing at attention on the porches of the remote rural cabins. At noon in Rome the stores closed and the trolleys stopped running and the factories shut down; when in the early afternoon the train pulled into the station, bells began to toll all over the city. They got out of the train into the hot Georgia sun and a group of her relatives took the casket and put it in the hearse while the President looked at it with a strong fixed stare. They drove directly to the church where her father had been pastor and held a very simple service. There were two hymns and then the mourners formed up to go to the Myrtle Hill Cemetery. Schoolgirls in white, all holding myrtle branches, lined the way. Although the President had wanted as quiet a funeral as possible, almost the entire population of his wife's home town turned out and stood by as her casket was lowered into the ground. When the casket rested in place, it was suggested to the President that now he leave the cemetery, but he said that he wanted to wait until the work was completely done. The crowds moved back to leave him quite alone with the girls near a large oak, and a breeze came up and moved some of the flowers. The workmen began to pile earth on Ellen's casket where she lay with two rings on her hand, the first her wedding ring, the other a diamond one. His head bared, he stood by the men with their shovels, and a distance off the people of the town, the relatives and the Washington people shortly saw that once again the President was weeping because Ellen was gone.

2 The President sat by himself hour after hour on the observation platform of the train heading for Washington and the now unbearably lonely White House. "I feel so utterly alone," he said, and begged some of Ellen's relatives to stay with him for a while. They did so, and for long hours he talked to them, saying it was his ambition and his career that killed her. Her brother said to him that it was not so, but that even if it were Ellen would not have wanted it otherwise.

Ellen was dead, Jessie and Nellie were married, and Margaret was often away. There was no woman to take charge of the White House. He asked his cousin, Helen Woodrow Bones, who had been brought up by his mother and father, if she would step into the breach. She took up permanent residence with him, hoping also that her two pets, Sandy the Airedale and Hamish the sheep dog, would amuse him. But of course nothing was the same, and often he sat alone reading Ellen's favorite poems or went walking the corridors of the Corcoran art gallery to look again at paintings she had loved.

Ellen was dead. "I do not care a fig for anything that affects me," he wrote a friend, and to another indicated that it would come as a blessing if someone would assassinate him. "If I hadn't gone into politics she would probably be alive now," he told her sister, and took a great interest in hearing from the British Ambassador details of how British Foreign Minister Sir Edward Grey, when he lost his own wife, worked to submerge his grief in his love of the outdoors, of flowers and fishing. Even as Great Britain went to the war, Sir Edward took time to write the President a sympathetic note. The lonely man in the White House read it out loud to the people around him.

Cary Grayson saw his patient declining before his eyes and worked harder than ever to keep up the golfing and auto rides. The doctor also stayed many nights in the White House to be on hand if the President wanted someone to chat with. And often the gentle Helen Bones would sit by her cousin in silence, simply wanting him to know that she was there to help. In her eyes he was something like a Bengal tiger she had once seen in a cage; she thought him trapped by his own cage of high position that prevented him from seeking out friendships wherever he could find them. As summer turned to fall and spring of 1915 came, Helen Bones herself sickened in the depressing atmosphere of the White House, and Grayson began to worry about her. She was a shy person and quiet, and had hardly any friends at all in Washington. Grayson decided that what she needed was a woman friend to talk with, someone who could take her out of the White House now and then.

Grayson looked around for the proper person and decided to introduce Helen to the older friend of the girl he would shortly marry. Grayson's future wife was Alice Gertrude Gordon, who was called Altrude by her friends, and Altrude's friend was a forty-two-year-old widow who owned a Washington jewelry shop left her by her late husband. The shop was a profitable one and ran itself with little aid from its owner, who was able to travel widely, take a great interest in clothes, particularly Paris frocks, and drive around in an electric automobile which, she said, was the first ever owned and operated by a Washington woman. She lived alone save for two maids in a house on 20th Street, N.W., at New Hampshire Avenue. She was tall and imposing and had a beautiful smile and appealing dimples. Her family was one of the oldest in Virginia and her father had been a plantation owner, Confederate officer, lawyer and judge, but she had been brought up in the impoverished post-Civil War South and had but two years of formal education. She was a non-political person, not active in Society or charitable circles, and in almost twenty years of Washington residence had never been inside the White House. Her name was Edith Bolling Galt.

Miss Bones and Mrs. Galt soon became friends, going for outings in Mrs. Galt's electric (which she drove like an absolute madwoman) and for long afternoon walks along the paths in Rock Creek Park. The Galt home was only a few blocks from the park, and after their walks they would make for its library, where a fire would be lit and tea served. One day in March, after a long hike over muddy paths, Helen Bones invited her friend to come for tea in the White House instead of in the 20th Street library. "Oh, I couldn't do that; my shoes are a sight, and I should be taken for a tramp," Mrs. Galt said.

"Yes, you can," said Miss Bones. "There is not a soul there. Cousin Woodrow is playing golf with Dr. Grayson and we will go right upstairs in the elevator and you shall see no one." They went to the White House and to the second floor. As they stepped out of the elevator, they saw coming around the corner, attired in golfing clothes and muddy boots, the President of the United States and his physician. Mrs. Galt had time to note that the golf suits were tatty and not smart at all, and time to think to herself that if her own shoes were not clean at least she was wearing a Worth gown and a nice tricot hat. Then she was being introduced and Helen Bones was explaining that they had been for a walk and were going to have tea. "I think you might ask us," Grayson said, and it was agreed that the men would change while the women had their shoes cleaned up. They would then all meet in the Oval Room.

They sat down to tea and when they finished the President took Mrs. Galt to see a desk made from the timbers of the British ship *Resolute* which, icebound and abandoned in the Arctic, was found by an American ship and returned to England, where Queen Victoria had the desk made for President Rutherford B. Hayes. Then Edith Galt went home. In the short time she was with the President, her cheerful manner made him laugh twice, making Helen Bones wonder if she was hearing right. He had laughed. "I can't say that I foresaw in the first minute what was going to happen," Helen Bones said later. "It may have taken ten minutes."

A few days later Mrs. Galt came to dinner at the White House, and a few days after that went riding with the two cousins, she and Helen sitting in the back of the car while the President sat by the driver. He seemed very tired and hardly said a word while his cousin and her friend chattered away. Around five-thirty they drove back to the White House and he asked the guest if she would not join them for dinner. There was something plaintive in the way he told her he and Cousin Helen were entirely alone. After they ate he seemed far more lively and the three of them sat around a fire talking about books and their pasts in the South. He read aloud, as he always loved to do, and spoke feelingly of his father, who had drilled him in English and composition when he was a boy. He talked a good deal of that boyhood, of the time he saw Jefferson Davis, the prisoner of Union soldiers, being led past his home in Georgia. She spoke also of her family; she was a direct descendant of Pocahontas, who after saving Captain John Smith from execution married John Rolfe and was Mrs. Galt's grandmother seven times removed. They talked about the scrimping the parents of both had to do after the Civil War, and of Negro ex-slaves their families knew. She saw, she thought, boyishness and simplicity in him, and something crying out for human companionship.

In the days that followed, the President and Mrs. Galt went for frequent rides with his cousin as chaperone (along with the ever-present Secret Service men), and she came often to dine in the White House. He sent her a book, and read aloud to her in the Oval Room. She met Margaret and Nellie, and he asked Dr. Grayson to come for dinner with Altrude. On April 30 in that spring of 1915 the four dined together, with Grayson performing the duty of picking up the ladies at their homes. The President earlier sent each a corsage of roses, golden ones for Mrs. Galt and pink for Altrude. Grayson came by at seven forty-five to pick up the older woman, she in a Worth black charmeuse gown with golden slippers, and the two drove together to get Altrude. Altrude, only twenty-one, was found in an unready state: she had decided the pink roses did not go with the dress she planned to wear and was changing in-to another one. Grayson, on edge and anxious that his friend make a good impression on the President, went into a panic at the idea that they would be late. "Make her come on," he begged Mrs. Galt, and urged that the finishing touches be done in the auto—he would turn his head. They went to the car and Altrude and Mrs. Galt spent the time of the trip in deciding whether the pink roses should be worn at the side of the shoulder or the waistline. (Finally they chose the shoulder.) The dinner went off splendidly and on

May 4 Mrs. Galt (in white satin and green slippers) was back to dine with the President, Aunt Annie and her daughter, Helen, Margaret and Grayson. It was a warm night and the party adjourned to the South Portico for their coffee. Soon everyone else drifted away, Grayson leaving and the other women taking a stroll on the south lawn. Mrs. Galt was alone with the President. He moved his chair closer to hers and said, "I have asked Margaret and Helen to give me an opportunity to tell you something tonight that I have already told them." And he said he loved her.

She was astonished. They had known each other two months; they were still "Mr. President" and "Mrs. Galt" to each other. "Oh, you can't love me," she said. "You don't really know me. And it is less than a year since your wife died."

"I know you feel that," he said. "But, little girl, in this place time is not measured by weeks, or months, or years, but by deep human experience; and since her death I have lived a lifetime of loneliness and heartache. I was afraid, knowing you, I would shock you; but I would be less than a gentleman if I continued to make opportunities to see you without telling you what I have told my daughters and Helen: that I want you to be my wife." He went on, saying any relationship between them would provoke gossip but that they would have to bear it and that it would be best for her to come to the White House rather than for him to call on her, but that if she cared for him as he cared for her she would accept these things. And the girls and Helen would act as chaperones.

They talked for more than an hour, and at the end she said that if she must that night say yes or no she would have to say no, that she needed time to decide what to do. He and Helen drove her home.

The next day Helen came for a walk in the park. No mention was made of the previous night, but when they sat down on some stones for a rest Helen observed that Cousin Woodrow looked really ill that morning. "Just as I thought some happiness was coming into his life!" Helen snapped. "You are breaking his heart!" Mrs. Galt explained she thought she was being fair to both parties in saying they ought to move slowly, and was certain she was right in trying to stand off from the situation and thus see it more clearly. This would have to be accepted as her attitude.

The next meeting between the couple was upon the occasion of a Presidential review of the Atlantic Fleet in New York. The outing had been planned before his proposal of marriage, and she decided to go ahead with it even if the circumstances were difficult. They sailed down on the Presidential yacht *Mayflower* with Aunt Annie and her daughter, Margaret, Helen, Joe Tumulty, Grayson and Altrude. From Chesapeake Bay to New York a violent storm raged. Helen hid in her cabin, telling everyone to leave her alone in her agony, and Altrude simply lay down on the deck while the pale Grayson, naval rank notwithstanding, reeled and gagged. The President's valet tried to bring brandy and ice for Altrude but could not raise his head and collapsed in the dining saloon. Mrs. Galt went below and took the liquor from him. She carried it part way to the deck but ran out of good health in the hatch and lay on her back with her eyes closed, clutching the brandy bottle to her chest. The President found her so and could not help laughing at the sight; that made her laugh too, and she felt better. At lunch only she and the President and Joe Tumulty appeared. When lamb with peas was served Tumulty turned a color Mrs. Galt thought similar to that of the peas and disappeared. When the yacht was finally docked in the Hudson, Tumulty and Margaret quickly announced that urgent matters made it imperative that they return to Washington at once by train. The others on the way back found the water calm and the spring weather very fine, and they anchored in the Potomac and went ashore to see Robert E. Lee's birthplace. By that time the President was talking about his work and problems to Mrs. Galt, and she was torn by the desire to help him and the fear that really she was unqualified to do so.

She worried about what to do, but she continued to see him for drives and dinners, with Margaret, Nellie or Helen invariably being their companions. She introduced her own family into the situation, bringing her sister Bertha to tea on a day when Helen and Margaret did not appear and the President brewed the tea himself, with the result that the drink, to her taste, was more like lye than tea. Afterward the three of them walked in the garden, which was glorious in the early summer weather. He had rented a summer place in New Hampshire and Margaret and Helen asked her to visit. She did so, driving up with Helen via Princeton, where Helen acted as guide on a tour of his former haunts. They went on for shopping in New York and then to the summer place, where they were joined in a few days by the President and Grayson. Margaret came up also. Jessica, the middle daughter, and her husband, Francis B. Sayre, came over from Massachusetts, where he was teaching at Harvard. The party went for drives and picnics, and Francis Sayre was struck by the ease and informality of the way the President acted in the rural surroundings. They ate out in the open and went for long walks as they had in the Princeton days when Sayre first met the President and Jessica, even though of course in those earlier times there were no Secret Service men always very close at hand.

Many of the members of the party stayed on after the President and Grayson went back to Washington for a while, and Helen and Mrs. Galt transferred their walking tours to these new surroundings, going out every day. But to the latter the house seemed a dead place when its temporary owner was not there.

Still she could not make up her mind to marry him while he was in office, although she said she would do so if he was defeated in the 1916 election. In July she left New Hampshire to visit some friends in upstate New York, carrying with her the memory of his figure standing in the open door, dressed in white flannels and looking after her as she drove away. On September 3 she returned to Washington and found flowers awaiting her along with a note of welcome reminding her that she had promised to dine with him at the White House on her first night home. She went to find the President was meeting with Secretary of War Lindley M. Garrison. Helen and Margaret were in the Red Room, however, and had a good deal to say to her about keeping him in a state of suspense about the romance. Finally he came in from the Blue Room and in her eyes he was so distinguished-looking in his evening clothes that when she put her hands in his and met his gaze something changed in her and she knew they would marry. After dinner Margaret went out and Mrs. Galt and the two cousins, Helen and the President, went for a ride through Rock Creek Park. He talked about the problem of keeping the United States out of the war and ended by saying that he had come to understand her reluctance to assume the responsibilities his wife must necessarily have during such difficult times. The car had as passengers a Secret Service man and the chauffeur, and Helen was sitting right beside her, but despite them she put her arms around his neck and said, "Well, if you won't ask me, I will volunteer." So it was decided. The next morning they told Margaret and Nellie they were engaged.

Edward Mandell House was a thin, small, retiring Texan who always talked in almost a whisper. He had inherited a sum of money that made it unnecessary for him to work for a living and he interested himself in politics, becoming adviser to a succession of Texas governors, one of whom made him an honorary colonel—a title by which most people came to address him. When Governor Wilson of New Jersey was named candidate at the Democratic convention of 1912, House struck up a friendship with the nominee, who found him a singularly agreeable man. The candidate was elected President and the relationship grew even warmer, with House suggesting Cabinet members and overseeing political fence-mending. In time it was said that the Colonel's ear was the one to reach if you had something to say to the President, and it was true: the President relied upon House in many ways.

William Gibbs McAdoo was a self-made financial wizard of great drive and force who did much good work in the 1912 Presidential campaign. A widower, he was named Secretary of the Treasury when the new President took office in 1913, and he soon bore a new relationship to the White House: son-in-law. Although he was years her senior and had a daughter practically her age, Nellie Wilson fell in love with McAdoo and married him in a White House ceremony held a few months before her mother's death.

Both these men were very clever in a political sense and both had very acute reactions to the activities of their President. In the summer and fall of 1915 those senses and those reactions were moved very strongly by the fact of Edith Bolling Galt's existence. For stories about the Presidential romance began flying around. (Washington, a city whose only preoccupation is politics, has always been a fertile place for the development of stories concerned with the doings of the occupant of the White House.) And what was being said in Washington in the fall of 1915 was that the President and this Galt woman had conspired long ago to get Ellen Wilson out of the way so that they could marry, and that the loyal Dr. Grayson had poisoned the First Lady. It was also said she died after a beating at the President's hands. Also that he had scandalously neglected to provide care for her grave in Georgia and weeds were growing all over it, along with cornstalks, but that he was so occupied with his new love that he did not care. Rumor had it that so taken with Edith Galt was he that official business was utterly ignored and stacks of neglected matters were piled high on his desk. Even if these stories could be handled or combated, there was still a political factor in the romance that could not be brushed away: the sympathy the country felt for a recently bereaved President would vanish immediately he married the gay and smiling Mrs. Galt.

While McAdoo and House worried about these issues, they had even more frightening facts to deal with. The President during his Princeton days took—alone, without Ellen—a trip to Bermuda and there met a stylish, cheerful, good-looking woman vacationer with whom he spent much time; she visited him at Princeton and the White House and received from him more than two hundred letters; as President he sent her $7,500 of his own money; all this was in general known to the President's political enemies, and—most terrifying of all—it was said this woman was going to play the role of jilted paramour and reveal the whole story if the President married Mrs. Galt.

The woman, born Mary Allen, had married a Mr. Peck. After his death she married a Mr. Hulbert, and when the marriage ended in divorce she resumed her former married name. Mrs. Peck was now living in California, and rumors were floating east that the letters were up for sale to anyone who wanted to buy them and make their contents known the moment the President remarried.

McAdoo and House saw political ruin ahead. They, and others, decided the President should not marry. Or if he must do so, then he must at least wait a year, until after the 1916 election.

The question was, how was the President to be told this? Various candidates were sought out to perform the task, but no one accepted the job. So McAdoo and House worked up a scheme that McAdoo carried out. Lunching with his father-in-law, McAdoo said that an anonymous letter from California had been received. The letter (which existed only in the minds of McAdoo and House) said Mrs. Peck was talking about the $7,500 and showing the President's letters to all interested comers. The President, as expected, was horrified. He said the letters were of a totally innocent nature, the

$7,500 was a loan he gave Mrs. Peck against some mortgages she held, and as far as the relationship being illicit in any way, his late wife had known everything he ever did with Mrs. Peck, and Ellen herself had enjoyed reading the letters replying to his. He was astonished that his friend Mrs. Peck would act in this way, but her doing so meant there was only one thing he could do about his relationship with Mrs. Galt.

He went to his desk to write a note telling Mrs. Galt that he would not expose her to slander and publicity that would hurt her in a way he could not prevent but also could not ask her to accept. For a long time he sat seeking the right words. Grayson came into the room and saw the President was pale, his lips tightly pressed together. The hand holding the pen shook. He did not write anything for a long time and then he put down the pen. "I cannot bring myself to write this," he said. "You go, Grayson, and tell her everything and say my only alternative is to release her from any promise."

Grayson went to Mrs. Galt. She sat silently when he finished speaking. "What shall I tell him?" Grayson asked. "Tell him I will write," she said.

She sat for many hours, and night came on, and dawn. She wrote:

Dearest . . .

I will stand by you—not for duty, not for pity, not for honour—but for love—trusting, protecting, comprehending love . . .

I am so tired I could put my head down on the desk and go to sleep—but nothing could bring me real rest until I had pledged to you my love and my allegiance.

Your own
Edith

All of that day passed with no reply from the White House. The next day and the next brought no answer. She was shattered. It appeared the romance, at his wish, was over. But on the third day Grayson appeared. He did not even shake hands with her before he began to speak. "I beg that you will come with me to the White House. The President is very ill. It is a desperate situation. Neither Miss Margaret nor Miss Bones is here, so I will have to act as chaperon." She said, "Did the President ask you to come?" "No, I told him I was coming, and he said it would be unfair to you and weak in him to ask it. If you could see him you would not hesitate. He looks as I imagine the martyrs looked when they were broken on the wheel."

She asked Grayson to wait and stepped out of the room. Her letter! What had happened to it? What was he doing to her? But she had written, "I will stand by you." She rejoined Grayson and went with him to the President's room. He was lying in bed. His face was pale. He held out a hand and it was cold. She took it and clasped it in her own. When she released it the waiting and the doubts and fears were gone forever from them both. Later it would be whispered that she bought off Mrs. Peck with giant sums and that Louis Brandeis was appointed to the Supreme Court because he was the intermediary who carried the money; later it would be said Colonel House took Mrs. Peck to Europe to get her out of the way and that she was on a regular salary from McAdoo's Treasury Department in order to insure her silence; later it would be rumored Mrs. Peck was about to institute a breach-of-promise suit against the President; later all these things and more would be said and wits would call him Peck's Bad Boy, but these stories did not touch them because they loved each other and always would. And she would learn, months later, when he confessed it to her, that he had not had the courage to open her letter. He carried it in his pocket until their honeymoon, when he drew it out, the envelope worn and frayed, and read what she had written: "I will stand by you for love."

On October 7, 1915, they announced their engagement via Joe Tumulty, who handed out typed sheets to the reporters assigned to the White House. To Ellen's brother the President said that Ellen told him before she died that she wanted this, and the brother said, "That is just the way she loved you." An old friend of the family, with a sister the President addressed as "Cousin," said to him that she had prayed he would be comforted and took this as an answer to those prayers. "What do you think, Cousin Mary?" he asked her sister. "To tell you the truth, I was a little shocked at first," said the woman. "So was I," said the President. He wrote another friend, "The last fourteen months have seemed for me, in a world upset, like fourteen years. It is not the same world in which my dear Ellen lived; and one of the last things she said to me was that she hoped that what has happened now would happen. It seemed to me incredible then, and would, I think, have continued to seem so if I had not been brought into contact with Mrs. Galt." He even wrote Mrs. Peck, saying he knew she would rejoice for him in this "blessing."

The afternoon the news was released he went to call on Mrs. Galt's mother for the first time, and he asked her, along with a sister and brother of the prospective bride, to come to dinner at the White House. The next day the mother and daughter went with him to Philadelphia for the opening game of the World Series. The crowds cheered her; her dimpled smile was enchanting. On October 10, for the first time he dined with her alone at her home.

They set the wedding date for December 18. In the remaining two months of their official engagement they talked constantly on a direct telephone line from the White House to her home, went golfing together (she consistently won), and took long walks and drives. The Secret Service men, who, embarrassing though it was, had to follow everywhere, agreed among themselves that she was a stunner with a wonderful figure complete with the prettiest ankles. They also said it was hard to believe the President was almost fifty-nine years old, for he acted like a boy, dancing off the curbs when he walked from the White House to her home and leaping over obstacles on the golf course. He whistled, tapping time with his feet. He was animated and gay; he played the fool for her, bending over with arms dangling to shuffle along like an ape when she put a golf club across his shoulders, and then leaning forward so that it slid over his head, to be caught with a flourish. He was proud to show her off and had his Princeton class of '79 come to dinner in the White House so they might meet her and, as it turned out, elect her an honorary member. They went to the Army-Navy game at New York's Polo Grounds and she marched with him across the field at half-time. There was a roar of applause and she thought to herself that everyone was her friend and his.

The wedding was to be at her house and they did not send invitations, feeling this would make it clear to all public officials and others that no gifts were to be given them. But when the State of California sent a gold nugget with the request that the wedding ring be fashioned from it, they accepted the present and had a plain band made. A minister from his Presbyterian church and an

Episcopalian from hers would perform the ceremony and only a very few old friends and servants would join the families as witnesses. The head usher of the White House, Ike Hoover, took over the decorating of her home and arranged the catering of the buffet supper with an outside concern. Hoover had all the furniture removed from the lower floor of her home and in the drawing room, where the ceremony would be, he put a wedding bower made of a background of farleyense and maidenhair fern extending from the floor to the ceiling, with overhead a canopy of green arranged in the form of a shell, Scotch heather forming the inner side. There was a mirror framed with orchids and the corners of the canopy were also caught up with orchids—*Dendrobium phalanopsis, Vanda coerules* and *Laelia anceps alba.* Above the mirror were South American *Cattleya trianae,* and sheaves of long-stemmed American Beauty roses were on both sides of the canopy. In the dining room there were roses and ferns; a small band of U.S. Marine musicians would furnish the music.

December 18 was clear but crisp and bracing. At eight in the evening the President came to Mrs. Galt's sitting room, alone save for a Secret Service man, and a while later Hoover tapped on the door and said, "Mr. President, it is eight-thirty." Bride and bridegroom smiled and both called out, "Thank you," and they went downstairs together. Margaret, Jessie and Nellie were there, of course, and both sons-in-law, and Aunt Annie and her daughter, and Ellen's brother and Altrude and Grayson. Some of Mrs. Galt's relatives through her first marriage were there, and all of her brothers and sisters with their wives and husbands. She wore a black velvet gown with a velvet hat trimmed with goura; her only jewelry was a brooch of diamonds the groom gave her. The President wore a cutaway coat and grey striped trousers.

When the minister asked, "Who giveth this woman to be married to this man?" Mrs. Galt's mother took the hands of both of them and put them one in the other. And so they were married. The buffet supper was served and then they left for their honeymoon at The Homestead in Hot Springs, Virginia. They went out of her house past aged Negro servants of both families standing in the hall calling, "God bless you, Miss Edith and Mr. President." Her mother's old cook, who as a slave had belonged to her grandfather, cried out, "Take Jesus with you for your doctor and your friend!"

Twentieth Street was roped off and they slipped into a car and with only Secret Service men along drove to the Alexandria station instead of Washington's Union Station in order to avoid possible crowds. Snow from the previous day's fall was still on the ground and they thought it lovely in the clear moonlight. At Alexandria a private car was waiting filled with flowers, and some sandwiches and fruit stood on a table. Around midnight the train pulled out.

The next morning at seven one of the Secret Service men, Edmund Starling, stepped into the car as the train came into Hot Springs. As Starling went into the narrow train corridor a figure came out of the car's sitting room. It was the President, in top hat, tail coat, and grey morning trousers. He was facing away from the Secret Service man. As Starling watched in silence, the President's hands went into the pockets of his trousers and his feet came flashing up in the air to click heels. He began to whistle a popular song. The heels came leaping up to click again and the whistling changed into outright singing:

"Oh, you beautiful doll, you great big beautiful doll; oh, oh, oh, oh, OH, YOU BEAUTIFUL DOLL!"

3 At thirty years of age he was teaching history and political science to the girls at Bryn Mawr College. He did not enjoy his work, for the students could not be expected ever to vote or play a part in the governing of the nation, and their girlish ways did not stimulate him to do his best lecturing. They admired him and faithfully wrote down his jokes in their notebooks, but their response to constitutional law was limited.

He threw himself into the writing of a college textbook, *The State*, and supplemented his $1,500 a year salary by delivering lectures at Johns Hopkins. But when Wesleyan College asked him to join its faculty, he was happy to leave Bryn Mawr; he was "hungry for a class of *men*," he wrote a friend. In his new post he taught political economy, the histories of France, England and the United States. In 1890, getting on to thirty-five, he returned to his alma mater, Princeton.

He stayed there twenty years. As a professor, he was one of the most popular in the university's history, and the highest-paid of his day. He was a wonderful classroom orator, precise, artful, knowledgeable. He related his lectures to the doings of the times as he illustrated the developments of political institutions, and his jokes and dramatizations were marvelously apt. Often the students applauded and stamped their feet at the end of the class. He worked with the boys on extracurricular activities, coaching the debating societies and helping out with the football team. At home during his free hours he wrote extensively—essays, political treatises. Also short stories. (Everything else sold well, but his attempts at fiction brought only rejection slips.) He wrote books about the political history of the country, a life of George Washington, a five-volume history of the American people. He rode a bicycle from his home to his classes. At home were the three little daughters growing up, and in the classrooms were hundreds of young men who would leave Princeton thinking him the finest teacher they had ever seen. When in 1902 the head of Princeton resigned, the university trustees unanimously picked as replacement the head of the Department of Jurisprudence and Political Economy.

Head of the university, he gave up his writing and teaching and turned to administrative duties, but still he remained extremely popular with the students. He told them he was not to be addressed as Professor or Doctor° but simply as Mister. He performed well at one of the most important tasks—getting money from the alumni—and he revised and strengthened the curriculum, modernizing it and making it far more demanding. The old Princeton way of gracious living vanished; one disgruntled student wrote home the place was "getting to be nothing but a damned educational institution." That was what the plan had been.

The tutorial system was instituted at the university. Fifty young men, preceptors, were hired to work with students in an intimate and personalized manner. The standards of the university rose even higher, and many inadequate students fell by the way. One such boy was expelled for cheating, and his mother came to plead for his reinstatement with the man who had passed upon the expulsion. She said she was undergoing serious medical treatments and that the shock of having her boy expelled might well bring those treatments to naught. The answer was, "Madam, you force me to say a hard thing, but if I had to choose between your life or my life or anybody's life and the good of this college, I should choose the good of the college." But he could eat nothing at luncheon that day.

Hazing bothered him; he came upon some sophomore forcing a freshman to pick up twigs with his teeth and acidly said, "Isn't that a fine occupation for a gentleman?" The rather snobbish fraternity-like eating clubs of the university also bothered him. He

---

° His Ph.D. was from Johns Hopkins.

proposed to abolish the clubs and their anti-intellectual approach in favor of a plan which would have the students of all backgrounds eat, study and live together in dormitories. Princeton graduates loyal to their old eating clubs fought the proposed move, but to the public at large which became aware of the controversy, it seemed as if the head of the university were fighting the battle of democracy in his attempt to shatter the citadels of Princeton's socially elect. He failed in the battle, but popular opinion in New Jersey and elsewhere translated him into the champion of the poorer boys struggling with the richer.

Another argument began. It concerned the graduate school. The university's head wanted the graduate students to work and study on the campus itself and not, as some others desired, in separate buildings some distance from the heart of the campus. The first idea became associated with the conception of a democratic mingling of the graduates and undergraduates, the second idea with that of a standoffish aristocracy.

The question was fought with violence. The head of the university lost. He resigned his post. But he left with the aura of a man who fought for the democratic way. It was 1910, and faced with a gubernatorial election, the New Jersey political bosses chose him to run on the Democratic ticket. He seemed to be very much the college professor; to the politicos he looked to be malleable. They saw him as a dupe, but he saw himself as the agent of Reform. After the bosses of Jersey City and Newark pushed through his nomination, he went campaigning, saying to the people who heard him, "If you give me your votes I will be under bonds to you—not to the gentlemen who were generous enough to nominate me." He was elected and to the disillusionment of the politicians proved that he meant what he had said. They termed him an "ingrate," but it did not matter. As Governor he pushed through reform measures to destroy the boss system and end corruption in state elections. He set up a public utilities commission to establish fair rates for transportation and communications, and laws were passed regulating the work of children and women, the handling of food, the schools. New Jersey had been the very symbol of the complacently corrupt turn-of-the-century business corporation's fief; now the bosses were driven away and the corporations tamed.

In 1912 he was nominated for the Presidency. His election was a certainty, for the Republicans were split, with the incumbent President, Taft, running on the regular party ticket, and the former holder of the office, Roosevelt, campaigning as a Progressive on the "Bull Moose" ticket. The returns in, the President-elect went vacationing to Bermuda. He went bicycle riding with his daughters and turned his head sideways to look at the ocean because someone told him the view was best from that angle. The cable system to the United States was out of order for five days, and he said that made him happy, for he needed peace to think. But he was a public figure now, and reporters dogged his footsteps. He came back from a ride with Jessie and asked the photographers not to take her picture while she was wind-blown from the exertion; when a camera popped he rushed at the man who ignored him and raised his fists as he threatened to chastise him physically.

Back at Trenton, he received a steady stream of visitors seeking appointment to high posts, but he kept his own counsel and refused to be hastened into making known his selections for the Cabinet. (Those who came, however, were generally ignored when the time came for him to announce his choices. He did not think it seemly that men should so nakedly seek power.) In the end his Cabinet was generally marked down as a weak one.

As President he did not consult with the Senators and Representatives. When he wanted to tell them something, he sent for them. There was little give-and-take when they appeared. He explained what was desired, and dismissed callers. When men offered information he already possessed, he cut them off by saying, "I know that." He could not abide callers who meandered about without coming to the point; they wearied him with their palaver and proffered good-fellowship. With his Cabinet he was pleasant and even affable, but he did not care for long extended discussions, preferring written memorandums. At the Cabinet meetings he offered cigars—although he did not smoke himself—and told jokes, but did not get involved in the minor problems of the various departments. When something important came up, he digested the memorandums on the subject with remarkable speed, sent for the Secretary in question, analyzed the problem in a few sentences, and recommended a solution. No one ever had trouble understanding him, and no one had to wait long for a written reply to a written question. (It rarely took more than a day for a Secretary to get an answer to a query.) No one ever dictated to a stenographer faster and more surely than the President. Few of these dictated replies ever needed doing over, for everything he said was right the first time. He was like that in his verbal habits also. Each sentence was gotten out correctly; there was never any stumbling or beginning again. He could not conceal his impatience with men who began to say something, stopped, and took off in a new direction.

At table there was never any business discussed, and never any guests who would talk of public matters. All the conversation was erudite and cheerful. In the Congress they criticized him for this and said that what he wanted was a few tough-minded sons instead of the gay and easygoing daughters. The sons would throw things back in his teeth, Senators told each other, and make the President less inclined to ignore the advice of other people. On the golf course, also, there was no business talk. No Senators or Representatives went along on the auto rides, for the rides were for relaxation. The President said he had a certain amount of energy and was not going to squander it by taking up business matters when he was not in his office during working hours.

In his first year he did more than most of his predecessors had done in complete terms. Tariffs were lowered, the Federal Reserve System was born, and the Federal Trade Commission and a strong anti-trust law. Personal income taxes were levied to make up for the losses in tariff revenue. The rights of laboring men were strengthened, and vocational schools were given federal assistance. At his inauguration he had motioned to an empty space in front of the Capitol and, indicating the men and women held back by police, said, "Let the people come forward." That was the theme of his administration; that was the meaning of the New Freedom.

In 1916 he was renominated. In order to receive his formal notification on a spot not the property of the government, he rented a New Jersey estate and was there through Election Day, when it seemed that Charles Evans Hughes was the winner. The apparent loss did not ruffle the President; he went to bed early after remarking that it seemed his programs had not been completely understood by the voters. The morning after (legend has it) a reporter calling at the Hughes home was told that President Hughes could not be disturbed. The tally was that close. It came down in the end to how California would go, and when the last returns from the mountain polling places were in, the state was in the Democratic column.

By then, by 1916, the domestic program was in the background, for the talk was all of whether the United States would go to the war. A Democratic slogan, "He Kept Us out of War," was credited with the President's victory, but he knew best of all that a German lieutenant looking through a submarine periscope could make nonsense of the slogan.

The Americans did not want to fight, not in the main. Nor did their President, who remembered from his youth what Sherman had done to the South. From the White House went unending notes to the contesting British and Germans as the President twisted one way and then another in his attempts to avoid the war. During the first half of his first term there had been a skirmish between American marines and some Mexicans at Vera Cruz, and when the handful of American deaths was reported to the President he whitened and staggered. To go to France in force would mean dead men in their tens of thousands. In the President's eyes the soldiers he would have to send to face machine guns and artillery shells were akin to his boys back at Princeton. That is what he usually called them—"boys," not "soldiers" or "men."

But the war, it seemed, could not be avoided. He sat before dawn one day in April on the South Portico, and the First Lady awakened and came to him with an overcoat, some biscuits, a glass of milk. In the rain of an April evening he went with the words he had written to the House Chamber of the Capitol. His fingers trembled as he turned the pages, and in the silences between his sentences the sound of drops could be heard hitting upon the roof. He said, "It is a fearful thing to lead this great peaceful people into war, into the most terrible and disastrous of all wars, civilization itself seeming to be in the balance. But the right is more precious than peace . . ."

On the plaza outside, cavalry Regulars from Fort Myer sat their horses to keep the crowds back and guard against disturbances of the kind which earlier in the day saw an anti-war pacifist strike Senator Henry Cabot Lodge of Massachusetts in the face. (Lodge hit back before the pacifist was dragged away.) Soon the Regulars would be indistinguishable from the farmers and clerks, the college boys and mechanics, and in the Oval Room of the White House the President would give off singing the nonsense songs of Princeton in favor of "Over There" and "There's a Long, Long Trail A-Winding."

". . . and we shall fight for the things which we have always carried nearest our hearts—for democracy, for the right of those who submit to authority to have a voice in their own governments, for the rights and liberties of small nations, for a universal dominion of right by such a concert of free peoples as shall bring peace and safety to all nations and make the world itself at last free."

(Something would have to come of it. America would bring the justice and peace of a just and peaceful nation to the world.)

"To such a task we can dedicate our lives and our fortunes, everything that we are and everything that we have, with the pride of those who know that the day has come when America is privileged . . ."

(Else what would it all be for, the dying boys and the sunken ships?)

". . . to spend her blood and her might for the principles that gave her birth and happiness and the peace which she has treasured.

"God helping her, she can do no other."

There was a moment of silence. Then a great roar of applause rolled up to him. Mixed in it were the high rebel yells of Southerners. The troops of cavalry formed up, and with Cary Grayson, Joe Tumulty and the First Lady he drove in silence back to the White House past the crowds of cheering people. "My message today was a message of death for our young men," he said. "How strange it seems to applaud that."

The Americans went to France and Pershing and his staff to a grave where an officer said, "Lafayette, we are here!" The way it got back was that the handsome and soldier-like head of the American Expeditionary Force said it himself, and that was right, because it was what he *should* have said. There was something different about the soldiers the Americans sent abroad under him in that AEF. Such soldiers, perhaps, were never seen before. They sang. They laughed a great deal. They believed in themselves, their country, their way. They were young, confident and open; to the Europeans it seemed that they were indeed godlike, untouched, sure of the sacredness of their mission, which was to give the world a new order and make the world clean and right.

And the war was fought and won. The New World had come to redeem the Old, and when it came time to ask for peace the enemy applied to the leader of that New World. And the guns stopped. That the night ended meant there must be a dawn, and that the dawn must compensate for the dead in their millions, for the girls who would get old and older and who would die as old maids whose lovers-that-should-have-been lay, forever young, in Flanders or Mesopotamia or Gallipoli. In parts of France the poison gas would cling to the roofs of caves for twenty years; the trench-system outlines under the fields could be seen from airplanes forty years later. The Sacred Way up to Verdun, the Lost Battalion, the Chemin des Dames, the Australians coming off their transports past the sunken *River Clyde*, the British boys in their 174 cemeteries crammed into the Ypres Salient, the Italian artillerists dueling with the Austrians in the snow; the English staff general going up forward for the first time and crying, "Good God, did we really send men to fight in that?", the Yank non-com with "Come on, you sons of bitches! Do you want to live forever?", the mules drowning in the shell holes, "Madelon"—it all had to be paid for, something must come out of it, it could not have all been done for nothing. The world was crying out for the price to be paid.

Three weeks after the Armistice was signed, on December 4, 1918, the President of the United States, the man who with his soldiers had brought the dawn, sailed for Europe to work on a final peace treaty and to form a League of Nations which would give the world justice and security and prevent war forever.

"You carry overseas with you," Ellen's brother wrote him, "the hearts and hopes and dreams and desires of millions of your fellow Americans. Your vision of the new world that should spring from the ashes of the old is all that has made the war tolerable to many of us. That vision has removed the sting, has filled our imaginations, and has made the war not a tragedy but a sacrament. Nothing but a new world is worth the purchase price of the war, and the comfort of millions of us is that you have the vision to glimpse it and the power to realize it in action."

Off Brest before dawn of December 13, at four-twenty in the morning, lights were sighted on the horizon and a welcoming fleet of American warships steamed up. By seven twenty-five, nine battleships were standing alongside the warship and five destroyers that had escorted the *George Washington* across the ocean. Each fired a 21-gun salute as it came by. Twelve destroyers followed the battleships. A little after ten Brest could be seen by the President and the First Lady standing on the bridge with Cary Grayson and the First Lady's secretary, Edith Benham. As they headed in, two French cruisers and nine French destroyers came up from the south firing salutes, the black puffs of smoke visible in the air moments before the roll of the guns could be heard. By eleven-thirty they were fifteen miles off shore, with the *George Washington* leading and the *Wyoming*, the *Pennsylvania*, the *Arkansas*, the *Florida*, the *Utah*, the *Nevada*, the *Oklahoma*, the *New York*, the *Texas* and the *Arizona* ranging behind in double column. The French squadron and the American destroyers followed through a calm sea and under a sky brightening after a dark morning. At one o'clock they entered the narrow strait into the harbor, and the shore batteries in the ten forts on both sides of the cliffs began firing salutes one after the other. The fleet below returned the honor gun for gun, and the booming from the heights and from the water mingled with the clouds of black smoke pouring forth. As the *George Washington* went in, military bands on top of the cliffs crashed into *The Star-Spangled Banner* and *The Marseillaise*. The pounding of the guns was deafening, but when they reached the harbor the noise grew even greater as the sound of the continual firing mixed with the whistles and sirens of the shore craft, ships dressed and yards manned.

A little after one-thirty the *George Washington* dropped anchor a mile off shore, and the escorting and welcoming fleets took up stations around it. As far as the eye could see across the mile-long harbor, ships were standing to, and weaving through them came boats carrying welcomers. Margaret, who had been abroad singing for the troops, came on board with Pershing and a contingent of French officers and dignitaries who bore bouquets and clicked their heels as they bent to kiss the First Lady's hand. Admiral Sims walked up to Pershing, whom he had not seen in some months, and made them all laugh: "Hello, Jack, how the hell did you do it?

I didn't know you had it in you." Two hours later, after lunch, they went ashore in a tender, the President standing by the French Ambassador to the United States, Jules Jusserand, who pointed out the sights. All along the terraced shore they could see fishermen in wooden shoes, velvet coats and flat hats, and women in colorful Breton headdresses and peasant bodices. They reached the quay, where a specially constructed platform was waiting. It was covered with masses of greens and flowers, and as the tender came to it a French marine band burst into the National Anthems of first America and then France. The tender was made fast and the party went ashore, the First Lady escorted by Pershing and the President coming last, walking up the gangplank alone with his silk hat held in his hand in response to the cheers rolling toward him. The French troops and the Americans presented arms, hands slapping smartly on the rifles, and the Mayor of Brest stepped forward to present the President with a large parchment roll made fast with a ribbon of red, white and blue and containing the greetings of the Brest City Council. The Mayor's seven-year-old daughter handed a bouquet to the First Lady and received a kiss in return.

The visitors got into open automobiles and began to ascend the steep road up the cliff to the railroad station, where the private train of President Poincaré of France waited to carry them to Paris. All along the route American soldiers stood at attention, and Ike Hoover, the White House usher, thought he could see their chests swell with pride to be so near their President. Above the road, over the troops and the shouting Bretons and cheering children waving American flags, hung printed signs: HAIL THE CHAMPION OF THE RIGHTS OF MAN. HONOR TO THE APOSTLE OF INTERNATIONAL JUSTICE. HONOR AND WELCOME TO THE FOUNDER OF THE SOCIETY OF NATIONS. The President held his hat in his hand and smiled even though he took note that the sign about the founder of the society of nations was a little premature. At the railroad station there was a pavilion decorated in red silk and the Mayor made a speech, saying destiny brought the American leader to release the people of Europe from their tortures. The train had huge armchairs and picture windows, and at four o'clock they pulled out of the station. Just before they left, the Mayor's little girl came in again with a bouquet which she shyly pushed forward. The President made as if to take the flowers and hand them to the First Lady, but the child hung on and finally got out, "Pour Mademoiselle Veelson," and Margaret bent laughing to kiss her. All along the line to Paris people stood waiting to shout greetings. And in the capital itself the next day there waited the largest throng in the history of France. The weather ever since Armistice Day had been rainy and muddy, but on the day they arrived there was a soft and clear autumn-like sky and a brisk west wind. It seemed the whole of France stood in the streets. From the Madeleine to the Bois de Boulogne not a square foot of space was clear. Stools and tables were put out by the concierges of houses along the parade route, with places on them selling for ten, twenty or fifty francs, depending upon the affluence of the customer. Carpenter horses and boards were arranged into improvised grandstands, and men and boys clung to the very tops of the chestnut trees. The housetops were covered with people. Captured German cannons were ranged along the line of march and the cannons were covered. Lines formed of thirty-six thousand French soldiers, the cream of the Army, stood fast to hold back the crowds; they parted only to allow wounded comrades in wheel chairs to gain places inside the lines so as to see the visitor. The people had gathered hours before the train was due in Paris and stood waiting and looking down toward the station, a tiny bandbox on the edge of the Bois reserved for official arrivals of visiting royalty.

Past them went the chasseurs in blue berets and the spahis in scarlet and white robes, the President Poincaré and Premier Clemenceau. The military bands along the route formed in compact groups and stood silent, and in fact a great silence fell all over Paris and the hundreds of thousands of people, a silence that grew ever more deep, so that when the time came for the train's arrival only the chomping of the cavalry horses could be heard in the completely jammed streets. Then at ten o'clock the first booming of the batteries on Mont Valérien was heard off in the distance: the train was in Paris. Moments later the sound of *The Star-Spangled Banner* came floating up the boulevards from the station and a stir went through the waiting multitudes. After the guns and the music came a new sound, like the distant rumblings of thunder, and it grew louder in turn to the ears of those who stood waiting at the

Porte Dauphine and on the Champs Elysées and Pont Alexander III, in front of the Chamber of Deputies and in the Place de la Concorde: "*Wil-son. Wil-son.*" And then he was in the streets of Paris in a two-horse victoria, sitting by the President of France, with the Garde Républicaine, swords on shoulder and plumes dancing, going on ahead, the cheers coming like waves as he moved. "Vive Wil-son! Vive Wil-son! Vive Wil-son!"

Never, even on Armistice Day, had such cheers been heard. From the windows poured roses, violets, forget-me-nots, holly, greens. The people screamed in holy fervor to the man standing in the victoria and holding outstretched his tall hat. He went under draped flags, and bunting, and an immense electric sign: WELCOME TO WILSON. The military bands beat on their drums and the bugles sounded; the noise was lost in the roaring cheers for the man who would save France from another 1870 and another 1914. The air was filled with coats and jackets thrown aloft after the hats. A huge banner stretched across the Champs Elysées: HONOR TO WILSON THE JUST. Flowers rained down onto the First Lady, so that people could barely see her as she rode in the carriage behind her husband. The President of France looked dazed and pale; he seemed terrified almost by the emotion before him. The American Secret Service men were in a frenzy of fear for their charge, but it was impossible to do anything; the crowds were too enormous, the noise too loud, the press of bodies too great. People grew giddy; women wept as they screamed his name.

"No one ever had such cheers," wrote the journalist William Bolitho. "I, who heard them in the streets of Paris, can never forget them in my life. I saw Foch pass, Clemenceau pass, Lloyd George, generals, returning troops, banners, but Wilson heard from his carriage something different, inhuman—or superhuman. Oh, the immovably shining, smiling man!"

It seemed the Arc de Triomphe would fall before this cascade of sound. His carriage went under it—the first time within the memory of living man this had happened. The Premier of France said, "I do not think there has been anything like it in the history of the world."

Later in the day the President spoke at a luncheon, exchanging toasts with the French President: "All that I have said or tried to do has been said and done only in the attempt to faithfully ex-

press the thoughts of the American people. From the very beginning of this war the thoughts of the people of America turned toward something higher than the mere spoils of war. Their thought
was directed toward the establishment of the eternal principles of
right and justice."

That day French soldiers joined hands to drag German cannons
down the street at a run; French girls screaming with laughter went
along as passengers. That day the overloaded branches of a tree
near the Madeleine broke and half a dozen doughboys tumbled all
over the sidewalk—but it was a day when nothing could go wrong
and they all jumped up unhurt and trooped away, laughing. That
day *Le Petit Parisien* headlined: VIVE WILSON! VIVE WILSON! and *La
Liberté* said Paris had given to him all its fire and all its heart. That
night Paris was ablaze with illuminations and the boulevards were
thronged with singing, dancing, confetti-tossing crowds.

He went to England. French ships escorted him to mid-Channel;
British craft took up the duty there. At Dover the Lord Mayor in
wig and robe greeted him, and little English schoolgirls draped in
American flags threw flowers in his path. In London a wintry haze
hung in the air, but the flags and bunting and triumphal arches
made of choice flowers, richly berried holly, and gilt golden eagles
in front of Charing Cross seemed to glimmer as the guns in Hyde
Park and the Tower pumped off blanks to announce his coming.
A detachment of the Scots Guards was at the station, and the band
of the Grenadiers, and of course the King in field marshal's uniform. They went out over red carpets to the great high red-and-
gold royal carriages drawn by beautifully groomed bays with red
harness and silk on their manes and surrounded by a Sovereign's
Escort and postilions and footmen in royal livery. The people fill-
ing the Strand broke out into a roar for the man who would save
England from another Continental war with its horrors of gas and
mud, and they got under way, the carriages, the Royal Standard
Bearer, the clattering horse escort going by Venetian masts, by the
National Gallery almost hidden by flags and bunting, by the rigid
ranks of the Coldstream Guards. For blocks in all directions the
streets were completely jammed; the newspapers said two million
people stood to see him. From Hyde Park Corner down Constitution Hill the lampposts were draped in scarlet with flags and emblems bearing Imperial and civic emblems. The Royal Horse

Guards band was at Hyde Park Corner to crash into *The Star-Spangled Banner* when the carriages came to it, and bells and chimes rang out over all London. He stood not simply to raise his hat but to wave it boyishly. They went to Buckingham Palace, where the Welsh Guards band waited, and from the balcony looked over at the crowd reaching all down the Mall to the Admiralty half a mile away, overflowing St. James's Park on one side and the Green Park on the other. The crowd screamed for him to speak and waved tiny American flags hawked all through the city that day—"a penny each and all silk"—and he laughed and waved his hand to say no, there would be no speech, and went inside but in a few moments had to go out in answer to the immense rolling sound of hundreds of thousands of voices chanting in unison, "WE WANT WILSON." The First Lady waved a Union Jack as she stood with her husband and the King and Queen. Never had London heard the cheers that reached up toward them.

A royal state dinner, the first held since Great Britain went to war, was given in the palace. Everything on the table was of gold— the candelabra, dishes, forks, spoons, knives. On three different sides of the room were hung gold dishes not used during the dinner; many were the size of tea trays. Beefeaters from the Tower stood in their red uniforms holding in their motionless hands unmoving halberds. Liveried servants were everywhere. The King's hands trembled as he read off a toast; the President replied extemporaneously, addressing his host as "Sir" but not "Your Majesty."

They left London and went up to Carlisle near the Scottish border and to the little church in which the Reverend Thomas Woodrow, his grandfather, had preached. He stood in front of the communion rail, declining to stand in the pulpit, and spoke to the congregation of the little girl who had worshiped in this church before she went to America and womanhood and ultimately motherhood, and of her sense of duty and of what she had taught her son. He spoke of what that son believed: "We shall now be drawn together in a combination of moral force that will be irresistible . . . it is from quiet places like this all over the world that the forces accumulate which presently will overbear any attempt to establish evil." He went along into the vestry to sign the book and the First Lady was glad for his moment of seclusion, for she saw what it meant to him to be in this church.

They went back to Paris and from there to Italy on the royal train of that country. At ten-thirty on the morning of January 2, 1919, they crossed the Franco-Italian frontier at Mentone to the accompaniment of cheers from the Italian troops lined up by the barriers. They headed south, their way at night lighted by blazing bonfires of welcome. In Rome an Alpine infantry guard of honor waited along with the Mayor's Guard in crimson and gold and silver helmets with plumes. In the royal carriage they rode with the King and Queen to the Quirinal Palace. Airplanes roared and a dirigible drifted over the streets covered with golden sand brought from the Mediterranean in compliance with an ancient way of honoring heroes. From the windows of the old houses hung rare old brocades and velvet with coats of arms embroidered upon them, and flowers rained down as swords, handkerchiefs, flags, hats, epaulets flew up into the air. The great cheers rebounded off the Baths of Diocletian and seemed to stir the banners crying HAIL THE CRU-SADER FOR HUMANITY and WELCOME TO THE GOD OF PEACE. Triumphal arches were emblazoned with texts from his writings and in the shopwindows all over Rome his picture stood with burning candles before it. The officials kissed the hand of the man who would return Italy to its former glory; his signature they pressed to their hearts. When he stood on the balcony of the Quirinal he threw kisses to the throngs and they in return hailed him as no one in Rome had ever been hailed, not Caesar and his legions returned from the conquest of Gaul, not anyone. *Epoca* said: "He launched his country into the great conflict with the sole aim of making justice triumph. He comes to Rome and will walk up the Capitoline Hill, whence were dictated to the world the laws of right and justice." The *Corriere d'Italia*: "We thought justice and right had disappeared from the world, when his figure arose." He went to call on Pope Benedict XV and en route to St. Peter's a child was knocked out of its mother's arms by the wild crowds. Margaret saw the accident and had the child, whose nose was scratched, brought to her. She fondled it and kissed the bruised nose and the people went mad, falling on their knees to kiss her hand and screaming, "Long live Miss Wilson! Long live America!"

They left Rome for Milan and again he blew kisses to the wildly cheering people gathered in what the newspapermen said was perhaps the greatest mass of people ever in one spot at any single time in the history of the world. He was gay and easy with the crowds; he waved his arms in time with a band. In Turin the students at the university begged him to speak and he put on one of their blue caps and wore it while saying a few words. The First Lady thought as she looked at him, How young and virile!

He returned to Paris as the man of whom it was said that he could bring to the earth that peace and good will of which the angelic choir sang upon the occasion of the birth of the Messiah at Bethlehem; of whom it was said that no such moral and political power and no such evangel of peace had appeared since Christ preached the Sermon on the Mount; of whom it was said that only Augustus nineteen centuries before had had such an opportunity to create a new world. In the children's ward of a Vienna hospital a Red Cross worker gently told the young patients that in that year of defeat for Austria there could be no Christmas gifts; they cried back, "Wilson is coming. Then everything will be all right." A French teacher asked her class to "describe President Wilson and give your own ideas about him," and one little girl wrote that he wore no beard so there would be more room on his face for the children to kiss. Another wrote, "I wish that President Wilson may never die." In the area of the Allied intervention in northern Russia his picture was almost as common in the peasant huts as the ever-present icon, and from Egypt an American wrote that the natives held him to be the Mahdi, the Mohammedan Messiah calling for revolt that would drive out the English so that he might send Americans to help govern the country. His name was recited as an incantation by the effendis, the harem women, the imams and mullahs; with tomtoms beating and pipes shrilling, crowds in the East cried for hour after hour, "Yahia Dr. Wilson." ("Long Live Dr. Wilson.") In the mountains of the Balkans the villagers settled petty disputes by saying, "President Wilson would have it so." Shakespeare, Caesar, Alexander—two thirds of the earth's inhabitants never heard these names, wrote William T. Ellis, but his name and creed "have found lodgment in a greater number of human minds than any platform or name save Jesus or Mohammed."

On the *George Washington* coming over, the President once grew pensive. "What I seem to see—with all my heart I hope I am wrong—is a tragedy of disappointment," he had said.

4 Paris in the early days of the new year, in January and February of 1919, was filled with the great men of all the world, and behind them, going where they went, were their secretaries, financial experts, generals, admirals. The torn world sent them to Paris pulsing with the conviction that the price of the war be paid by the body and by the purse of the losers. Europe was consumed by more than a score of violent territorial disputes between Russia and Sweden, Belgium and Holland, Italy and Yugoslavia, Albania and Greece, the Czechs and the Poles, the Rumanians and the Hungarians, the others. In the Far East and in Africa the cry was the same: the peace treaty must give justice, the lands and the reparations must be equitably distributed, all wrongs must be righted.

One of the great men of the world had no corps of assistants trailing about with him. Sometimes he took a particular expert to sit beside him as he conferred with the Europeans, but more often he sat alone save for perhaps one secretary at his elbow as he talked and argued with the other great men attended each by half a dozen aides. All day and into the night the conferences over the fate of the world went on; in between there came to see him delegations to tell of their troubles which he might, if he would, cure. The Committee of Mutilated and Wounded Soldiers of Milan came, and the National Union of Railwaymen in England, and the Worshipful Company of Plumbers of London. Prince Charoon of Siam came, and the Carpatho-Russian delegation, the President of the Provisional Government of Albania, the Celtic Circle of Paris, the representatives of the Parliament of Kouban, the Archbishop of Trebizond. Other great men could go golfing on weekends outside Paris, but when they returned, always they saw lights burning in the anterooms and inner chambers where the President's questioners and petitioners waited.

There was no end to the problems that the war brought. The Bolsheviks possessed Russia; it was said they would march into Germany and then into France. Along the areas east of Berlin irregular armies fought nasty pocket wars; in the Orient the Japanese moved into China. For eighteen hours a day, day in and out, the President, the great man of the great men, worked and conferred, often holding several meetings in different rooms at the same time, walking swiftly from one to the other. But no amount of work could change reality, which was that no country, no matter how enormous its losses in the war, could get all that it wanted. And so in the newspapers there appeared criticisms of the way things were going, and the other great men became argumentative. The President began to tire under his load. He developed a nervous habit of talking too much and too definitely, and with the new assertiveness came a nervous little chuckle with which he would interrupt himself. But the problems of who would get what remained.

Besides the foreigners, there were the Americans. "Come home and reduce the high cost of living," wired twenty Democrats of the Massachusetts legislature. Suffragettes sent demands that women deserved the vote; Californians wrote they did not want Japanese men to bring Japanese wives to produce Oriental citizens of their state. Adherents of the Socialist Eugene V. Debs, jailed for sedition, sent petitions asking his release. The President got up at dawn to deal with the questions confronting him, and before breakfast worked two hours. Afterward there would be a conference on a French contention limiting the size of the future German Army, or a Japanese one dealing with racial equality, or an English one concerned with the money to be paid out by Berlin. At lunch there would be guests with axes to grind. Then more sessions, more conferences—who would rule Vilna and who Danzig? At dinner—he gave up changing into evening clothes for the meal— there would be more talk. Afterward the journalist Ray Stannard Baker would come to talk of what news should be given out to the clamoring American reporters. Then there would be several hours of reading the petitions and looking at the maps and studying the reports. There was no time for golf and none for auto rides. He became gaunt, haggard and pale. Under the stress of wartime Washington the President had developed a twitching around one eye, and now this new tension made not only the eye but half of his face jerk up and down in a spasmodic fashion. Secretary of the Navy Josephus Daniels came over to try to help out his chief; he found the strain such that ever after he said he spent a whole year in Paris in one month.

In February, after two months abroad, the President briefly returned to Washington in order to take care of pressing matters. He stayed a few days in America and then sailed back to France and the unending talks and meetings, the interminable arguments and compromises and arrangements. The normal haggling of an American Congress, or of any Parliament, was nothing compared to the Paris of 1919 wherein met the men who spoke for hundreds of millions of people certain that any abridgment of their claims meant that the entire war had been fought for nothing. The God of Peace and Apostle of International Justice, the great man of the great men, began to shrink in the eyes of those who dealt with him. He said that perhaps Italy was not entitled to territories Yugoslavia wanted, and in Rome his picture was torn down. He opposed a partition of Germany that would give France full sway over thousands of miles of undoubted German territory, and the French Premier accused him of favoring the late enemy at the expense of the French people who had sacrificed so much. Explosive rumors sprang into being in the Paris salons; the statesmen reacted to them, or passed them on, and, at once, frightened and angry men came to the President to cry that Evil was attempting to despoil their people and their ideals. "God knows I wish I could give them all they hope for, but only He Himself could do that," the President sighed.

"Everyone seems to look to him, big and little," wrote home Ike Hoover, the White House usher brought to take charge of the President's living quarters, "and yet no one seems to really wish to help him. It is a selfish world we are living in, especially over here. Everyone seems to be trying to further their own interests and to the Devil with the other fellow. It is a selfish bunch."

Hoover fell ill in the closely confined life they all led, and so did the First Lady and her secretary, Edith Benham, and so did Cary Grayson.° But more than illness, a pall of depression slowly descended upon the Americans. The cheers had been so great and the promise so fine, and now there came all the talking and arguing and the long discussions. . . . It all seemed meaningless. To Ray Stannard Baker the whole business seemed futile, boundlessly futile. He felt himself surrounded by ancient European hates, suspicions and fears, and came to think that perhaps it was all a profitless thing that they had ever gone to the war and to Paris. "I'm going to get the willeys if this keeps up!" said the President's stenographer, Charles Swem.

And the President grew thin and gray and his hair seemed to whiten day by day. The twitching of his face was continuous. During the infrequent moments when he was away from his work he would sit silently, or play solitaire, a bent man no longer young, shuffling and dealing the cards. His temper grew short; he could refer to Lloyd George and Clemenceau as "madmen" and bitterly say that the Irish petitioners for home rule were devoted only to "miserable mischief-making." "Logic! Logic! I don't give a damn for logic!" he burst out. He seemed worn and old and his only exercise came when Grayson would stand him before an open window and grasp his hands to pull him vigorously to and fro so that at least a little color would come to his cheeks. At night when Baker would come he found the President utterly exhausted and worn out and growing grayer and grayer and grimmer and grimmer, with the lines in his face deepening beneath his eyes. He looked tired all the time; he said he felt as if he could go to sleep standing up. "I get so I cannot understand why he does not crumble up," Hoover wrote home. "I wonder if the Doctor notices it as I do." Grayson did notice, of course, and he begged the President to slow down. "Give me time," the President answered. "We are running a race with Bolshevism and the world is on fire. Let us wind up this work here and then we will go home and find time

° Grayson at this time held the rank of Rear Admiral, promoted by Presidential request despite complaints from certain anti-Administration Congressmen.

for a little rest and play and take up our health routine again." The killing work went on. His voice grew hoarse, he suffered from indigestion and heartburn, and he developed headaches; one blinding one he attributed to "bottled-up wrath at Lloyd George" and the Prime Minister's demands for impossible reparations from the Germans.

He could not go on in this way. On April 3 a fit of coughing seized him. All day his voice had been husky and by evening he could hardly talk. Grayson took his temperature: it was 103. The doctor was terrified, thinking to himself that the President had been poisoned. Such was the rumor that flew over Paris: he had been poisoned by germs slipped into the ice in his drinking water. He took to his bed. The coughing was frighteningly violent and so severe that he could not get his breath for long moments at a time. Grayson sat with him all night and the First Lady acted as nurse, but he could not keep food down and suffered violent diarrhea. To Dr. Grayson the situation seemed very serious; it was influenza, he decided. The fever kept up and the President could not sleep, he who had always been able to sleep—to "pull down the curtains of my mind"—no matter what aggravations were his. When he dozed off for a few minutes he came awake to racking coughs that Grayson could not stop. His entire digestive system was completely out of control and his face grew alarmingly thin, its gauntness emphasizing the luminous eyes.

He insisted on getting back to work and sent word to the Premiers of France, England and Italy that unless they were afraid of catching his disease he wanted them to come to his room for more conferences and more arguments. They came and he sat up in bed to go over with them yet once again the questions of who got what. Grayson and the First Lady were outside the door, telling each other he should never have gone back to work so soon, and Grayson cabled Joe Tumulty in Washington that the President was working too hard in spite of the illness: "This is a matter that worries me." Tumulty cabled the President a plea that he not strain his constitution and the President sent back a grim joke in reply: "Constitution? Why man, I'm already living on my by-laws."

There came a night of burning fever and Grayson, backed by the First Lady, absolutely forbade any more work. The patient had no strength with which to fight. For three days he slept—a fitful slumber.

When he awoke, he sent for his reports and his papers, he held his conferences. And he ruled that it was over, the fight was lost. The Italians were too wild in their demands, the French greedy, the British unreasonable. He told Grayson to order the captain of the *George Washington* to prepare for an immediate return to the United States. "I will retire in good order; we will go home." At once the Europeans came flying to promise moderation and compromise. Clemenceau might privately say the President was like a cook who keeps her trunk ready in the hall, and the French papers might say he was like a spoiled child threatening to run home to Mama, but the demands were scaled down and conciliatory gestures made.

He stayed. But in the American delegation they could no longer understand their chief. He became obsessed by the idea that the French servants—the waiters, the porters, the cleaning women—everyone—were all spies who spoke perfect English and reported to their government every word he said. It was useless to point out that three quarters of them knew no more than a few words of English, for he insisted it was not so. He locked all his documents in a safe he kept near him.

At the same time he began to worry about the furnishings of the Paris house in which he was staying. He wanted everything itemized; he said things were being stolen. "Coming from the President," Ike Hoover wrote, "these were very funny things, and we could but surmise that something queer was happening in his mind." He began to check very carefully on the use of the delegation's automobiles, ordering they be used only for strictly official trips even though, before, he had urged the cooped-up staff to go for relaxing drives and trips. Suddenly, also, he decided the furniture in a room was wrongly arranged and spent half an hour with Grayson moving the couches and tables back and forth. And quite as suddenly he turned on Colonel House. House suggested the President spare himself some of his labors by making better use of aides instead of trying to carry the load alone; it meant House was trying to plant spies by his side and subvert him.

His tone and his attitude toward the Europeans and his own Americans alike bespoke a disturbing secretiveness and dourness. He spoke to the former in what they considered an infuriating fashion: they thought him the schoolmaster criticizing errant boys all over again, and they suspected his motives. "I never knew anyone to talk more like Jesus Christ and act more like Lloyd George," said Clemenceau. The Americans he largely ignored. He dismissed the views of Secretary of State Robert Lansing and lectured his experts on their own fields of expertise. He was extremely impatient in his dealings with people, kicking his legs in irritation and walking fretfully about the room. The criticisms of the French press angered him and he threatened to force the transfer of the entire business to another country. There was a petulance in the way he labored over his typewriter on his reports, as if to indicate no secretary could do it right. His work in a way was brilliant, for he was able to compress scores and hundreds of difficult problems in his mind and come up with answers to them—perhaps no one else in the world could have done it—but that he was doing it more and more by himself exposed him to the great dangers of forgetful mistakes.

Through it all, though—the irritability and ill-health which made him if not cool to his wife (for he could never be cool to her), then unresponsive to her cheeriness; through the highhandedness to his colleagues—he clung to one great central idea: the establishment of a League of Nations which would be a forum for the dispensation of justice for all men and wipe out the threat of war forever. If the peace treaty possessed flaws—and who could say it would not?—then the League would exist to remedy those flaws. As a boy in a barn near his minister-father's church he had composed a set of rules by which his boys' club would be governed, and as a man he had for decades studied the problems of how men can live with one another within the framework of laws. Now as a President and most powerful man in the world he worked for a League of laws and intelligence to deal with whole nations standing before a bar of international justice.

In this he never wavered. He talked about it on Memorial Day of 1919, on May 30, when he went to the American Army graveyard at Suresnes to speak over the dead boys in their freshly dug graves. He attempted in that speech to say what it was they died for and to give meaning to those deaths, and the journalist Ray Stannard Baker, listening, thought to himself it was the greatest speech he had ever heard in his life, it was so perfectly turned, so sure, so musical and so appealing in that hour in that place. Another speech of another war President came into Baker's mind—the speech made at Gettysburg.

In the acacia groves on a hillside from which one could gaze off to the valley of the Seine and to Paris, he stood bareheaded under a hot, bright sun near the old fortress of Mont Valérien, dust from the new cemetery rising from under the feet of the listening thousands, many of whom were wounded soldiers, and said:

"So it is our duty to take and maintain the safeguards which will see to it that the mothers of America and the mothers of France and England and Italy and Belgium and all the other suffering nations should never be called upon for this sacrifice again. This can be done. It must be done, and it will be done. The great thing that these men left us . . . is the great instrument of the League of Nations...

"If we do not know courage, we cannot accomplish our purpose and this age is an age that looks forward, not backward; which rejects the standard of national selfishness that once governed the counsels of nations and demands that they shall give way to a new order of things in which the only questions will be, 'Is it right?' 'Is it just?' 'Is it in the interest of mankind?'

"Ladies and gentlemen: we all believe, I hope, the spirits of these men are not buried with their bones. Their spirits live. I hope—I believe—that their spirits are present with us at this hour. I hope that I feel the compulsion of their presence. I hope that I realize the significance of their presence. Think, soldiers, of those comrades of yours who are gone. If they were here, what would they say?

"They would remember America . . . they would remember the terrible field of battle. They would remember what . . . they had come for and how worthwhile it was to give their lives for it.

"'We command you in the names of those who, like ourselves, have died to bring the counsels of men together, and we remind you what America said she was born for. She was born, she said, to show mankind the way to liberty. She was born to make this great gift a common gift. She was born to show men the way of experience by which they might realize this gift and maintain it.'

"Make yourselves soldiers once for all in this common cause, where we need wear no uniform except the uniform of the heart, clothing ourselves with the principles of right, and saying to men everywhere: 'You are our brothers and we invite you into the comradeship of liberty and peace.' Let us go away hearing this unspoken mandate of our dead comrades.

"If I may speak a personal word, I beg you to realize the compulsion that I myself feel I am under. By the Constitution of our great country, I was the Commander in Chief of these men. I advised the Congress to declare that a state of war existed. I sent these lads over here to die. Shall I—can I—ever speak a word of counsel which is inconsistent with the assurance I gave them when they came over? It is inconceivable. There is something better, if possible, that a man can give than his life, and that is his living spirit to a service that is not easy, to resist counsels that are hard to resist, to stand against purposes that are difficult to stand against, and to say, 'Here I stand, consecrated in the spirit of the men who were once my comrades, and who are now gone, and who left me under eternal bonds of fidelity.'"

The First Lady, on crutches because of an infected foot, sat in a car. Near her was her secretary, Edith Benham, and in the crowd were Miss Benham's two young servicemen assistants, whom she sent to the ceremonies because she wanted them to have something, some ideals, a memory, to take home and make a part of their lives. Listening, she wondered if the boys would care for the speech. She found later that they were so moved they did not know if they ought to stand still or applaud at the end; that sitting next to one of them was a "little roughneck motorcycle driver" and that the driver cried.

At the end the President took a wreath sent by the Boy Scouts of America and moved to place it by the graves. A Frenchwoman came up to him; she said, "Mr. President, may I be permitted to add these flowers to those which you have just deposited here as a tribute to the American dead who in sacrificing their lives saved the lives of thousands of Frenchmen? My two boys were killed in battle."

A month later, work done, the Versailles Treaty and the Covenant of the League of Nations completed, the President and First Lady sailed for America.

On July 10, 1919, the President came before the Senate of the United States to present to it for its approval the treaty and the Covenant. Two of the Senators refused to stand up when he entered.

In the eyes of most of the men before him as he began to speak he was the schoolmaster incarnate raised to unthinkable heights from which he flung down not requests but dictates. In the most recent election, that of November of 1918, days before the Armistice, he had asked the country to give him a Congress dominated by members of his own party. The request seemed unfair, partisan, to many voters; a Republican House and Senate were elected. But the President ignored the verdict and the implied suggestion that Republicans should have something to do with the peace and treaty-making and took no Republican of stature with him to Paris. Once there, he consulted only with himself. And in fact he had always been a self-contained thinker and planner, always treating politicians, even those of his own party (let alone the opposition) with suspicion. It was futile to spend much time with them, he said. No Senators were ever asked to a sociable lunch at the White House; their opinions were rarely requested under any circumstances. If given gratuitously, they were ignored.

Now he stood before them as the world figure of his time. He had burst all narrower confines. Looking down at him from the press gallery, the journalist Henry L. Stoddard, shocked somewhat by the pallor of his face and his worn look, thought to himself that below stood a being utterly suffused with arrogance and the certainty that as he had dictated the laws and remade the map the job must needs have been done right and that therefore upon it these Senators must stamp, and quickly, their approval. There was a sureness about the speaker, Stoddard thought, that was the confidence of one who saw world Utopia as the result of *his* labors. Looking up at him from their seats, the Senators—human beings, after all—saw with senatorial eyes their dignity being shredded by a President who seemed to be saying to them, and bluntly so, that as he had redone the world, so now it was their duty to approve his work and then be gone. He was in their eyes

the man who, when the war was over, had the government take
over the oceanic cables so that the American people at home would
learn just what he, and he alone, wanted them to learn about the
Paris negotiations. And those negotiations in the end, many Senators thought, repealed the Declaration of Independence and took
away the liberty of action of the United States and surrendered
its rights and made it, as Theodore Roosevelt's daughter Alice put
it, "merely a pawn in Mr. Wilson's campaign for the Presidency
of the Federation of the World."

And now this would-be emperor aping the Hohenzollerns and
Hapsburgs stood before the Senate demanding a rubber-stamped
"Yes!" upon his treaty and his League. All wartime unity and re-
straint gone, Senators opened fire. "Britain's tool—a dodger and
a cheater"° sought with his League to open "Pandora's box of
evil" to "empty upon the American people the aggregated calam-
ities of the world and send the Angel of Death into every American
home, embargo our commerce, close our exchanges, destroy our
credits, leave our merchandise rotting on our piers, shut the Isth-
mian canal, order Congress to declare war, levy taxes, appropriate
money, raise and support armies and navies, dispatch our men to
any part of the globe to fight because an alien Council so willed."°°
This was the man who spoke so much of sacrifice but made a great
ship his pleasure yacht for European jaunts, lived in the palaces of
princes and accepted "presents from foreign diplomats worth hundreds of thousands of dollars"°°°—"more than a million."† He was
"trying to impose his arbitrary will on the nation . . . seeking to
hand over American destiny to the secret councils of Europe" or to
the black races, or the Pope, or "greedy, conscienceless England."††
"I feel as if I had been wandering with Alice in Wonderland and
had tea with the Mad Hatter."†††

Above all the Senators, the most powerful, the most brilliant,
stood the Majority Leader: Henry Cabot Lodge of Massachusetts.
As a young man working as editor of the *International Review*, he
had accepted an article sent in by a Princeton University senior

° Senator Borah
°° Senator Sherman
°°° Senator Reed
† Senator Penrose
†† Senator Johnson
††† Senator Knox

who never before had published an article in a non-college magazine. The author of the article, which was titled "Cabinet Government in the United States," went on to become a college professor, college president, Governor of New Jersey and President of the United States. Editor and author met when the latter came to Washington as President. They met and clashed, each during the war publicly intimating the other was a liar. Once the President refused to sit on the same platform with the Senator for a ceremony honoring the hundredth anniversary of a Washington church; it was said the Senator was infuriated by the fact that before the President took office the Senator was "the scholar in politics" and that afterward he was "*a* scholar in politics." Henry Cabot Lodge saw the President as thinking steadily of a third term; the President's friends said the Senator hoped to remodel the League in his own image and so gain his party's nomination for the Presidency in 1920. Senator Lodge did not hide his hatred of the President. "Shifty," he said.° He agreed with his best friend, Theodore Roosevelt, when Roosevelt spoke of the President's "hypocrisy, his inefficiency, his rancorous partisanship and his selfish eagerness to sacrifice all patriotic considerations to whatever he thinks will be of benefit to himself politically."

Together with Roosevelt, Lodge had conspired, even as the President sailed to Europe, to defeat any League of Nations that might be brought back. Frustrated and bitter, his death but weeks away, Roosevelt lay on his sickbed and with Lodge sitting by planned that defeat. Even earlier, before the President left, Lodge handed Henry White, the only Republican member of the Peace Commission, a memorandum saying that the American people and Senate were against the planned League. White was secretly to give this memorandum to the Europeans, Lodge explained; it would strengthen their own doubts about the League. (White did not do as Lodge asked.)

While the President was in Europe, Roosevelt died. But when the President returned, Lodge was waiting. He had said that he never expected to hate anyone as he hated the President. The President could match him. He held the Senators opposing him, par-

---

° He also summed up his view of the President's intellectual attainments by saying: "Not a scholar in the true sense of the word."

ticularly Lodge, to be "contemptible . . . narrow . . . selfish . . . poor little minds that never get anywhere but run round in a circle and think they are going somewhere . . . I cannot express my contempt . . . If I said what I think about those fellows in Congress, it would take a piece of asbestos two inches thick to hold it." °

These, then, were the two forces which must merge and agree before the United States would enter the League of Nations. The President held that the Senate must ratify what he had brought back without changing a word of it; the majority of Senators took the position that changes were needed and that they would put them in before they ratified anything. Senator Lodge worked out a series of stipulations as to what conditions the United States would demand before entering the League, and his backers said those amendments or reservations would guard American rights and sovereignty. The President refused to budge on the rules and regulations worked out in Paris. He pointed out that if the United States entered only under special stipulations every country would also have the right to attach its own conditions and that the result would be chaos. He had signed his name as President, he said, and had given his word in the name of the American people. He could not take back that signature nor rescind that word. Colonel House counseled compromise, but his words no longer held any influence. The President told House you get nothing worthwhile in this world without fighting for it and he would fight for the League.

Washington's summer of that year saw the President try to convince individual Senators to come over to his side. He was not yet ready to fight. Son-in-law McAdoo said the speech presenting the treaty and Covenant to the Senate was noble but that it was a case of "casting pearls before swine," and although the President may have agreed, he tried face-to-face meetings in an attempt to elicit senatorial promises to vote for the League as it stood. But the endeavor did not appear to be succeeding and meanwhile Senator Lodge, chairman of the Foreign Relations Committee as well as

° In the years since 1919, many people have come to believe that the President termed the League enemies a "little group of willful men." But the remark was made years earlier and concerned senatorial opponents of a ship-arming bill.

Majority Leader, gathered headlines as his group considered what to do. He began his committee hearings by reading aloud, personally, the entire text of the treaty and Covenant. The task took him two weeks, his voice droning on in a committee room entirely empty save for one clerk who had to take down what he said. After that the committee had before it witness after witness to paint black pictures of what the League would do to the formerly free and independent United States.

Realizing he was not doing well with his conferences with the individual Senators, the President turned to the idea that the men in the Capitol, the politicians, would not do the right thing unless they were bludgeoned into it, and that the only force capable or able to do that job was the united voice of the American people. He had always said that most of the Senators in Washington did not know the real thoughts of their constituents anyway. He began more and more to speak of taking a speech-making trip across the country to the West Coast to arouse the people's opinions and voices that would brush away senatorial objections and put the United States, unencumbered, into the League meant to bring peace to the world for all time to come.

While he considered such a move, he tried to relax and recuperate from the exertions and sickness and tenseness of Paris. There were still deep lines of exhaustion in his ravaged and weary face, and Grayson and the First Lady worked to smooth them away. They took him to play golf every day, and in the hot Washington evenings they went with him for long slow drives. Constantly he was still meeting with Senators, but the trend was against him and he grew impatient. In Europe the Rumanians were invading Hungary and the Armenians were battling Soviet and Turkish troops advancing from opposite directions, and the Poles were fighting the Ukrainians, and still his United States was not in the League nor hurrying to get into it. In the power and machinery of the League lay the cure for every injustice, he said—but the Senators kept talking.

The President began to speak as though his tour were inevitable, calling it the "appeal to Caesar"—the people. And increasingly it appeared that the tour would be necessary. For above the Senate, and above Lodge's level Brahmin voice in the committee room, there lived in the country the American fear and contempt for the Europeans and their everlasting wars and intrigues. The essence, the very life, of American diplomacy for two centuries had been aloofness from European involvement. In the little towns where the paving ended at the limits where the trolley made its turn-around, and in the cities lying inland from the Eastern seaboard all the way to the Pacific, Europe was strange, foreign, different—bad. The President once said that it was the men talking in the grocery stores of a thousand towns who formed American public opinion, and now he knew those men were saying that America had made the world safe for democracy and perhaps that was all America should be expected to do. In the White House the President of those men and their families said America must do more, and that the men in the grocery stores must know that and understand it and endorse it.

But there was the question of his health. His wife and doctor, with all their strength and fear, fought against the picture of a jolting train and poor sleeping arrangements, of irregular hours and endless parades and talks and receptions, the heat of summer and the pumping hands of admirers, the noise, the excitement. The President went so far as to say he would go in August, but Grayson persuaded him to cancel the idea temporarily. All through the hot and terrible summer of Washington the President kept returning to the idea of rallying the moral opinion of the country to the League. He had Senator Watson of Indiana in and asked him, "Where am I on this fight?" and Watson replied, "Mr. President, you are licked. There is only one way you can take the United States into the League of Nations." "Which way is that?" "Accept it with the Lodge reservations." Fire came into the President's eyes and he said, "*Lodge* reservations? Never! I'll never consent to adopt any policy with which that impossible name is so prominently identified." Watson left, the President's last words staying with him: "I'll appeal to the country."

The journalist H. H. Kohlsaat came to see him in the Blue Room one morning and found him looking unwell and weak as he talked of his proposed tour. "You are too ill to take that long trip," Kohlsaat said. "The heat will be intense in Ohio, Indiana, Illinois, Iowa and Nebraska. You will break down before you reach the

Rockies." The President seemed to be trembling. "I don't care if I die the next minute after the treaty is ratified," he said.

Finally it seemed as if he had decided in his mind that it must be done. Grayson went to see him to make the final appeal of a doctor telling his patient that he could not be responsible for the consequences. He walked into the President's study and found him writing there. The President looked up. "I know what you have come for," he said. "I do not want to do anything foolhardy, but the League of Nations is now in its crisis and if it fails I hate to think of what will happen to the world. You must remember that I, as Commander in Chief, was responsible for sending our soldiers to Europe. In the crucial test of the trenches they did not turn back—and I cannot turn back now. I cannot put my personal safety, my health, in the balance against my duty.

"I must go."

Grayson bowed and left the room.

5

On Wednesday, September 3, 1919, at six-forty in the evening, they left the White House to go to Union Station—the President, the First Lady, Grayson, Tumulty. Two dozen reporters would be with them, eight Secret Service men, a corps of aides and a valet for him, a maid for her, a double train crew. The train was seven cars long; the President's blue car, the *Mayflower*, last in line. They would be traveling 9,981 miles, almost to the Canadian border, almost to the Mexican. Every state west of the Mississippi except four would be visited, and it would take twenty-seven days, with twenty-six major stops and at least ten rear-platform speeches a day. All through the planning stage Grayson and the First Lady pleaded that some rest days be scheduled —perhaps a week at the Grand Canyon—but the President would not allow it: "This is a business trip, pure and simple."

Tumulty was also concerned about the omission of any relaxation periods, thinking to himself as they stood on the railroad platform just before getting under way that never had he seen the President—"Governor" to Tumulty since their New Jersey statehouse days—look so weary. In those Trenton years, in his secretary's eyes, he was vigorous, agile, slender, an active man with hair only slightly streaked with gray. Now he was an old man, gray and grim, to Tumulty's mind like a warrior determined to fight on to the end. The President said to him, "I am in a nice fix. I have not had a single minute to prepare my speeches. I do not know how I shall get the time, for during the past few weeks I have been suffering from daily headaches. But perhaps tonight's rest will make me fit for the work of tomorrow."

The three men and the woman went into the *Mayflower*'s sitting room and ordered cool drinks. Out to serve them came a tiny Negro White House servant, "Little" Jackson (sometimes "Major" Jackson), wearing a gigantic mushroom-shaped chef's hat almost as big as he. It sheltered him like a toadstool, the First Lady thought. They all burst into laughter—which pleased Tumulty, who had gone to some trouble to get the hat made.

They halted for a moment in the Baltimore train yards and some Red Cross workers gathered around to wish them luck and offer cigarettes and sandwiches. The cigarettes the President declined by saying he never smoked; he also said he wouldn't take any food as they had just dined on the train and he was "about filled up." Shortly after, they all went to bed. In the morning the reporters came for a press conference, but they distressed the President. "They ask me such foolish questions," he sighed. They stopped for a few minutes at Dennison, Ohio, where a new locomotive was attached to the train, and some thirty or forty persons gathered beneath the *Mayflower*'s rear platform to hear the President say good morning, glad to see you, how are you, as he shook hands all around. An old man looked up and said, "I wish you success on your journey, Mr. Wilson. I lost two sons in the war; only got one left and I want things fixed up so I won't have to lose him." The people broke into applause.

They headed for Columbus and his first speech and before noon they were there. The COLUMBUS WELCOMES YOU sign at the railroad station was enlarged to include OUR PRESIDENT, and the city's school children had been dismissed from classes for the day. On Broad Street hundreds of them were assembled to wave American flags. They broke ranks and came running through the police lines and Army band that led the slow-moving automobile parade to trot along beside his car, where he stood wearing a straw hat although Labor Day was past. Airplanes from Ohio State University's landing field zoomed overhead and dropped flowers on the crowd. At the hall where he would speak he waited backstage for a moment while the First Lady, in blue dress and Russian sable scarf and with a checked coat over her arm, went out before the people. There was considerable applause for him when he appeared, but it was not the applause he had heard in Paris, London and Rome months before.

"My fellow citizens," he began, "it is with great pleasure that I greet you. I have long chafed at confinement in Washington and I have wanted to report to you and other citizens of the United States. It has become increasingly necessary that I should report to you." He spoke with no notes, saying, "This is what the League of Nations is for: it is to prove to the nations of the world that the nations will combine against any nation that would emulate Germany's example. When you are told that the League of Nations is for any purpose but to prevent war, tell them that it is not so." He smacked his hands together when he spoke of the war and said, "The League of Nations is the only thing that can prevent the recurrence of this tragedy and redeem our promises. And when this treaty is accepted, as it will be accepted, men in khaki will not have to cross the seas again!"

Outside the hall his car was halted for a few minutes while escorting Army troops fell into line. People jammed up against the vehicle. He stood up and waved his hat and the crowd clapped hands, but the reporters thought the applause relatively restrained. And the crowds were not as large as expected. Perhaps it was because the Columbus trolleymen were on strike and the streetcars from the outlying areas were not running, but perhaps also it was because all over America that September railroad men, plumbers, rubber workers, machinists, cigar makers, chorus girls, potters, shoe workers, electrical workers, all these and others were on strike and there were people in Columbus (and elsewhere) who felt that a President ought to be doing something about the worst labor situation in the country's history instead of gallivanting about, talking of the troubles of far-off places and (in the eyes of some) laying the groundwork for his Presidency of the World or of the United States for a third term.

Just two hours after they arrived they left Columbus, ten minutes of their time having been spent beside the waiting train greeting the local dignitaries presented by the Mayor and a former Governor. An Army veteran told the reporters he had been in Paris when the President entered the city: "I never will forget that day. All Americans were princes and Woody was King." But the man also thought the President looked a lot older now.

They headed for Indianapolis, halting for a few minutes at Urbana, Ohio. "You will beat them," a man called out. "Their case is so weak they are not hard to beat," the President answered. They went on. Earlier the day had been overcast, but now the sun came out, baking both the lush fields around them and the jolting cars of the rolling train. At Richmond, Indiana, he spoke from the rear platform for six minutes: "Shall we or shall we not sustain the first great act of international justice? The thing wears a very big aspect when you look at it that way, and all little matters seem to fall away and one seems ashamed to bring in special interests, particularly party interests." The Secret Service men were in a semicircle, holding the people back, and he was up on the platform crying, "What difference does party make when mankind is involved?"

Outside Indianapolis a local reception committee came aboard to ride in on the *Mayflower*, and he talked with them in the lounge compartment. They pulled into the station at six in the evening and went at once in a motorcade to the Indianapolis Coliseum. The Indiana State Fair was in session and people came streaming in from the midway, deserting the prize cattle and the exhibits to jam the arena. The crowd was unruly and seemed, in the eyes of the reporters, to view the President and First Lady—she in a gown with a gray georgette bodice and a dark blue velvet skirt—as simply an added attraction to the fair. The Governor of the state began an introductory speech, but the crowd did not quiet down even when the Mayor of Indianapolis got up to ask that they do so. Finally the President arose. "I am making this journey as an American and as a champion of the rights which America believes in——" But still the crowd was noisy and those in the back, unable to hear him, made for the doors, which added to the clamor. A state official got up and told those who wanted to leave that they should do so at once; afterward police would bar the doors. Several thousand people in the rear walked out and his speech went on: "If it is not to be this arrangement, what arrangement do you suggest to secure the peace of the world? It is a case of put up or shut up."

They left at ten and went on to St. Louis, a pilot engine running two minutes in front of them. They arrived at four in the morning and at eight a dozen youths of the Junior Chamber of Commerce came to volunteer to carry baggage or do anything needed. Behind them came a reception committee to greet him with yells when at nine he came down from the train in a straw hat. He went to the Hotel Statler in a motorcade, waving. But the cheers were not boisterous and there were no children: school was open in St. Louis that day. In the hotel lobby there was a band that burst into *The Star-Spangled Banner* as he entered, and he came to attention for it and then went up in the elevator to a room where he met with members of the reception committee brought in by twos and threes to pump his arm up and down and hear him say that St. Louis was a wonderful city and he was charmed to be there. He went downstairs to a businessmen's luncheon in the hotel ballroom where he spoke of his Senate opponents, saying they were "contemptible quitters" did they "fail to see the game through." Cigar smoke drifted up to him from the thousand men and made more intense the headache he had had all day. He cried, "America was not founded to make money; it was founded to lead the world on the way to liberty." At the end there was a dash to get on line so that every man could tell his children he shook hands with the President, and then he went upstairs to work on the speech he would give that night.

It was twilight when he went to the hall to sit on a platform in a hard steel chair from which he rose to cry out to the thousands of listeners that "if we keep out of this arrangement war will come soon. If we go into it war will never come." From the hall they drove to the station, arriving there at nine-fifteen. Crowds gathered by the *Mayflower*, and when Grayson and the Governor of the state appeared on the platform they were greeted by shouts of "We want Wilson!" He came out to bow and when at eleven the train pulled out the people got another glimpse of him through the window of the car, sitting at his desk in the evening warmth and working on his next speech, typing, typing. The next morning he was up early when the train stopped to kill some time in Independence so as not to get to Kansas City before the scheduled arrival time of eight o'clock. Housewives came running from their homes when word spread that the President was there, most of them wearing big cottage aprons and Mother Hubbards. One apologized, saying they would have dressed up had they known beforehand he would stop in their town, but he said he was glad to see them "just as you are." They asked if the First Lady would not come out, and she did so and the women burst into applause. In Kansas City at eight the heat was already quite intense and he had to shout at the reception committee in order that his words be heard above the hubbub of the crowd gathered outside the *Mayflower*. There were flowers for the First Lady—"Oh thank you, they're beautiful"—and clicking movie cameras. The headache was worse.

Kansas City, the voice hoarse: "I have come to fight a cause, and that cause is greater than the U. S. Senate!" At noon they were back on the train with its white "special" flags flying from both sides of the locomotive. He turned to the milling crowd behind the police lines and cupped his hands to shout, "I've had a great time here!" Between smiles, the reporters noticed, his face wore the most serious of looks; the headache was continuous for most of the hours of the day.

They hurried north as the second section of the regular train. At St. Joseph they stopped for three minutes and a crowd shouted, "Speech! Speech!" but Grayson asked him to spare his voice, so he only leaned down over the platform rail, almost bending double, and shook some of the dozens of hands thrust up at him. Fathers held their children on their shoulders to see, and a group of Red Cross women got him and the First Lady to sign their roster. Newspaper people from Des Moines came aboard to ride the train into their city, and at eight that night they pulled in to where the reception committee waited—representatives of the Commerce, Trades and Labor Assembly of the city, the Grand Army of the Republic post, the Ladies of the Grand Army of the Republic, the Spanish-American War Veterans, the Rotary, the City Federation of Women's Clubs, the War Camp Community Service, the Salvation Army, the Red Cross, the Soldiers Fathers League, the League to Enforce Peace, officials of the City of Des Moines and the State of Iowa, the Greater Des Moines Chamber of Commerce, people from the Des Moines *News,* the *Register and Tribune,* the *Capital.* He shook hands all around and went to stand before ten thousand people in the Coliseum and cry out—there were no mechanical devices to project his voice—that "the world is waiting,

waiting to see not whether we will take part, but whether we will serve and lead, for it has expected us to lead."

That night they slept at the Hotel Fort Des Moines, their first night off the train, and he told his people he felt like taking three baths to wash off the train grime. The next day, Sunday, the reporters went driving and to play golf and tennis while he complied with the rule of his church that there be no work on the Sabbath. But of course there were the forthcoming speeches to be worked on, and when he and the First Lady went to the Central Presbyterian Church there were crowds hoping to shake his hand and, inside, people stretching in their seats to see the visitors. Meanwhile a Missouri priest said the League was a Wall Street plot. The clergyman was echoed by the Socialist Victor Berger of Milwaukee declaring it was a "capitalist scheme" to bring "more wars and more armaments."

At midnight they left Des Moines for Omaha. Originally it had been intended to arrive there at five in the morning and for the party to remain sleeping in the rail yards until the reception committee came at nine, but Grayson felt the President would rest better in some quieter place and so the train halted by a siding near Underwood, Iowa, fifteen miles northeast of Council Bluffs. They slept there by a quiet cornfield. At Omaha there were sirens, noisemakers, auto horns blaring to welcome him, and a battery of photographers. "Stand by your guns," the President said to them, and they in return said, "Please have Mrs. Wilson turn this way and smile." "I have no control over that little lady," he answered. He looked better, the reporters traveling with him thought; the quiet Sunday and the night by the cornfield seemed to have done much good.

Omaha: "I predict there would be another world war within a generation if no pains were taken to prevent it. If this guarantee is not lived up to, I want to say that in another generation or two we must have another and far more disastrous war. If I felt that I stood in the way of this settlement of the world's affairs, I would be glad to die that it might be consummated." After his talk people came rushing up past the guards and jumping over the press table to grab his hand. At the train a crowd was yelling "We want Wilson," and he told the Secret Service men to form them up into a line so that he could shake hands with several hundreds of them. By noon they were on their way north to Sioux Falls, South Dakota, stopping along the way, as always, for him to make brief talks from the rear platform.

They spent two hours in Sioux Falls: out of the train; the motorcade with the cheers and his responding wave; the speech: "America may have the distinction of leading the way! . . . I sometimes think, when I wake up in the night, of the wakeful nights that anxious fathers, mothers, and friends spent during the weary years of the awful war, and I hear the cry of the mothers of the children, millions on the other side and thousands on this side: 'In God's name give us security and peace and right'"—and then they were again in the lurching autos and back to the train and going on. He tried to sleep as they went through the night to St. Paul, but it was difficult for him. In the morning at the St. Paul station fifteen hundred girls of the War Camp Community Service waited, and as soon as he appeared on the *Mayflower*'s platform they burst out into a nonsensical get-up-in-the-morning war song: "Good morning, Mr. Zip-Zip-Zip, with your hair cut just as short as mine, rise up and shine, good morning, Mr. Zip-Zip-Zip, you're surely looking fine." He stood with a fixed smile on his face and then went to the cars standing behind troops of the 4th Minnesota National Guard who led him to the state capitol.

After that it was Bismarck, North Dakota, crying "The whole world is waiting on us," and an auto tour of the city. During the day they stopped for a few minutes to walk from the train a short distance to where there was a wonderful view of some waterfalls. It was the first, literally the first, quiet exercise of any kind since Washington.

When they returned to the siding the Secret Service men made their usual check of the train and flushed out two hobos who were planning to hitch a ride under one of the cars. When the men found out whose train this was, one asked a Secret Service man, "Do you think he would shake hands with fellows like us?" The President stepped forward and did so, and even offered a lift. But the hobos said no, they would not trouble him, he had troubles enough, and they would wait for the next train coming through. The First Lady shook hands with them and then the train pulled away. Looking back, the President waved to the two and they bowed and waved their shabby hats in return. Edmund Starling glanced at the President and, seeing a wistful smile, thought to himself, he envies them.

And indeed there was much about the two tramps that the President could envy. For it was likely they slept well at night and were free from a constantly more severe headache and free also from the sneezing and coughing that resulted from the train fumes and the cigar smoke blown up at him in the crowded halls where he spoke, and from the serious asthma attacks the high altitudes were bringing on in spite of the sprays and medications Grayson gave him. The President's poor appetite in the murderous September heat also worried the doctor, and he prescribed predigested foods and lots of fluids to help his patient, but the reporters could not help but notice that although the President in public smiled and waved he seemed to sag as soon as he was out of sight of the crowds. They also noticed the serious, intent look that rarely left the face of the usually cheery First Lady and the tense, worried appearance of Grayson.

Billings, Montana: "I am just as sure what the verdict will be as if already rendered, and what has convinced me most is what plain people have said to me, particularly what women have said to me. When I see a woman dressed with marks of labor upon her and she says, God bless you, Mr. President, and God bless the League of Nations, then I know the League of Nations is safe. I know the League of Nations is close to those people. A woman came to me the other day and took my hand and said, God bless you, Mr. President, and turned away in tears. I asked a neighbor, What is the matter? and he said, She was intending to say something to you but she lost a son in France. That woman did not take my hand with the feeling that her son should not have been sent to France. I sent her son to France. She took my hand and blessed it but she could not say anything more because a whole world of spirit came up in her throat. Down deep in the heart of love for her boy she felt that we had done something so that no other woman's boy would be called upon to lay his life down for a thing like that."

As the train pulled away from the station some little boys came running after it. One had an American flag and he reached up to the rear platform of the *Mayflower* and handed it to the First Lady. "Give it to him," he said. A boy running by his side had no flag, but he reached down into his pocket and then stretched out his hand with something in it. The child was running as fast as he could, holding out his hand, and Starling hooked a leg through the platform railing and leaned out to reach him. "Give him this," the boy panted. Starling opened his hand. A dime lay in his palm.

They kept going, up into the Northwest. Meanwhile, back in Washington, Senator Lodge dispatched men to speak out against the League, "that evil thing with the holy name." Senators Johnson, McCormick and Borah went to Chicago. Johnson cried to a crowd of ten thousand sitting with coats off and ties loosened in the steaming Coliseum, "I have heard of men placing themselves in the hands of their creditors, but never have I heard of a man placing himself in the hands of his debtors. The United States is the greatest solvent power on earth and they ask us to enter into partnership with bankrupts!" Borah hooked his thumbs under his arms and stalked across the stage. "Is there an American who wants a foreign nation to say when and where the Monroe Doctrine should apply?" he asked. "No, no," the crowd yelled. "England has suggested—all England has to do now is to suggest—that we send 100,000 men to Constantinople," the Senator said. "Don't let 'em go," the crowd cried back. Who betrayed the American soldier and the American ideals? the Senator asked. "Wilson! Impeach him! Impeach him!" roared the crowd. Johnson the next day went on to Indianapolis to say the Europeans were filled with "duplicity unequaled in the history of the world. But when the President seeks to keep up the duplicity by binding our sons to guarantee it, I say it shall not be!" "No!" roared the crowd. In the Senate at Washington, Senator Sherman stood to say, "He is no longer Wilson the American President of the United States. Now he is Wilson the internationalist, aspirant for first President of the World's League of Nations." Senator Reed, a Democrat, went into New England and waved a sheet of paper over his head, crying that it was the Covenant of the League. "I have it here and I seem to see the bloody footprints of John Bull tracking all over the dastardly document."

The train went on: Helena, Coeur d'Alene . . . Outside Coeur d'Alene, Borah's town, a woman held up a baby for the President to see. The First Lady leaned over the platform railing and took the child. "It's a boy," the infant's father proudly said, "and his name is Wilson." They went on to a circus tent, cowboys in Western regalia riding before, and he told the people, "My fellow countrymen, we are facing a decision now in which we cannot afford to make a mistake."

The crowds were getting more enthusiastic now with every stop, but at night in the hot dry air the President could hardly breathe. It became necessary for him to try to sleep sitting up in an easy chair of his compartment in the jolting and swaying train; that way, it was not as difficult for him to catch his breath. Fighting the splitting headaches, he would sit with his forehead resting on the back of another chair and dictate by the hour to his stenographer, Charles Swem.

Tumulty kept coming in from each stop with a stream of telegrams sent on from the White House and dealing with the Russian situation, the actions of U.S. troops on occupation duty, petitions about the high cost of living, the question of what American decoration should be awarded the King of the Belgians, who would soon be coming to the country on a state visit, and the labor disturbances breaking out all over the country—including the police strike in Boston, which saw mobs free of interference breaking windows, shooting craps on Boston Common, molesting women in the street. The telegrams had to be dealt with even as he planned ahead for his next speech.

They made their way up to the State of Washington, moving slowly through wooded mountain country and under a drizzle and low-lying mist that turned the atmosphere suddenly cold. It was the chilliest spell for that season that the area had experienced in years, and for the first time the heat in the train was turned on. At Rathdrum, Idaho, the train stopped for a few moments to change engines and a band appeared to play for him. He went out on the platform very much bundled up against the penetrating damp cold and spoke for a few minutes to the people, some of them Indians, standing by their muddy trucks. "A League of Nations will not make war impossible but it will help to prevent war. You do not want war. You want world peace. . . ." A mounted policeman put his horse through a bucking exhibition.

In Spokane two hours later the weather was boilingly hot; the reporters came from the train in panamas. The crowds were, despite the heat, the most enthusiastic of the entire trip. Marching troops of the 21st Infantry led the motorcade through twenty-three blocks filled with people, some sitting atop big delivery vans parked in the side-street intersections. Flags hung across the hot streets and a canopy of white and red dahlias woven into a wire screen stretched above the main thoroughfare. Bouquets sailed out of the crowd toward him, and the Secret Service men on the running boards leaped high to catch them. At each side of his nose there were heavy dark lines leading down to his mouth, and when he stood up in the car to wave his hat the people noticed that the First Lady, in navy-blue jersey cloth and a small toque of dark gray velour, reached up her hand to steady him.

They went to a park to be seen by hundreds of massed school children, and then to his speech: "Isn't 10 per cent insurance against war a pretty good thing?" "You bet it is," a man called out. "Well, the League of Nations will give you 98 per cent insurance against war." Two hours after arriving at Spokane they pulled out. A policeman asked him how he liked the city and he said, "Fine! Fine! I have always wanted to visit Spokane, I have heard so much about it. This is the first opportunity I have had." His headache made him actually see double. The policeman held up a child to shake his hand.

They made for Tacoma and paused for a moment at Pasco, Washington, so that he might say a few words. After his talk he remarked to the little throng that theirs was a dusty area. Someone joked, "Yes, we have to have a lot of grit to live here." As the train pulled out a man came dashing down the track. The President looked at him curiously. "Don't mind me," gasped the man. "I only promised to get the last look at you from Pasco and now I've done it."

Tacoma's crowds were enormous and uproarious: TACOMA GREETS AMERICAN LEADER. ". . . . If it fails every woman should weep for the child at her breast who when he grows to manhood will have to go forth to fight . . ." He talked about the little boy who had given him the dime: "I would like to believe that dime has some relation to the widow's mite—others gave something; he gave all that he had."

At Seattle they found Secretary of the Navy Daniels and his wife, back from a trip to Hawaii, ready to take them at once to a formal review of the Pacific Fleet in Puget Sound. The street crowds unleashed deafening cheers; at Union Street the employees of a store had constructed a confetti gun, and when they fired it he and the First Lady, who held him with one white-gloved hand, disappeared from view in the paper pouring down on them. Japanese school children waved flags and shrieked while auto horns blared.

He was standing up in the car waving a high silk hat—it was the first time on the trip he had worn one—when with terrifying suddenness all the noise and cheering ended. Standing by the curb in long lines were men in blue denim working clothes. Their arms were folded and they stared straight ahead, not at the President, but at nothing at all. They did not hiss or boo but motionless, noiseless, simply stood there. In their hats they wore signs saying RE-LEASE POLITICAL PRISONERS. They were members of the International Workers of the World—the Wobblies—gathered from all over the state to demonstrate their anger at the imprisonment of radical leaders on sedition charges and to embarrass Seattle's Mayor Ole Hanson, their sworn enemy. They lined the building fronts to the curbs, and only a few children pushed and yelled for the President, making the silence and immobility of the men even more awesome. From the streets over which the motorcade had come there were heard the bands playing and the crowds noisily breaking up, but where the IWW's were there was not a sound but the put-putting of police motorcycles. The President was standing and smiling when he first reached the IWW's, but in a flash the smile vanished and a flabbergasted look came over his face. He stood in the terrible silence for two blocks, the hand holding his hat hanging by his side, and then he sank down onto the car seat beside the First Lady. He put his tall hat on his head, a little to one side, and it seemed that he sat in a crumpled-up way. His face was white.

For six blocks the statue-like men lined the street. When the car had gotten past the silent, terrible blocks there were more cheering people, but the President did not again rise in the car; he simply waved his hand and weakly smiled. They went to the harbor and boarded an overcrowded launch that lurched violently and collided with another craft before taking them to the *Oregon*. They sailed several miles through the bay alive with warships firing salvos of twenty-one guns each and flinging across the water the strains of the National Anthem.

At seven in the evening, after speaking at a Seattle Hippodrome dinner, he went to the Seattle Arena for a second talk and found wildly enthusiastic mobs ringing it on all sides. While he was speaking inside, the people outside noisily shouted his name and cheered, making it hard for the listeners to hear him. "If there had been a League of Nations in 1914, whether Germany belonged to it or not, Germany would never have dared to attempt the aggression she did attempt," he cried out over the clamor from outside. Secretary Daniels felt his chief had put his last ounce of strength forward, and Jonathan Daniels, his son, thought the President had made a great speech. But a Navy admiral said to the boy's father, "Something seemed to be wrong with President Wilson. He appeared to have lost his customary force and enthusiasm."

That night the President sat in darkness with the First Lady in a little roof garden of the Hotel New Washington and looked down to where the fleet stood at anchor with all lights blazing. It was a beautiful sight, and all of a sudden in her eyes he looked good again, delighted as a boy with the ships and the beauty and quiet of the night. But later for hours from their suite in the hotel they heard below the roistering sounds of sailors off the ships playing guitars bought on shore leave in Honolulu and twanged in the street as a tribute to the Commander in Chief. With the noise and his extreme difficulty in breathing, he was up most of the night, and the next morning, Sunday, when Secretary Daniels and his wife came to pay a call, they were told the President had a terrible headache and must beg to be excused.

Later, however, he pulled himself together to break his rule about working on the Sabbath and received the leaders of the terrible silent men of the six blocks. A delegation of five men came, two wearing the caps they had been issued during their Army service. Jack Kipps, a Socialist and the head of the International Workers of the World in the Seattle area, led them into a room where the President stood by a long table, one hand holding the edge. "Good morning," the President said, stepping forward. Kipps thought to himself that the President was smaller than his pictures made him appear and that his head seemed heavy on his neck. "And he looked old—just *old*." They shook hands and Kipps found the President's was dry and shaky. His voice also trembled. He waited for the men to speak. He did not look at them. The delegation and the President stood in silence for a moment and then one of the men got out something about a petition they had for him asking that all imprisoned radical leaders be released. The President said he would read it and they handed it to him. His face seemed terribly long and gray to them. Again there was a long silence. Kipps said they had a thousand signatures on their petition but that if they had had more time they could have gotten ten thousand. The President's hand was shaking so much that he gripped the lapel of his coat with it. For a few moments he closed his eyes —the headache that had prevented his seeing Secretary Daniels was all but unendurable—and the men started to leave. Again he shook their hands and got out a thank-you. They went to the door and he took a few steps after them and stopped in the middle of the room and bowed. He looks like a ghost, Kipps thought. The men went down and got into a streetcar. "Christ Almighty," one of them breathed. "What a mess he was!" Kipps said.

That night the travelers went to the train and headed for Portland and a drive around a race track where ten thousand people roared for him and to the Hotel Portland for a luncheon after which the cigars of the men in the banquet room sent clouds of thick smoke drifting up to him. His voice was very hoarse. "I have lived to see a day in which, after saturating most of my life in the history and traditions of America, I seem suddenly to see a culmination of American hope in history; all the orators seeing their dreams realized, if their spirits are looking on; all the men who spoke the noblest sentiments for America heartened with the sight of a great nation responding to and acting upon those dreams, saying, 'At last the world knows America as the savior of the world.'"

That day there was bad news from Washington. Testifying before Senator Lodge and his Foreign Relations Committee, William C. Bullitt, who had been attached to the American delegation at Paris during the Peace Conference,* said that Secretary of State Robert Lansing had told him outright that the League of Nations was a terrible idea. Reading from notes he said he had made of the conversation, Bullitt quoted Lansing as saying, "I believe that if the Senate could only understand what this treaty means, it would

---

* And was later to be Ambassador to Russia and France.

unquestionably be defeated, but I wonder if they will understand what it lets them in for . . . I believe that the League of Nations at present is entirely useless."

The newspapers headlined the story and added that Secretary Lansing, on vacation in upstate New York, returned from a day of bass fishing and said he had no comment on Bullitt's statement. The implication of the Secretary's silence clearly was that he was not going to deny that he made the remarks to Bullitt. The revelations of his Secretary of State's attitude threw the President into a rage. "Read that," he rasped at Tumulty, "and tell me what you think of a man who was my associate on the other side and who confidentially expressed himself to an outsider in such a fashion! Think of it! This from a man whom I raised from the level of a subordinate to the great office of Secretary of State of the United States! My God! I did not think it was possible for Lansing to act in this way!" Senators Borah and Johnson traveling behind him damning the League and Senator New in the Senate saying his dreams were "scarcely less visionary than the hallucinations of Don Quixote" were one thing, but for his Secretary of State to say the same thing was quite another. He could not get it out of his mind, and there was something desperate in his face as they went south into California behind three engines pulling the train up over the Siskiyou Mountains.

They spent two days in the San Francisco area and he made five major addresses. There was a men's luncheon, a women's luncheon, a trip by ferry across the bay and a talk at the Greek Theatre of the University of California at Berkeley. Margaret Axson Elliott, Ellen's younger sister, came with her husband, an assistant to the President in Princeton days, and stayed with them at the Hotel St. Francis in San Francisco. Sitting with the Mayor of Oakland and the President and First Lady as they drove in one of the unending motorcades, Margaret—"Madge" to the family—saw a child fall off the curb and get dragged back by its father. The Mayor of Oakland saw it too. "Those are the little chaps for whom you are fighting, Mr. President." "God help them, yes!" the President said. Often on the trip he repeated that—"I am the attorney for these children." At the end of their stay Madge drove with them to the train. "Take care of yourself. This trip is pretty strenuous," she said. He nodded. "It is! I shall be ready for a rest when it is over."

The Far West's September weather was hot, steamy, draining—
he seemed to be weakening hour by hour, but there was no let up
in the reception committees and politicians and the pushing and
screaming crowds that were everywhere, along with the bands that
awakened him in the morning and blared long into the night. Always there were more hands to shake, more people wanting just a
moment of the President's time, his ear for just a second or two.
"They mean so well—but they are killing me," he groaned. They
went down to San Diego and to the stadium, where with the assistance of then-novel loudspeakers he spoke to a crowd of more than
forty thousand madly enthusiastic and vociferous persons shielding
themselves with umbrellas from the sun.

As they headed north to Los Angeles, Grayson had the train
halted so that the President might get off and sleep in an inn.
The doctor also argued that there must be no more rear-platform
speeches and handshaking, but in the Los Angeles station a be-
grimed Mexican rail-yard worker reached up to shake. Although
the Secret Service men leaped forward to bar others from doing the
same, the crowd set up three cheers and would not take no for an
answer. So he had to shake what the reporters estimated to be a
thousand hands in a matter of minutes.

There was a dinner for him, the First Lady wearing black and
silver brocade and a velvet hat trimmed with sapphire tulle fastened
with a diamond and sapphire, and at the Shrine Auditorium there
were seven thousand to hear him while three times that number
stood outside. Cheers drowned out the voice of the Mayor as he
tried to make the introduction, and when the President stood up
the people increased the enormous volume of sound. As soon as
the cheers began to diminish, a man waving a large American flag
urged the people to redouble their efforts, and so he stood for a
long time before he began his speech. LOS ANGELES SHRIEKS APPROVAL
OF THE PRESIDENT, said a local paper, and the New York *Times* correspondent on the train wrote the traveler was "now getting the
cumulative effect of his missionary work." Correspondent David
Lawrence, who earlier in the trip had been struck by the lack of
enthusiasm, now wrote the President would leave the West Coast
"triumphant."

The second day in Los Angeles was a Sunday and in the morning
he drove to a shabby street where there lived a woman who as a

young girl had been very close to Miss Elly Lou of Rome, Georgia. When the parents of the girl—"Janie" in the long ago—died, Ellen's people took her in and raised her as their own. The two girls shared Ellen's room, went to the same school, grew up to be young ladies. Then Janie married a man who took her west and to a financially very difficult life. She and Ellen never met again but corresponded regularly through the years. Now Ellen was dead, but her husband went to Janie in her small bungalow in a down-at-the-heels neighborhood. In San Francisco, Madge Axson Elliott heard of it and something caught at her throat. "His heart is turning to his young Ellen," she breathed.

In the afternoon there came to the hotel someone else from out of the past: Mrs. Peck, invited for lunch by the First Lady. She came by streetcar to the Hotel Alexandria and went in through the great crowds to Grayson, who brought her to the President and First Lady. She had not seen the former in four years; the latter she had never met. Mrs. Peck thought the First Lady handsome and Junoesque with a charming smile; the First Lady thought her sweet-looking but faded.

Mrs. Peck told of her troubles with the President's enemies who sought to buy the letters he had written her, of how her room had been searched and of the large sums offered. "God, to think that you should have suffered because of me!" said the distressed President. She told of her financial difficulties, of how she sold encyclopedias door to door and worked as a movie extra sipping tea in the background of a garden-party scene, of her suffering because of the gossip about them. In an apparent attempt to smooth over a difficult situation by making a joke, the First Lady said, "Where there's so much smoke there must be some fire."

It was an unwise remark to make to a woman who, she once had told a friend, still kept the lace for the dress she had intended to wear at her White House wedding. She flared out some sharp things to the First Lady, but the tiff was passed over when the President talked about his fight for the League. Several times people came in to ask if the President would not greet the crowds outside the hotel, or this delegation or that, and once Grayson came in to ask if the First Lady would not say hello to a women's group, and finally the President went out to meet with some League supporters.

It seemed to Mrs. Peck that he was like a man being drawn into a maelstrom.

Finally it came time for her to go. The President put his hand on the First Lady's and asked, "Isn't there something we can do?" Mrs. Peck did not fail to note the First Lady's silence and said, "Not for me; not for me. I am quite all right." The First Lady went to tell a valet to bring Mrs. Peck's wrap and the President walked with his visitor to the hall. She quoted from a poem: "'With all my will, but much against my heart, we two now part.'" The elevator came and she was gone. They would never meet again.

Going across the Sierras, finally heading in the direction of Washington, they ran into forest fires that scorched the sides of the train cars and filled the long mountain tunnels with choking gas fumes. He could not sleep at all and the headaches, formerly located at the back of his head, now seemed to be moving into the very center of his brain. The sharp changes of altitude were the worst thing possible for his asthma, and when they moved out of the mountains into the dust of the Western desert the twitching of his face was more pronounced and continuous for hours on end. In Washington a resolution was introduced in Congress directing the State Department to furnish a "list of all presents of any kind whatsoever that were tendered" the President from "any King, Prince or Foreign State." Rumors were spread that "women and liquor" were aboard the train.

At Reno, Nevada, the crowd called for the First Lady and he brought her out on the train platform. "Here is the best part of this traveling show," he said. A man below called, "Mr. Wilson, I would like to make a statement: I am very much pleased with your better half." Everyone laughed. They drove to a theater: "Answering those who fear the League will get the United States into trouble, I want to get into any kind of trouble that will help to liberate mankind!" The talk was piped over telephone lines to megaphones set up in three other theaters in the town.

They went on toward Salt Lake City, stopping at Ogden for a one-hour drive through crowded city streets after rolling through the small desert towns where the entire populations turned out to call his name, the children singing, Indian squaws standing with papooses on their backs, people clinging to dust-covered telegraph poles along the right of way. At Salt Lake City the speech was to be in the Mormon Tabernacle at eight in the evening. At six Tumulty came to the hotel where they were resting and said the Tabernacle was so packed that the police had locked the doors. Looking from the hotel windows, they saw thousands of people milling about in the streets, and when they went down, a police escort had hard work getting them through the crowds.

Inside, fifteen thousand people sat in an unventilated building on a very hot night; the heat and fetid air made the First Lady feel sick and blind. They went up on the rostrum, where the hot thick air was even more stifling, and she thought she was going to faint. Her maid saw her getting white and passed up a bottle of smelling salts which she gratefully inhaled and then poured onto a handkerchief for the President. He was in agony from the terrible pain in his head and choking from the asthma and the poor air, and when they got back to the hotel his clothing was soaked through with perspiration. The First Lady and Grayson got him into dry things, but within five minutes they too were sopping wet. All night on the train he could not keep dry.

The next day at Cheyenne two troops of cavalry from Fort Russell gave him a saber salute as he stood at attention for *The Star-Spangled Banner* before the parade to the Princess Theater and an hour's speech. Four hours later, at eleven at night, they pulled into Denver. They had wired ahead asking there be as small a reception committee as possible, giving the explanation that this was a security request from the Secret Service, but when they got there they found the entire city ablaze with special lights strung up by the Denver Gas and Electric Light Company. The streets were jammed. Thousands of yelling people escorted them to their hotel, where they talked with his cousin Harriet Woodrow Wells, whom as a boy he had loved but who had rejected his proposal of marriage.

When he tried to sleep, he could not. The First Lady was desperate, terrified of the way he looked and what lay ahead. "Let's stop," she begged. "Let's go somewhere and rest. Only for a few days." "No," he said. "I have caught the imagination of the people. They are eager to hear what the League stands for. I should fail in my duty if I disappointed them." She was so downcast that he tried to make light of the situation: "Cheer up! This will soon be over. And when we get back to Washington I promise you I'll take a holiday."

In the morning they went to the state capitol grounds to greet school children and then to the City Auditorium for his speech. The acoustics were very bad and he had to shout. By eleven in the morning they were on their way to Pueblo, Colorado. They lunched on the train and his appetite was bad, as usual. As the train approached Pueblo he asked what the arrangements were and was told the schedule called for a drive to the fairgrounds to greet a crowd before going to speak in the Memorial Auditorium. The idea of a long standing-up auto tour to the fairgrounds seemed too much for him. "Who authorized such an idiotic idea?" he snapped. He was told it was listed in the plans he himself had approved. "Send for Tumulty and tell him to bring the original program," he ordered. Tumulty brought it and showed the President where he had signed an approving "W.W." The President sighed. "Any damned fool who was stupid enough to approve such a program has no business in the White House."

He said he would not go to the fairgrounds. But when they arrived in Pueblo the reception committee pleaded that he make the trip, saying ten thousand people were waiting for him. Reluctantly he agreed and drove around in front of the crowd, waving his hat. When they went to the auditorium for his speech he seemed to stumble at the single step of the hall's entrance. The Secret Service man Edmund Starling caught him and almost lifted him up over the step. Always before the President had refused any suggestion of physical assistance when his party was battling its way through the enormous crowds of the trip, but this time he did not object. He went out onto the platform. It was a little after three in the afternoon, September 25, 1919. Passing the newspapermen, he said, "This will have to be a short speech. Aren't you fellows getting pretty sick of this?"

He went up to the cheering and yells and began to speak. His voice was not strong, but he did well enough until suddenly he stumbled over a sentence. "Germany must never be allowed——" He stopped and was silent. "A lesson must be taught to Germany——" He stopped again and stood still. "The world will not allow Germany——" Reporter Joseph Jefferson O'Neill looked up from his notes. This had never happened before in any of the speeches. O'Neill looked at the First Lady and saw terror on her face. Edmund Starling thought to himself the President was about to collapse and tensed to step forward and catch him. But the President gathered himself together, although his voice was very weak, and went on. He spoke of Memorial Day at Suresnes, of the soldiers alive and dead at the cemetery, and of how he wished that some of the Senators opposing the League might have been there on that day. As he spoke of the dead boys in the graves at Suresnes, Joe Tumulty, standing in the wings of the auditorium, saw down in the audience men and women alike reaching for handkerchiefs to wipe their eyes. "There seems to me to stand between us and the rejection of this treaty the serried ranks of those boys in khaki, not only those boys who came home, but those dear ghosts who still deploy upon the fields of France."

He halted. The people looked at him and he at them.

The President of the United States, standing before an audience of some several thousands of his fellow citizens, was crying.

He had come to the last words of his speech. He said:

"I believe that men will see the truth, eye to eye and face to face. There is one thing that the American people always rise to and extend their hand to, and that is the truth of justice and of liberty and of peace. We have accepted that truth and we are going to be led by it, and it is going to lead us, and through us the world, out into pastures of quietness and peace such as the world never dreamed of before."

He turned away and the First Lady came to him. Their tears mixed.

They went to the train but traveled only a few miles when Grayson asked him if he thought a stroll in the open air might do him some good. He said he would like that, and word was sent to the engineer to halt the train. The brakes went on. The engine stood panting with steam up and the reporters were told that the President and the First Lady and Dr. Grayson were going for a little walk. They had come down out of the mountain country and were in beautiful prairie land with no houses in sight and evening coming on. It was very pleasant. The reporters got out and lay down on the grass to relax and watch the long, lovely September twilight.

The trio walked slowly down a dusty road with Starling idling behind at a little distance. They came to a bridge and paused on it, looking down at the thin Arkansas River, hardly more than a stream at that point. They went on in the comfortably warm Colorado air and saw a farmer in a small auto driving down the road. He came to a stop when he recognized the walkers and took out a head of cabbage and some apples, saying he hoped they would eat them "for dinner tonight." They thanked him and he drove off, raising a little cloud of dust as he went.

A man and his wife and their friend, they strolled down a silent country road. They came to a field cut off from the road by a fence. Some distance back from the road was a frame house with a soldier in uniform sitting on the porch. The President said, "That fellow looks sick to me." Grayson said, "Yes, he certainly is." They climbed over the low fence, Starling following, and went across to the boy and said hello. The soldier's mother and father and brothers came out and for a few minutes the visitors talked with the farm people. Then they said good-by and, carrying the cabbage and apples, strolled back toward the setting sun.

About an hour had elapsed when the reporters on the grass saw the four specks, three together and one in the rear, coming toward the train. When the group was about a hundred yards away from the *Mayflower*, Grayson and the President broke into a dog trot and ran by the men on the grass. Reporter Morton Milford said, "Pretty good! I don't know whether I could do that myself or not." The President was smiling as he went up on the rear platform.

That night the First Lady's maid came to her room in the rolling *Mayflower* to brush her hair and give her a massage. The two spoke in the lowest of tones, for the President's compartment was next door and the First Lady thought he was asleep. But about eleven-thirty there was a knock on the intervening door and she heard his voice: "Can you come to me, Edith? I'm terribly sick." He was sitting on the edge of his bed with his head resting on the back of a chair. "I can't sleep because of the pain. I'm afraid you'd better call Grayson." She sent her maid to the doctor's room. He was not there, and although it was only a few minutes before he was located, it seemed to her that hours passed. But when he came there was nothing he could do to ease his patient. The tiny sleeping room oppressed the President; he said he could not stay in it; he must move about. They went into the room that he used as a study and office. His typewriter stood on the Pullman table. They brought in some pillows and tried to make him comfortable, but he could not stay still and twisted about to try to find a position that would lessen the splitting agony in his head. The hours passed as the train rushed eastward, and about five, sitting propped upright by the pillows, he fell asleep.

The First Lady motioned Grayson to go to bed and sat alone opposite her husband, breathing as quietly as she could for fear she might awaken him. Dawn came as she sat motionless, staring at him. The room grew light. He awoke, stood, and said he must shave, for soon they would be in Wichita, Kansas, for another speech. Grayson came in and spoke with her and went to Tumulty's compartment. He knocked on the door and told Tumulty to get up and come quickly, the President was seriously ill.

The two men hurried through the train and as they moved Grayson tersely said something was terribly, terribly wrong and that to continue the trip could be fatal but that Tumulty's support would be needed to convince the President. They went in and joined the First Lady. A few minutes later the President came out of the bathroom, freshly shaven and dressed, and Grayson thought to himself that no one else would have shaven himself while in such a condition. The men said to him that he must cancel the tour, but at once he said no, no, he could not do it. As he spoke saliva came down from the left side of his mouth and they saw that the left half of his face was fallen and unmoving. His words were mumbled and indistinct.

Grayson told him that continuing was out of the question, but he said, "I must go on. I should feel like a deserter. My opponents will accuse me of having cold feet should I stop now." It was difficult to understand his words. Grayson said, "I owe it to the country, to you and to your family not to permit you to continue. If you try to speak today you will fall down on the platform before the audience." Still the President insisted he would go on. Tumulty urged him to obey the doctor. The President turned to him. "My dear boy, this has never happened to me before. I don't know what to do." "You must give up the trip and get some rest," Tumulty said. "Don't you see," said the President, "if we cancel this trip

Senator Lodge and his friends will say that I am a quitter, that the trip was a failure. And the treaty will be lost." Tumulty reached over to him and took both of his hands in his own. "What difference, dear Governor, does it make what they say? Nobody in the world will consider you a quitter. It is your life we must consider."

The President was sitting with Tumulty holding his hands; he tried to move closer but found his left arm and leg refused to function. But he said, "I want to show them that I can still fight and that I am not afraid. Just postpone the trip for twenty-four hours and I will be all right." Grayson began to protest, but the President interrupted. "No, no, no. I must keep up."

Finally the First Lady spoke and said to him that he must give up, that he could not go on, that he must not let the people see him as he was this day. Ever after she felt it was the hardest thing she had done in her life, to tell him the truth that morning even as the train slowed down at the Wichita outskirts. And when she had said what had to be said he finally understood. "I suppose you are right," he said. He burst into tears and the two men went out to tell the reporters. She sat with her weeping husband and she thought, I will have to wear a mask—not only to the public but to the one I love best in the world. For he must never know how ill he is and I must carry on.

I

From left: Mrs. Ellen Wilson, Jessica, Margaret and Eleanor

Additional information about these pictures can be found on page 250

II
Inauguration Day, 1913

III
Opening day of the 1916 season,
six months after the Presidential marriage.
The President is flanked by Edith Wilson and Dr. Cary Grayson.

IV
Grayson

V
Tumulty

VI
Europe, 1918

VII
Europe, 1918

VIII
Lodge

X
The West, 1919

XI
The West, 1919

XII
Spring, 1920.
The President, the First Lady and the doctor

XIII
Spring, 1920

XIV
Inauguration Day, 1921

XV
At the funeral of the Unknown Soldier

Courtesy Washington "Post"

XVI
S Street, 11:10 A.M., February 3, 1924

PART TWO

The Second Mrs. Wilson

And I must carry on

6 Tumulty said, "Gentlemen, we are not going to Wichita. The President is very ill. It will be necessary for us to start back for Washington as soon as the railroad arrangements are completed, and we will go through with no stops other than those that are imperative." He turned to Grayson. Grayson said, "The President has suffered a complete nervous breakdown. It is altogether against his will that he give up his speech-making tour. He did not wish to disappoint the people of Wichita. In fact, he was insistent that he would be able to take part in the parade and make his address. But my judgment as a doctor and the judgment of Mrs. Wilson and Mr. Tumulty is that we must not allow him to exert the slightest effort of any kind, and that we must get him, as soon as possible, into the restful atmosphere of the White House." The reporters ran to get off the halted train and to telephones.

Grayson also got off and headed for a little grocery store close to where the train was standing. He made his way through a small crowd of poorly dressed Negroes, for the train stood in the heart of a colored shanty-town district, and went into the store of Mr. and Mrs. W. B. Rankin. He asked Mrs. Rankin for the number of the local telegraph office and for a moment she hunted through her telephone book for it and, not finding it, asked the operator to make the connection. Grayson then took the phone and started dictating telegrams to Washington and the President's daughters. Margaret was on a visit to New London, Connecticut, and

Jessie with Frank Sayre at Harvard. Each was wired: RETURNING TO WASHINGTON. NOTHING TO BE ALARMED ABOUT. LOVE FROM ALL OF US. Tumulty wired a man at the Los Angeles hotel where Nellie and her husband were shortly expected: PLEASE TELL MR AND MRS MCADOO THAT THE PRESIDENT IS RETURNING TO WASHINGTON BUT THERE IS NOTHING TO BE ALARMED ABOUT. He also wired a niece of the President, who had planned to board the train at Memphis: THE PRESIDENT IS OBLIGED BECAUSE OF SLIGHT ILLNESS TO RETURN IMMEDIATELY TO WASHINGTON AND IS VERY SORRY NOT TO BE ABLE TO SEE YOU AS PLANNED.

Meanwhile, neighborhood people clustered around the train. The Secret Service men deployed to prevent them from approaching too closely and asked them not to make any noise. But when their numbers increased, it was decided to get the train under way and circle the city for the period needed by the railroad officials to plan a route east. In Wichita itself, fifteen thousand people gathered at the municipal auditorium were told there would be no speech. Disappointed, they filed out as a quartet sang "Smile Awhile" and for the most part went down to the main depot to learn more about the reason for the cancellation. They were joined by many of the one hundred thousand waiting for the motorcade and composing the largest crowd in the history of the city. Grayson rejoined the train before it began to move and the reporters came back to ask for more concrete information than they had so far been given. Grayson told them he hoped the President would need only a short rest and that it was certain he was not seriously ill. He added there was nothing organically wrong with the President's physical or nervous system. He would say no more than that.

After two hours of slowly circling Wichita, the route was laid out, the tracks ahead were cleared, and the train picked up a pilot engine and headed for Washington, seventeen hundred miles away. But the President seemed unwilling to admit the tour was over. When Grayson urged him to try to sleep, he said, "I won't be able to sleep at all, Doctor, if you say I must cancel the trip." He was unable to doze off, although the use of his arm and leg was returning, and so he sat with the First Lady in the office compartment of the *Mayflower*. She got out her knitting and tried to make small talk with him, but he could not be diverted and her chatting lapsed. They roared on, going at a speed greater than that of most expresses, the train whistle moaning to warn back the people gathered by the tracks in hope of seeing the President. All across Kansas and into Missouri crowds stood by and during the few necessary stops they came up to peer into the *Mayflower*'s windows. Their curiosity was unnerving and so the blinds were drawn. The darkened car was like a funeral cortege and the silence was oppressive after all the noise and cheering of the past weeks, and the President and First Lady sat together, alone. His hands were trembling.

In the club car up front, however, the reporters broke out whisky bottles—wartime prohibition notwithstanding—and celebrated their return home. For more than three weeks they had been living out of suitcases, and they had had enough of it. Most of them thought the illness to be some sort of indigestion or at the most a not unexpected reaction to the rigors of the trip. Several of them argued that the whole thing was a ruse and that the President was not sick at all, but this view was generally discounted. "It's a fraud, a ruse; he's shamming," the reporter from the New York *Sun* said, but reporter David Lawrence answered by saying, "He's not feeling well; that's that. The doctor says he's sick; he must be sick."

With no real work to do, the reporters passed the time playing cards and singing as they sped east. Grayson issued a bulletin for them and they dropped copies of it out of the train for station telegraphers to send to their papers: "The President has exerted himself so constantly and has been under such a strain during the last year and has so spent himself without reserve on this trip that it has brought on a serious reaction in his digestive organs." For later editions Grayson issued: "President Wilson's condition is due to overwork. The trouble dates back to an attack of influenza last April in Paris from which he has never entirely recovered. The President's activities on this trip have overtaxed his strength and he is suffering from nervous exhaustion. His condition is not alarming, but it will be necessary for his recovery that he have rest and quiet for a considerable time." Nothing more could be learned from the doctor, so the matter had to be left at that.

In the early hours of September 27, Saturday, as they approached St. Louis, the First Lady sent for the Secret Service man

Starling, who all along had planned to leave the train in that city in order to pay a visit to his ailing mother. She told him neither she nor the President wanted the President's condition to interfere with Starling's plans and said to him that he must stay with his mother until he was assured she was well. She added that the President wanted to say good-by to Starling and took the Secret Service man into the office, where the President, wrapped in a dressing gown, lay on a couch. It seemed to Starling as he walked up that the left side of the President's face had fallen a little, but when he looked more closely he decided he was mistaken. The President offered his right hand and Starling took it and pressed it but did not shake it, thinking that perhaps the motion would be painful. "I want you to know how sorry I am," Starling said. "I will be praying for you until you recover and I am sure it will be soon." The President smiled wanly and Starling saw his original thought was correct. Only the right side of the President's face was moving. "Thank you, Starling," the President said. "I want you to take something to your mother for me." He gave Starling a shawl. The First Lady also had a gift—two large boxes of candy. Starling found himself unable to speak. He shook the First Lady's hand and left the *Mayflower*.

At three-thirty in the morning the train reached St. Louis and halted there to take on water and change engines. The Secret Service men, minus the departing Starling, were joined by police who stood in a cordon to keep the area as quiet as possible. But still the President could not sleep and the pain was intense as ever it had been. He could not force himself to eat and had no desire for anything but strong black coffee.

For the remaining day and a half of the trip Grayson's bulletins were very similar: "The condition of the President shows no very material change . . . he still suffers from headaches and nervousness. . . . The President's condition is about the same. . . ." At every brief halt scores of inquiring telegrams were delivered, and Tumulty answered them in vague terms. As they neared Pittsburgh the train's speed was reduced to save the *Mayflower* from jolting too strenuously around curves and other switches, and it was not until eleven on Sunday morning, forty-eight hours after leaving Wichita, that Washington's Union Station was reached. Perhaps one thousand people were there, and Margaret stood on the platform. She linked her arm with that of her father and together they walked down the long train shed to where White House cars waited. He talked to his daughter quite casually and indicated that all he needed was a little rest. He nodded to the watching people and even smiled when photographers approached. He was pale and his smile was somewhat uneven and lopsided, but to the eyes of the people behind the police lines there did not seem to be anything seriously wrong.

When they came out into the plaza in front of the station he got into an open car and they headed for the White House. Because it was Sunday morning the streets were practically empty. But as they rode the President reached up and took off his hat and bowed as if he were returning the greetings of a vast throng. Enough people saw what he had done to send flying through Washington the information that the President is physically all right but salutes empty sidewalks. He has lost his mind.

The White House staff was waiting when the car pulled up at the door. Ike Hoover, the usher, thought the President looked a little peaked and spiritless, otherwise he seemed all right. But to the woman's eye of Elizabeth Jaffray, the housekeeper, there was something definitely wrong. It was something about the way he wore his clothes that made Mrs. Jaffray think him different from the careful and methodical man who had left for the trip. The staff was told the President had suffered a collapse and would be "somewhat restricting his schedule." No details were offered.

Lunch was served with John Randolph Bolling, the First Lady's brother, sitting at table along with Margaret. Afterward the President said to Grayson that he would want to go to a church service, it being a Sunday. Grayson said perhaps he had better not but encouraged him to go for a drive and get some fresh air—it would help him sleep. With the First Lady, Margaret and Bolling, he toured Rock Creek Park and Chevy Chase, returning to the White House at twilight.

Although he could use his left arm and leg, still the ghastly headaches tortured him. He could not work or even read, and wandered the White House second floor, the family living quarters, drifting from the study at one end of the hall to the First Lady's room at the other. At night he could not sleep.

The next day, Monday, he went motoring with the First Lady and Margaret from three in the afternoon until four-thirty. At five the First Lady had in for tea a dozen of the reporters who had covered the trip, explaining that the President regretted he could not join them. She made the reporters laugh when she told them that at one point on the trip, while driving in a motorcade to visit an Army post outside a town, she had thought she heard a cheer and, turning to bow and smile, found only a mooing cow looking at her.°

So passed a few days. He signed some bills, a few unimportant Congressional resolutions, dictated a handful of letters. Most of the time he stayed in his room and study and did not go to the business offices of the White House. He saw no officials, including Tumulty, but he dined downstairs with members of the family and even played some billiards. He appeared reasonably bright and cheerful even though he was still weak and in pain and had trouble sleeping. On the evening of October 1 there was a movie in the East Room and afterward he seemed so well that he said he would read aloud to the First Lady from the Bible, as he had done every night during the war. He stood under the chandelier in her room with his Bible, a small khaki-covered type given to soldiers, held in one hand. His voice was strong. When he finished he put his Bible down on a table and talked with the First Lady for a few minutes. As they chatted he wound his watch. A little after he went to his own room the First Lady noticed he had left the watch on the table and took it in to him. "That worries me, to have left that watch there," he said. "It is not like me." "Nonsense," she replied. "What difference does it make? It is what I do all the time—forget things."

That night, as she had since their return, the First Lady did not sleep well, arising often to look into his room to see how he was. At dawn she found him sleeping normally. It was after eight before she looked in again. She found him sitting on the side of his bed trying to reach for a water bottle. As she gave it to him she noticed his left hand hung loosely. "I have no feeling in that

---

° Telling the story may have been a way of impressing the reporters with the fact that saluting a cow—or, more to the point, empty sidewalks--is not necessarily a sign of insanity. This is, however, only the author's speculation.

hand," he said. "Will you rub it? But first help me to the bath-room." She got him on his feet with difficulty. Every move seemed to cause him great pain. Once he was in the bathroom, she asked if she could leave him long enough to call Grayson at home. He said yes and she went to a telephone and rang the Usher's Room downstairs. Ike Hoover answered and she said, "Please get Dr. Grayson. The President is very sick." Hoover at once telephoned Grayson and dispatched a White House car to the doctor's home. Meanwhile, upstairs, the First Lady heard a slight noise in the bathroom. She rushed in and found the President lying uncon-scious on the floor. Her first thought was to keep him warm. She snatched a blanket from his bed and while she was putting it over him he moved his head and asked for a drink of water. She gave it to him and put a pillow under his head.

After calling Grayson and sending the car, Hoover went up-stairs into the hall. All the doors were closed, and although servants were working in the area, none knew that anything was amiss. After a few minutes Grayson arrived and tried the knob on the President's door. It was locked. Grayson knocked and the First Lady admitted him. Together they lifted the President and put him on his bed. Ten minutes after entering the room Grayson came out. Hoover was still standing in the hall. "My God," Grayson gasped, "the President is paralyzed." He named a doctor and nurse and told Hoover to send for them at once. It was a little after nine in the morning.

Word soon spread in the White House that the President was ill, but beyond that nothing could be learned. Within a few hours three other doctors had joined Grayson, and two nurses were in attend-ance. No servants were allowed in the room, but Hoover was asked in to help rearrange the furniture. As he helped move things about, Hoover looked at the President lying in the enormous bed that Abra-ham Lincoln had used and thought to himself that the President looked as though he were dead. There was not a sign of life. Hoover also thought he saw a cut above the President's temple and another on his nose and assumed these had been a result of a fall.

All day the President's room was filled with doctors and nurses. The First Lady did not leave his side for a minute. Below, the serv-ants could find out nothing. But word reached the reporters in the

White House press room, and for them Grayson issued a bulletin: "The President had a fairly good night, but his condition is not at all good this morning." Later he issued a second: "The President is a very sick man. His condition is less favorable today and he has remained in bed throughout the day. After consultation with Dr. F. X. Dercum of Philadelphia, Drs. Sterling Ruffin and E. R. Stitt of Washington, in which all agreed as to his condition, it was determined that absolute rest is essential for some time."

There was no hint of what the condition might be. The New York *World*, a paper very friendly to the President, had earlier said "one thousand rumors" enveloped Washington; now, if possible, the number doubled. Suddenly people noticed that bars were in place on one window of the White House, and at once it was said they were there because the President, insane, was trying to escape and run out into the street. Other rumors had him a prisoner, unconscious, sulking. One particularly strong one was that he had contracted syphilis during a dalliance in Paris and that the effects of the disease were now making themselves felt. That Dr. Dercum was a professor of nervous and mental diseases at a Philadelphia medical college was widely held to confirm the bars-on-window theory. °

All day and all night Washington seethed. The next day, Friday, October 3, the bulletin was simply, "The President's condition is about the same, with a slight improvement." The Cabinet members were all bewildered. Tumulty, in tears, told Secretary Daniels, "We must all pray." Nothing more. Secretary of Agriculture David F. Houston saw Secretary of War Newton D. Baker at the Shoreham Hotel and Baker said, "I am scared literally to death." Houston thought to himself that Baker looked it. Later in the day the Cabinet men were all telephoned through the White House switchboard and told that by request of the Secretary of State there would be a special Cabinet meeting on Monday. That day, also, a rumor arose in New York that the President was dead. At once stock prices began dropping sharply. Calls were put in to the White House and the rumor was denied. It was decided the story was put into

---

° Although the rumor has lasted into the present day, there is irrefutable medical proof that the President never suffered from a venereal disease. The window bars were almost twenty years old and had been put in place to protect the glass from Theodore Roosevelt's ball-playing children.

motion by the sight of flags half-staffed because of the death of the Manhattan Borough President.

The bulletins continued bland. In the White House diary for Saturday, Ike Hoover wrote: "Consultation of doctors at 10 A.M. Condition said to be improving. Dr. Grayson remained all night." The First Lady was handed a note: "My little girls tomorrow morning are offering their communion for him. God will not desert us in this critical hour of need. Please let the President know that we all think of him every minute of the day and that my poor, humble prayers are lifted up each day for his early recovery. Sincerely your friend, Tumulty."

On Sunday, Secretary of the Navy Daniels called at the White House and spoke to Tumulty and Grayson. Grayson told Daniels the truth: the President was completely paralyzed on his left side. He also told him that the President was bravely asking for a stenographer to take some letters but that he was dissuaded from getting one on the basis that Sunday was a day of rest. Grayson was frank to say the excuse was a ruse and that it would be impossible for the President to do any work. Daniels was so shaken by the information that he found himself almost unable to think. He could not bring himself to tell even his wife that the President was paralyzed. It hurt too much.

Secretary of Agriculture Houston also talked with Tumulty, the latter speaking in strictest confidence, and learned the truth. He and Tumulty agreed it would be "one of the tragedies of the ages" if the President remained incapacitated. In the Shoreham Hotel at lunch, later, Houston saw the Vice President, Thomas R. Marshall. Marshall was terribly distressed and said to Houston that he was completely in the dark. He begged Houston to give him any information he had, but Houston was unable to repeat what Tumulty had told him in confidence. Marshall appeared terrified by the turn of events and was bitter at the doctors who were keeping the situation a mystery from him. He said it would be at best a tragedy for him to assume the duties of President and an equal tragedy for the American people, that he knew many men who knew more about the affairs of the government than he, but it would be especially trying for him if he had to assume the duties without warning. There was nothing Houston could say to him.

On Monday at eleven, in compliance with Secretary of State

Lansing's request, the Cabinet met in the Cabinet Room. The other Cabinet members probably did not know it, but the Secretary of State had already done some spade work for the gathering. On Friday he had called upon Tumulty, bringing with him a book which contained the text of the Constitution. Lansing pointedly read aloud to Tumulty the passages saying that in case of the removal of the President from office, or his death, resignation, or inability to discharge the powers and duties of the office, the same should devolve upon the Vice President.

When Lansing finished reading, Tumulty coldly said, "Mr. Lansing, the Constitution is not a dead letter with the White House. I have read the Constitution and do not find myself in need of any tutoring at your hands of the provision which you have just read." He then asked Lansing who could certify to the President's disability. Lansing intimated it was a job for either Grayson or Tumulty himself. Tumulty burst out that the Secretary could rest assured that while the President was "lying on the small of his back" Tumulty would not be a party to "ousting" him. "He has been too kind, too loyal and too wonderful to me to receive such treatment at my hands."

At this point Grayson walked into the room. "And I am sure," Tumulty went on, "that Dr. Grayson will never certify to his disability. Will you, Grayson?" Grayson said he most certainly would not. Tumulty then hotly said that if anybody outside the White House circle tried to certify the President as disabled within the Constitution's meaning, he and Grayson would stand together and repudiate the attempt. He added that if the President were in a position to know of Lansing's remarks it was certain that very decisive measures would be taken.

At the Cabinet meeting, Lansing, presiding, said it was necessary to decide whether or not the government was going to be carried on. He added there was nothing to guide the Cabinet as to who would decide the question of the President's ability to discharge his duties. Somebody said that if the question had to be considered at all it should be done only after the Cabinet received authoritative word as to the President's condition. They decided to send for Grayson, and a messenger was sent to ask the doctor to come to the Cabinet Room. While they waited, they discussed the situation.

"The business of the Government must go on," Lansing said. He read out the same constitutional provisions he had propounded to Tumulty. Someone pointed out that President Garfield had been shot in July of 1881 and had not died until September and that Garfield's secretary ran the government during that time. But someone else mentioned that Congress was not in session during the period, as now it was, and that, had it been, serious questions otherwise ignored would have had to be faced.

Grayson came in. Lansing said, "Dr. Grayson, we wish to know the nature and extent of the President's illness, and whether he is able to perform the duties of his office, so that we may determine what shall be done to carry on the business of the Government." Grayson said the President was suffering from a nervous breakdown, indigestion and a depleted system, that it was "touch and go," the "scales might tip either way and they might tip the wrong way" if the President were harassed by business matters. The President should be bothered as little as possible; any excitement would kill him. Grayson also said that when moments before he left the sickroom the President asked what the Cabinet wanted and by whose authority it was meeting.

There was no immediate answer to this implied question, for several Cabinet members said at the same time that they were meeting to get information and take up business matters arising since their last meeting prior to the President's trip. Secretary of War Baker made a point of saying that the Cabinet was very anxious that Grayson express the sympathy of all the men to the President. More efforts to get something out of Grayson—"tell us more exactly what was the trouble"—elicited nothing beyond "His condition is encouraging but we are not yet out of the woods." The meeting ended.

For days the bulletins were all the same: "The President had a very good night, and if there is any change in his condition it is favorable. . . . The President had a restful and comfortable day. . . ." There was absolutely nothing concrete given out, and for the first time in his career Tumulty had no off-the-record information for the White House reporters. Soon it was said all over America that a madman raving in wild delirium sat at the head of the government, or an imbecile whose mind was completely gone. One paper said the Cabinet was on the verge of asking the Vice

President to take over the government; Tumulty denied it was so. Even the sympathetic New York *World* editorialized about the fact that only "vague generalities" were given out: "From the beginning of his illness to the present moment not a word has come from the sick-chamber that can be regarded as frankly enlightening. Mystery begets mystification."

The President's brother, Joseph Wilson, a Baltimore businessman, wrote Tumulty: "It has seemed to me that it would not be amiss at least for the attending physicians to make a more detailed statement than any that has so far appeared concerning the real cause and the extent of the President's illness, in order to satisfy the public mind and to refute the numerous rumors which are afloat." The suggestion was not complied with. But heavy traffic was diverted from streets near the White House, and the musicians of a hotel band a block away were asked not to play loud numbers.

On October 12 papers all over the country carried the text of a letter sent by Senator George Moses of New Hampshire to a friend and released by the friend to a New Hampshire paper. Moses wrote: "Of course he may get well—that is, he may live—but if he does he will not be any material force or factor in anything. . . . There is no possibility that Mr. Wilson would be able to perform the functions of his office either in the immediate or remote future." Grayson refused to make any comment on the letter, saying that if he answered every rumor he would have no time to attend to the President's health. The *World* reluctantly had to point out that this did not answer the rumors. When Attorney General A. Mitchell Palmer went to speak at a Philadelphia Columbus Day celebration, he was surrounded by reporters before he went onto the Academy of Music stage. "What is the President's condition?" he was bluntly asked. "You read the papers, don't you?" he answered. "Don't you know any more than that?" "I do not." "Does any Cabinet member know any more about it than what he reads in the papers?" "No."°

° At about this time a worried official of the United Press asked the manager of the Washington bureau, "Suppose Wilson was running around nekkid on the second floor of the White House, and nobody could ketch him—how would you find out about it?" The bureau manager had to reply that for all he knew the President was in fact doing just what the UP official described.

Palmer was wrong in saying no Cabinet man knew anything beyond what a newspaper reader would know, but one man in Washington definitely had no more information than the newspaper reader. He was the Vice President of the United States, Thomas Riley Marshall of Indiana. Marshall had come to the governorship of his state after practicing law for a third of a century in Columbia City, Indiana, population three thousand, and was a rustic type, physically unimpressive, who often said very amusing things that made people laugh. (William McAdoo saw Marshall's best scene as a country grocery store where he could sit by the stove and tell stories with his cronies.) The Vice President was the greatest possible contrast to the President in every way besides geographically and so had been nominated in 1912 and again in 1916 to balance the ticket. His destiny was the traditional one of American Vice Presidents: like the sailor lost at sea, he was never heard of again. At least it was so in Washington that he was a completely discounted factor. But in the hinterlands he was known as a lecturer who would appear anywhere a fee awaited him. He had no substantial private resources beyond his $12,000 annual salary and found the lecture trail an attractive financial proposition.

The first Vice President ever to go lecturing, he explained he had either to give his talks, "steal, or resign." He always kept in his mind the advice given him by William Jennings Bryan, the acknowledged king of the lecture trail: "Always get your money before you step onto the platform. Don't be standing around later waiting for it. Don't step onto the platform unless you already have the money in your pocket." On his endless travels to keep his lecture dates he amused himself by spinning tall tales to his fellow passengers in the day coaches, few of whom recognized him. One such fellow passenger, complaining that business in the auto accessories line was slow, learned from Marshall that he was a dope peddler, a narcotics salesman. The man asked if this line wasn't against the law and Marshall told him that yes, it was, but he had a special arrangement with the authorities in Washington.

Upon the occasions when he was in the capital Marshall spent most of his time working at getting jobs for his cronies, telephoning people from his office, which, however, did not please him. He wanted one where he could put his feet up on the desk, and instead had to do with one that was too easily accessible and did not differ much "from a monkey cage, except that the visitors do not offer me any peanuts." A cigar was never absent from his face or hand, and of course he will always be remembered for the remark he made during a Senate debate: "What this country needs is a really good five-cent cigar."

After the first two or three terrifying days of the President's illness, the bland bulletins seemed to put Marshall's mind at ease, for his humorous inclinations did not desert him. On October 6, as Senator Borah bitterly argued about the League of Nations with the Democratic Minority Leader, Senator Gilbert Hitchcock of Nebraska, Marshall from his seat as presiding officer interrupted to put before the Senate a letter he had received. He had it read out by the Secretary of the Senate. It was from a brand-new father who wanted the Senate to help him choose a name for his baby boy. He sought, the man wrote Marshall, to name the boy after a Senator, any Senator. "The man who will give the baby the biggest prize can have the name . . . Mr. Marshall, see what you can do for me." (Sometimes the Vice President's levity shocked people.)

A few days earlier, when a delegation went by train to New York to welcome the King and Queen of the Belgians to America, the usual Washington attitude toward Marshall was demonstrated when the Secretary of State was given a private compartment on the train and Marshall and his wife were given two seats in a coach. (After the King and Queen and their son, the Duke of Brabant, later King Leopold III, learned of the President's illness, they announced they were abandoning their ceremonial tour of the country and would travel in a quiet way, incognito.)

Marshall had, it was true, sat in on a few Cabinet meetings at the President's suggestion in late 1918 when the President was in Europe for the Peace Conference. But soon he gave up his attendance, saying if he couldn't have the President's $75,000 a year he was not going to do any of the President's work. He added that he preferred his own job, anyway—"No responsibilities." But in October of 1919, Marshall was in the position, whether he liked it or not, of being liable to have to take over the President's duties at any moment. The Cabinet had not formally discussed the possible devolution of the President's duties upon the Vice President, but the thought was in everybody's mind. And yet for days nothing was said by anybody to the Vice President about the possibility.

Finally Tumulty decided Marshall should be told something of the situation he was in. Thinking that it would be unwise for anyone formally connected with the President to speak with Marshall —any direct statement might be used as proof of Presidential disability—it was decided to send a completely unofficial person to tell Marshall clearly that at any moment he might find himself President of the United States. The man chosen was J. Fred Essary, a reporter for the Baltimore *Sun*. Essary went to Marshall's office and sat by the Vice President's desk. As the reporter began to speak, Marshall lowered his head and put his hands on the desk. His teeth gripped his cigar. Essary said what he had to say, giving no details beyond what he himself had been told: the President could die at any moment. When Essary finished, he waited for Marshall to speak. But the Vice President, head bowed, was silent. Essary uncertainly stood up and waited. Marshall did not say a word. Essary went to the door, opened it, looked back. Marshall's head was still down. The cigar had gone out. He was looking at his hands. Essary went out and closed the door behind him.

7

The word "thrombosis" refers to a clotting of blood in a blood vessel. Such a condition can block the blood's normal movement in a part of the body. It is caused by a multiplicity of reasons and can be brought on by overwork and hypertension. It is not the same thing as a "stroke," in which the blood vessel ruptures, but the symptoms are very similar.

Some of the symptoms of a thrombosis in the human brain are violent stomach upsets—which are at first often diagnosed as resulting from indigestion or influenza—and hitherto unexperienced insomnia, twitching of the face, difficulty in using a pen, headaches, great weakness, and paralysis of one side of the body (which may come and then temporarily go).

These are the physical distresses, obvious to anyone who comes in contact with the patient. There are also more subtle mental changes. The victim often becomes unreasonable, apprehensive, irritable. He may become violently emotional—the most common characteristic is frequent crying spells—and lose a great deal of his judgment. One thrombosis in the brain may well be shaken off, but eventually there will be another, although the second may not come for months or even years. The process by which repeated clottings end the patient's life may, in some cases, take up to twenty or even thirty years. In effect, little bites, one with each thrombosis, are being taken of the brain. The brain is slowly dying. When there is one bite too many, the brain dies.

The great Louis Pasteur suffered a thrombosis and lived to do some of his finest work with two thirds of a brain. However, most doctors advise the family of a man who has suffered a serious thrombosis to retire him from business immediately and to guard him against temptations which formerly would not have interested him. Important businessmen, shorn of their judgment by the condition, have lost their fortunes in months. Clergymen have taken up with prostitutes.

In April of 1919, in Paris, the President of the United States suffered, according to all evidence available after the fact, a thrombosis in his brain. His illness was diagnosed as influenza by his doctor—a logical diagnosis at a time when influenza outbreaks were sweeping the world. When the President got up from his sickbed, certain strange things in him were seen—his sudden decision, later rescinded, that he go home; his worry about the furniture in the house he occupied; his suspicion of the French servants; his rapid banishment of Colonel House from his confidence; his insistence that official cars not be used for formerly permitted pleasure trips—but not too much attention was paid to these changes.

There were two reasons working to prohibit much inquiry. One was that he was under enormous strain during the peace negotiations and could logically have been expected to develop eccentricities; the second was that he was the President, a strong President and a strong personality, and there was not a person who could say him no. In any event, none of his actions were in themselves terribly objectionable—House, for instance, was disliked and distrusted by many people, including Cary Grayson and the First Lady, and perhaps the servants *were* spies and the cars overused.

So the Peace Conference ended and the President came home to fight for the League of Nations. But when on his tour he collapsed, one half of his face fallen and his arm and leg temporarily paralyzed, Dr. Grayson knew at once that serious brain damage had been sustained. Once back in Washington, there was reason to hope that with rest he might well throw off the effects of the thrombosis and get back to something approaching normal health. Then came the morning when he fell in his bathroom. After that he lay between life and death for several days. Only a tiny group of people, half a dozen, had access to his sickroom. The doctors called in as consultants could, of course, not dictate what the President should do in non-medical matters. Cary Grayson, in addition to being a doctor, was a naval officer on active duty, sworn to obey the orders of his Commander in Chief and therefore voiceless in policy matters. The President himself was desperately ill and unable to decide anything. There was only one person who could speak in his name and make use of, and make felt, his powers as President. Only one person could decide that he would continue in his job as though nothing had happened.

She made the decision. He would continue to function as President of the United States. No one was seeing him, not Tumulty, not Daniels, not Lansing, no Cabinet officer, no Senator, but he was still the President. In the Executive Offices of the White House, Tumulty bravely stalled off inquiries about the state of things by giving vague replies, but the staff saw him day after day looking more worried as he wandered from office to office, picking up papers and putting them down. At first documents and requests continued to go up to the second-floor family quarters for Presidential action, but when no answers were forthcoming and urgent letters simply vanished, the flow began to slow down. Things were put off and put off, but the officials began to wonder where all this was leading.

One day the chief mail clerk, a horse-race fan who often went to the track with Grayson, met the doctor in the hall and tried to buttonhole him with the mail situation. Unanswered letters were piling up, the mail clerk said; what was to be done? Grayson gave a vague reply and tried to get away. The clerk desperately said an important personal letter for the President had arrived. "I don't think anyone else can handle it." Grayson thought a moment and said, "I'll talk to Mrs. Wilson and see what we can do." Gratefully the clerk sent the letter up to the family quarters, bypassing Joe Tumulty completely. This was one way of getting things done and Tumulty never said anything about it.

Not long afterward there came a letter from Judge Learned Hand enclosing a letter signed by the head of the Bureau of Investigation of the Department of Justice—the later FBI—and containing very serious charges of graft against a high Administration official. The letter was for the President's personal attention. When the other staff people had gone home for the night, the chief mail clerk showed the letters to Charles Swem, the President's stenographer, and asked his opinion about what should be done. As Swem read the letters, Tumulty came in and looked over his shoulder. He took in the gist of the material at once and reached out his hand. "Let me have those." Swem snatched at the papers and said, "No, I'm handling this." Tumulty, bigger and stronger, got a good grip and pulled the letters out of Swem's hands. The chief mail clerk stayed back during the short struggle and said nothing as Tumulty went off with the letters. (Again, it was a way of getting things done and at least the thing was off *his* shoulders.) The clerk never did find out what, if anything, was done. Things in the office had almost come to a standstill.

Meanwhile, in the living quarters, a prostatic obstruction began to develop in the patient, blocking elimination from the bladder. Dr. Hugh Young, a specialist, was called in from Johns Hopkins and he made repeated attempts to dilate the muscles forming the contraction in hope that the bladder could thus be drained. He failed, and on October 17 all elimination ceased. The five consulting doctors and Grayson held a tense meeting. If the condition was not remedied there would be a progressive poisoning of the body, followed by irreversible and fatal uremia. The doctors talked in one room; in another room, the President's, the First Lady sat by as nurses applied hot packs to the distended bladder. The President's pulse slowed, then speeded up dangerously. His temperature rose.

After a time Grayson opened the door and beckoned the First Lady. She went out of the room to stand with him by a window looking over the south lawn toward the Washington Monument. He said to her that the other doctors felt there must be immediate surgery but that he himself felt an operation would be more than the President could stand, that it would mean his death. Grayson had walked around the block to get himself together in order to present the matter to the First Lady. "There is nothing else but for you to decide."

She thought to herself that it was like a chasm opening under her feet. But she said, "We will not operate. You know more than anyone else of the real chances of recovery. So go down and tell them I feel that Nature will finally take care of things, and we will wait." Grayson went out but was back in a minute with Dr. Young, who took a pencil and paper from his pocket and drew diagrams to try to convince her that there must be an operation at once. She walked blindly into her dressing room, Young following. Dr. Sterling Ruffin came in and backed up Young, and so did Dr. Francis Dercum. But she kept saying no, no, she was afraid of an operation.

As they tensely went over the situation one of the nurses came in and said the President was asking for the First Lady. She went toward his room; as she walked out Young called, "You understand, Mrs. Wilson, the whole body will become poisoned if this condition lasts an hour, or at the most two hours longer!" She went in and the President smiled as he always did and always would whenever she appeared. He reached out his thin white hand for her to grip. She stayed there holding him as the doctors and nurses bent over the bed and the hands of the clock seemed to fly. Every few minutes his temperature was taken, the reading each time higher. He tossed restlessly as the hot packs were applied, and for two hours they were this way until the muscles relaxed and normal flow took place. Exhausted, the President slept.

But the crisis weakened him. For some days prior to it the First Lady devoted ten minutes a day to keeping him up on the news, but now he had not the energy to concentrate for even that long. It was the worst possible time for him to be in this condition, for his attention was desperately needed by a country undergoing the violent stresses the war engendered. All over America it was said the radicals were rising in revolution, and groups of ex-soldiers banded together to attack street-corner speakers they identified with Lenin and Trotsky—in New York civilians joined three hundred policemen, half on horseback, to charge five thousand radical sympathizers gathered on Fifth Avenue and yelling "Down with the capitalists!"—but nothing was heard from the White House about the strife. (Instead, the Attorney General, A. Mitchell Palmer, began to think along the lines that would soon see him arresting hundreds of people without warrant and deporting them without hearings.) A series of terrifying race riots broke out all over the country—in Washington, Chicago, Omaha, Mobile, Gary—but the President could not speak out. (Secretary of War Baker tried to step into the breach and sent Army troops to various towns to quiet the rioters.) The conference called to try to adjust the widespread labor troubles met, but without the President's guidance it accomplished nothing, and the stock market reacted by plunging

THE SECOND MRS. WILSON   105

downward. A coal strike involving half a million miners began brewing, and although a Presidential statement was made saying the strike would be "unjustifiable" and "unlawful" no one believed the President wrote it. (He did not. Tumulty did.) Government injunctions against the strike were gotten and laboring people raged. A specially appointed arbitrator, the Secretaries of the Treasury and of Agriculture, as well as A. Mitchell Palmer and the now out-of-office William McAdoo, all worked to settle the acrimonious coal dispute, but their efforts appeared to be failing. Secretary Daniels mourned the bitterness that necessitated the dispatch of troops to the mining towns and said that if he were not ill the President would have nipped the whole thing in the bud. The rise in the price of mere existence was alarming—the letters "HCL" referring to the high cost of living were constantly in the headlines—and shops were boycotted by belligerent women attacking anyone trying to buy from the "profiteers"—a term become as familiar as "HCL." There were shortages in many basic foodstuffs and it was figured the price of food was up 88 per cent since 1913. Nothing was done by the White House. In the wake of the demobilization of the great Army and Navy enormous problems arose, with hundreds of thousands of ex-servicemen unable to get jobs—nothing was done.

If the Executive Branch of the government was motionless, the Congress likewise offered no leadership. One question obsessed it: Should the United States go into the League of Nations on exactly the President's terms or should the reservations and amendments worked out by Senator Lodge be attached to any entry? In the White House that was also the only thing that mattered. Most of the hours of the day the President lay dozing, too weak to attend to even his natural functions without aid, too weak to eat. Even to speak a word was tiring to him. But when he could muster his strength at all, it was to whisper hoarsely to the First Lady that she must allow no compromise with Senator Lodge.

Meanwhile the bland bulletins were assuring the country that the President was slowly getting back to normal. Secretary Daniels, a newspaperman before his government service, thought it a terrible thing to lie to the public this way. "If you would tell the people exactly what is the matter with the President," Daniels told Grayson, "a wave of sympathy would pour into the White House, whereas now there is nothing but uncertainty and criticism." "I think you are right," Grayson replied. "I wish I could do so. But I am forbidden. The President and Mrs. Wilson have made me promise to that effect." The stated rationale of this was the thought that the true news of the President's condition would encourage the League's enemies to new efforts. So Grayson, silent or vague to questioners, went about trying to help his patient.

That patient was the most disciplined and the bravest that a doctor could know. He was uncomplaining as he lay in his bed. There was never, ever, not then, not after, a word of complaint. He even preserved his sense of humor: a week after the bathroom fall, too weak even to swallow, he held up a finger to halt the First Lady's attempt to hold a spoon to his lips and gestured that Grayson should come close. The doctor bent over and the patient whispered, "A wonderful bird is the pelican; his bill will hold more than his bellican. He can take in his beak enough food for a week. I wonder how in the hell-he-can."°

Upon another occasion Grayson and Dr. Young stood by the bed and discussed shaving the President's face, which had not been touched by a razor since the morning of the fall in the bathroom. Young said that one of the doctors could do it: "You know, in the olden days the doctors were barbers. Doctors were really barbers in those days." There was a whisper from the man on the bed: "They are barbarous yet."

After perhaps two weeks had passed since the thrombosis, it was decided that the President could be lifted out of bed for a few minutes every day and placed in a chair by the window. On October 22, twenty days after the First Lady found him unconscious in the bathroom, he put his signature to four bills sent up by the Congress, and a few days later he vetoed the Volstead Act.°° The First Lady placed a pen in his trembling hand and steadied and pointed it as he signed his name where she indicated. The effort completely exhausted him. But the signature was a parody of his usual firm stroke. The o's of his first name were left open at the top and the slanting of the letters was completely foreign to his

---

° Grayson's retelling of the incident at the time perhaps gave rise to the widely believed rumor that the President's mind was a total blank save for an ability to recite childhood nursery rhymes.

°° The act was later passed over his veto.

former fashion. As soon as the signatures were seen by Senators familiar with his writing, debates in the cloakroom centered upon the question of who had forged the President's name. Most Senators said it was Tumulty's work; others thought the First Lady did it. A microscope was obtained to study the writing; a handwriting expert was hired and urged to express an opinion.

No resolution of sympathy was offered in Congress for him, but one Senator wanted to introduce a bill ousting the President "whenever for any reason whatsoever" he became "unable for a period of six weeks to perform the duties devolved upon him." Another wanted to give power to determine Presidential inability to the Supreme Court, that body to make an investigation when authorized by concurrent Congressional resolution. Senator Moses, who had written the widely publicized letter about the illness, took the lead in diagnosing the President's condition and soon his fellow legislators universally addressed him as "Doc." Senator Albert Fall of New Mexico violently declared in meetings of the Senate Foreign Relations Committee that the elected President was not in office. He pounded his fist on the table and shouted, "We have petticoat Government! Mrs. Wilson is President!" (He also said the Democrats ought to ask Congress to adjourn until there was a legitimate President in office.) Other people were talking about the First Lady and it began to be said that she was the "Presidentess" who had fulfilled the dreams of the suffragettes by changing her title from First Lady to Acting First Man.

Perhaps to counter the stories about him, the White House people wanted the President to receive the King and Queen of the Belgians, who, after touring the country incognito in respect for the President's illness, were now coming to Washington. When the royal couple and their son first planned the American visit, it was planned to have them as White House guests for several days, but now instead they stayed at the home of Breckinridge Long, Third Assistant Secretary of State, with Vice President Marshall (who was very resentful of the cost to him) acting as official host. (During the period of his term as official host, Marshall declined to preside over the Senate, explaining he could not perform the President's work as entertainer of royalty one minute and the Vice President's duties as head of the Senate the next. "Too much Jekyll and Hyde for him," Breckinridge Long wrote in his diary.)

The Belgians came on the afternoon of October 30, the first out-siders, save for the medical people, to see the President. The First Lady served them tea in the Red Room and then they went up to the President, bearing with them a gift for him, a set of eighteen beautiful plates showing Belgian scenes. They also had a fan, deco-rated with diamonds and sapphires, for the First Lady.

The President received them in bed. He wore a dressing gown. The King and Queen must have been surprised to see the Presi-dent's white beard—the doctors had decided not to shave him— but the visit went off pleasantly. After a few minutes the First Lady took them out and showed them through the White House. When the tour was over the Queen asked if she could not introduce to the President her son, the seventeen-year-old heir to the throne, who had waited below. So they went up again, to find the Presi-dent's dressing gown, clumsy in bed, had been changed for an old gray sweater purchased many years before on a visit to Scotland. The Queen was delighted to find him studying the scenes on the plates through a magnifying glass, and the President in turn greeted the young future King, apologizing for the old sweater.

At the front door a corps of reporters waited to fall upon the royal couple with questions about the President's condition. The answers blandly indicated he was fine, and the Queen remarked he had on a worn sweater. The reporters misunderstood and printed the information that the President received in torn clothing. The next day mail poured in from people eager to tell the First Lady she ought to be ashamed of herself for letting the President wear ripped things. Old ladies sent wool, saying she could use it for darning her husband's clothes.

One week later, Senator Gilbert Hitchcock of Nebraska, the Democratic Minority Leader, was received. Hitchcock, a newspa-per owner, was the not particularly brilliant nor strong leader of a party entirely dominated in the past by its very strong President. Understandably Hitchcock felt timid about his mission, which was to say clearly to the President that the Democrats could not raise even a majority of Senate votes for ratification without reserva-tions, let alone the necessary two-thirds count. He was shown into the bedroom where the President lay propped up in bed, with the First Lady and Grayson standing by. Hitchcock's first reaction was shock at the long white beard. He falteringly got out his opinion that the Lodge amendments must be accepted. Otherwise, it would be impossible to get the United States into the League, utterly impossible.

"It *is* possible! It *is* possible!" the President gasped out.

"Mr. President, it might be wise to compromise——" Hitchcock started to say.

"Let Lodge compromise!"

"Well, of course, he must compromise also. But we might well hold out the olive branch."

"Let Lodge hold out the olive branch!"

Hitchcock was shown out.

On November 13 there was another visitor: the Prince of Wales, later King Edward and Duke of Windsor, who was touring Canada and America. The Prince arrived ten minutes late for his appointment and apologized to the First Lady by explaining he had just come from visiting Mount Vernon, where he was detained by a "very charming young lady" who gave him flowers and engaged him in conversation. Actually the Prince was being gallant in describing the lady as "young," for she was a woman who insisted on telling him of his grandfather's tour of America half a century before, at which time, she said, the grandfather gave her a kiss. The attractive young Prince made the First Lady laugh with his explanation and after tea in the Blue Room they went up to see the President.

Prince Edward, little more than a boy, and boyish in his ways, came bouncing into the room. "I am very glad to see you again, Mr. President," he began, referring to their meeting in London during the President's visit there. There was silence. The Prince sat down by the bed and tried to find something to say. "My, what a magnificent bed this is, Mr. President," he got out. The President smiled with the right side of his face. But he was having great trouble with his speech that day. "This—is—the—bed—that—Abraham—Lincoln—" he said slowly, word by word, and talked about the bed while the Prince nervously pleated his trousers. The President mentioned the visit of the Prince's grandfather, the later Edward VII, and said the grandfather had slept in the Lincoln bed and one night slipped out the window for a social event not on his official program. This gave Prince Edward a chance to jump up and look out the window. "Do you think it was this window, sir?" The President said he unfortunately did not know.

The visit had important implications. They stemmed from the fact that the Prince, and only the Prince, was invited to call. For the British Ambassador had been desperately trying to see the President. The Ambassador was Viscount Grey of Falloden, who as British Foreign Secretary Sir Edward Grey had written the President a touching letter when Ellen Wilson died. Now old, sick, half blind, Lord Grey had come out of retirement to travel to America and lend his efforts toward getting the United States into the League of Nations under any conditions necessary. He arrived just as the President fell ill and, undergoing treatment for his eyes at Johns Hopkins in the interim, waited for the President to meet with him. He had no reason to think he was in personal disfavor with the President—or the President's wife—and of course before his appointment the British Government had asked if he was acceptable to the President and had been told he was "entirely" so.

But when Lord Grey arrived in America it was discovered that he had brought with him a British Army officer, Major Charles Kennedy Craufurd-Stuart, who had been secretary to the preceding British Ambassador, Lord Reading. Craufurd-Stuart was a musically gifted man of the world who composed songs ("At Gloaming Tide," "Make-Believe Land") and played the piano. He was very much up on gossip and he did not care much for Americans. During the last days of Lord Reading's reign as Ambassador, in late 1918, just before the President went to Europe, Craufurd-Stuart at a party, between piano renditions, combined love of gossip and distaste for at least one American and spoke very recklessly about the First Lady. The extremely knowledgeable Washington hostess Mrs. J. Borden (Daisy) Harriman marked him off as a crazy man, and so did other people, but word of his remarks about the First Lady—with all ramifications of the stories about her buying off Mrs. Peck—quickly reached the White House.

Lord Reading was asked to send Craufurd-Stuart home. When Craufurd-Stuart heard his chief had been asked to send him back to England, he at once went to the home of Secretary of State Lansing and begged that the Americans not insist on his banishment—it would destroy his career. Lansing told him he should be more discreet in his talk, and the pressure for his recall relaxed. Then the President went to Europe and Lord Reading gave up the ambassadorship and went home, accompanied by Craufurd-Stuart. That seemed to be the end of any American service for Craufurd-Stuart. It was a surprise when Lord Grey brought him back to Washington.

As soon as Craufurd-Stuart arrived with Lord Grey, the White House sent word through the State Department that the man was not wanted in America. Lord Grey asked why and got no reply. He insisted on an explanation and was told that Craufurd-Stuart had slandered the First Lady. Lord Grey did not believe the demand for the dismissal came from the President, and he did not send Craufurd-Stuart packing. State Department men from the Secretary down went to see Lord Grey, asking Craufurd-Stuart's dispatch home, and Cary Grayson appeared to say he should go on "an early steamship." Lord Grey refused, and the State Department, under heavy pressure from Grayson, threatened to declare the man persona non grata. Lord Grey countered by notifying the State Department that he was changing Craufurd-Stuart's status from British attaché accredited to the American Government to mere member of the Ambassador's household—a position not subject to dismissal proceedings brought by the Americans. Grayson gave up, but he noted in the First Lady's attitude something which indicated she did not think Lansing had tried hard enough to get rid of her alleged slanderer. Craufurd-Stuart stayed, but when Prince Edward went by invitation to the White House, he went alone. Lord Grey began to meet for talks about the League with Senators—including Senator Lodge.

Colonel House from his New York home viewed all this with apprehension. He wrote in his diary that the agitation against Craufurd-Stuart was the work of the First Lady, not the President. The President's illness of course made House very uneasy, and his discomfiture was increased when in response to his offers to be of any aid whatsoever the First Lady coldly wrote she could think of nothing for him to do. (His was one of the few letters to the White House that got an answer, and it was an answer the First Lady must have grimly enjoyed writing. She had not forgotten who it was that tried to stop her marriage to the President.) House was not entirely discouraged and, without any inside information, seemed to assume the cheering bulletins were accurate. He wrote again to the President and then sent his views about the League to the President, care of the First Lady: "Of course the arguments are all with the position you have taken and against that of the Senate, but, unfortunately, no amount of logic can alter the situation . . . Let Senator Hitchcock know that you expect it to be ratified in some form . . . Its practical workings in the future will not be seriously hampered . . . and time will give us a workable machine.

"To the ordinary man the distance between the treaty and the reservations is slight."

To these letters House received no reply, and the fact shook his faith in the bulletins indicating everything was quite in order at the White House. He had been accustomed to being called "dearest friend" by the President, and this new and sudden silence made him wonder who was in charge of his friend's household. Uneasily saying that it was possible a "bedroom circle" was keeping him from the President, he wondered if the First Lady even let the President see the letters. Actually he might have saved himself the trouble of writing at all, for some of his letters were never opened at all until the President's correspondence was deposited in the Library of Congress. That was in 1952, more than three decades later.

Early in the Senate battle over the League, the Republican Senator James Watson of Indiana said to Senator Lodge, "I don't see how we are ever going to defeat this proposition. I don't see how it is possible to defeat it." Lodge replied, "Ah, my dear James, I do not propose to try to beat it by direct frontal attack, but by the indirect method of reservations." In mid-November, visiting Lodge at his home, Watson said, "Suppose the President accepts the treaty with your reservations. Then we are in the League." Lodge smiled—a very confident smile, Watson thought. Lodge spoke of the hatred the President felt for him personally. "Never," Lodge said, "under any set of circumstances in this world could he be induced to accept a treaty with Lodge reservations appended to it." Watson was doubtful. "That seems to me to be a rather slender thread on which to hang so great a cause," he said. "A slender thread!" Lodge exclaimed. "Why, it is as strong as any cable with its strands wired and twisted together."

In the Senate there were those who came to agree with Lodge

in this estimate of the President's likely reaction, but there were those who also said that if the President's scholastic career had not been more distinguished than the Senator's everything would turn out all right. But still there was a chance something could be worked out. Colonel House tried one last time. He asked Stephen Bonsal, an aide of his during the Peace Conference, to talk to Lodge and get some sort of private promise on what Lodge would accept as final amendments. It was in House's nature to pacify— "The Yes, Yes, Man" was what the First Lady called him—and he thought that if the President would agree to accept terms privately given by Lodge, Lodge would accept this sop and let the League be passed. Bonsal got Lodge to write down what he would want in less than one hundred words of signed statement. Bonsal took it to the White House. It was never heard of again. Colonel House said the First Lady either destroyed it or did not bring it to the President's attention. Lodge, of course, took the White House silence as the final slap in the face.

As the time for a vote approached, Senator Hitchcock found there was utterly no possibility of carrying out the task the President had assigned him. The Senate simply did not contain enough men willing to follow blindly the dictates of the President. There were the "Irreconcilables," who would not vote for the League under any circumstances, and it was of no use to talk to them. But there were also the "Mild Reservationists," who wanted the United States in the League just so long as certain safeguards were taken, safeguards generally described as aimed at preventing too free use of American troops in policing the world. If these men could have their reservations, the United States would be in the League. But denied their reservations, they would vote nay. Other men outside the Senate knew this, and each day letters and telegrams poured into the White House begging the President to swallow the reservations and get the country into the League. Few if any of these pleas reached the man they were intended for. Joe Tumulty constantly sent up notes begging for compromise but got no reply beyond the First Lady's statement that no compromise could be permitted. Finally admitted to the sickroom to present his case for acceptance of the reservations, but warned not to excite the President, Tumulty was kept by the First Lady's glare from getting too emphatic.

On November 17, Hitchcock came again. All the men who had been at Paris were for acceptance of reservations; Bernard Baruch was for them, Herbert Hoover, almost every man in the Cabinet. It fell to Hitchcock to try to convince the President. "You haven't come to talk compromise, have you?" the First Lady said to him outside the sickroom. Hitchcock began to plead with her. Defeat would bitterly shake the President, the Senator pointed out. Wasn't it best to get at least half a loaf? She told him to wait and went into her husband's room. "For my sake," she said, "won't you accept these reservations and get this awful thing settled?"

He turned his head on the pillow. He took her hand. "Little girl, don't you desert me; that I cannot stand. Can't you see I have no moral right to accept any change in a paper I have already signed? It is not *I* who will not accept; it is the Nation's honor that is at stake." His eyes were gleaming. "Better a thousand times to go down fighting than to dip your colors to dishonorable compromise."

Hitchcock came in. He asked the President what was to be done. The reply was there could be no amendments, no reservations. Anything but a complete acceptance would constitute a nullification. The President dictated a letter to Hitchcock which the First Lady wrote down and handed the Senator: "I hope that all true friends of the treaty will refuse to support the Lodge reservations."

Thinking to himself that the President still heard in his mind the roaring cheers of the Western crowds, that in his ears rang the sounds of the last thing he heard from the American people, the shouts of the throng yelling for him in Pueblo before the quiet walk by the train standing still on the prairie, Hitchcock went to the Senate and delivered to the others the message the President had for them.

That afternoon the question of whether the Senate should approve the treaty with the Lodge reservations was put to a vote. It was defeated by those men who complied with the President's instructions. Then the Senate voted on the treaty as it was brought back from Paris. It was defeated by Senator Lodge's followers.

It was she, of course, who told him. He was silent for a long time and then he said, "I must get well."

8 On November 18 the members of the
Cabinet, meeting at the behest of Secretary Lansing, were able to
look from the Cabinet Room in the Executive Wing of the White
House and see, over on the South Portico, the man who had appointed them to office. Huddled in blankets and wearing a cap, the
President sat in a wheel chair. He was motionless. His wife and
doctor stood by him. He was gazing at the sheep brought in as a
wartime labor-saving move to crop the south lawn.

This was the President's first breath of fresh air since the fall
in the bathroom. His wheel chair was not the usual invalid conveyance, for when one of the standard types was tried it was found
to be useless for him: unable to sit upright in it, he slid down to
one side and would have fallen to the floor. Instead, the White
House usher, Ike Hoover, suggested a replacement—one of the
single-person rolling chairs used then and now on the boardwalk
at Atlantic City. A dealer in Atlantic City agreed to rent one out for
five dollars a week, and when it arrived Hoover and some White
House workmen changed the footrest part of it so that the President
was able to sit with his legs out in a straight line from the seat in a
fashion that afforded him more support. Seated in the chair, he
was taken down in an elevator and rolled out onto the portico. He
stayed perhaps fifteen minutes and then was taken back upstairs
and to bed.

If this quick glimpse was all that the Cabinet men were to be given of their chief, they yet were operating under his orders. His stenographer, Charles Swem, had found that the President was unable to dictate for more than five minutes at a time—at the end of that period the President would lose the thread of what he was saying and simply halt and fall silent as he gazed into space—but in the President's name dictates were given to his subordinates, the members of his Cabinet. Cary Grayson thought, correctly, that it would have been the part of cruelty to disturb the President with every detail of public affairs, and the First Lady fervently agreed, but there yet existed those questions for which decisions must be made. These questions were generally presented in written form upon the elegantly embossed stationery of the various government departments—The Secretary of State, Washington; The Secretary of the Navy—complete with circular seals of office. They were not presented in person, for when this was tried the callers found themselves confronted with a tall woman who said in response to all pleas for a personal interview, "I am not interested in the President of the United States. I am interested in my husband and his health."

Many of the letters delivered to the White House by messengers from the various departments not only needed answers but absolutely had to have them. But for most of the letters, for by far the greater percentage, there were no answers. It was as if, to draw a homey parallel, a man running a store falls ill. The store remains open. The customers come in, stand in line, order their goods— and then wait. Their orders are not filled by the wife of the owner standing behind the counter. They order again. They wait. But the proprietor's wife either ignores them or seems to forget the orders. Eventually the customers, bewildered, go home. And yet they live on. They borrow food, or use cans stocked up in the cupboard, or eat out—or something. They postpone doing the wash, or they eat off paper plates—or something. They live on. Secretary of the Navy Daniels, for instance, would write the President that he needed the President's endorsement of a considered decision to expel from the Naval Academy a number of midshipmen who got drunk on a Caribbean summer cruise and contracted "immoral diseases." The letter, citing applicable rules calling for what a responsible Secretary considered a desirable move, would be sent to the White House—and never heard of again. After a while Daniels would write Tumulty that the midshipmen involved, after having been told they were going to be expelled, were still in residence at Annapolis, where by their presence they were hurtful to the discipline of their classmates. Daniels would beg for "speedy action"— quick dismissal of the men. There would be no reply. Daniels would apply again. Then he would somehow adjust the problem as best he could. Perhaps the men could be pressured into resigning. Even if worst came to worst and they stayed, the Navy would not be destroyed. Life would go on. Or—another case—Herbert Hoover, who held a number of temporary wartime posts, would send in his resignations to the President. There would be no reply or acknowledgment. Hoover would technically still be in government employ, having never had his resignations accepted, but he would close his government office and go on living.

If Secretary Lansing was agonizing about what to tell the still unreceived Lord Grey, it would not destroy Anglo-American relations that the Secretary got no instructions. Latin-American good will would be damaged, but not wiped out, by the failure of the White House to say whether or not the United States was going to recognize the new government of Costa Rica. Every few weeks the Secretary or one of the Under Secretaries would write the White House saying recognition should be accorded, and always there would be silence for an answer. Tumulty would be asked to lend his good offices to getting recognition approved and he would send up a memo to the family quarters. There would be no answer. Dozens of appointment-to-office forms were sent up for signature and, unsigned, they piled up, although the men they concerned would be taken into government offices and assigned work. (Still unsigned, the forms would forty years later repose in files at the Library of Congress.)

Initially all applications for Presidential action were given to Joe Tumulty. He was the President's secretary—it should be noted he performed the work that in later Administrations would require scores of men—and it seemed logical to deal with him. But actually Tumulty was allowed very little access to the President, not seeing him in the flesh for more than a month after the bathroom fall, and he was in fact reduced even to asking Margaret Wilson "when you think fit" to get the President to give answers on various questions, including the selection of a new Secretary of Commerce to replace the outgoing William Redfield. (Tumulty was not consulted when eventually the choice was made; first Grayson offered the office to a man who declined it, and when another was found to take the job he was generally considered a poor choice.)

The loyal subordinate of a decade, Tumulty was slow to realize and admit that things were not as they had been. "Mrs. Wilson is keeping me from the President," he told very close friends; he did not seem able to face it that were he able to be with the President eight hours a day things would not have been much better. He continued sending his memos: when Postmaster General Burleson complained that the President had not acted on a series of Executive Orders concerning Post Office appointments, Tumulty dutifully sent the letter up to the family quarters. This one came back, at least, but it was hardly answered: "The President says he is waiting to discuss the matter with Mr. Burleson. E.B.W." Tumulty sent the letter and the First Lady's note back to Burleson: "I am enclosing a self-explanatory memorandum from Mrs. Wilson."

After a whole series of letters from Lansing and Tumulty ("Would you please let me know if the President has decided whether he will receive Lord Grey?") was ignored, Grey finally announced he was returning to England. He had been in the United States four months (so had Craufurd-Stuart) and was out of patience. Lansing wrote the President saying that although Lord Grey was never given a chance to present his credentials it might be wise for him to be informally received for a farewell chat. Lansing's letter was sent up with a note from Tumulty attached to it: "Dear Mrs. Wilson, What shall I say?" There was no answer from the First Lady. Lord Grey sailed. No good-by letter or telegram attended his departure. The veteran American diplomat Henry White, observing all this, wrote his half-brother, "The situation is a most extraordinary one. Only most urgent matters of routine are attended to. In fact there would appear to be almost a suspension of Government." The journalist Ray Stannard Baker wrote in his diary that it seemed to him "as though our Government has gone out of business."

And yet business of a kind was being transacted. By far the majority of all letters to the President were ignored, and dozens of bills were becoming law without his signature, but certain mat-

ters were acted upon. Over the wide left margins of an elegantly
typed letter, down to the bottom space under the typing, up the
right margin and then across the top, weaving in and out of the
title of the writer and his seal of office, there were each day penciled notes by a woman who had a total of just two years of formal
schooling and whose round and enormous script resembled that
of a twelve-year-old. The reader of these notes—Secretary of War,
of Labor, or whatever—would have to rotate his returned letter in
his hands and sometimes continue on to the envelope to find what
the message in the childish handwriting was. For each scrawl began, "The President says" or "The President wants" and there was
no one in the world to say that the President from his sickroom in
the southwest portion of the second floor did *not* say or did *not*
want. Secretary of State Lansing, a precise kind of man, found this
business of getting one out of a dozen letters answered, and that
one in such a fashion, an intolerable thing. The President, he told
his friends, was in "such a condition that he was utterly unable
to attend to public business." He added that often he, Lansing,
sent "memoranda reduced to the simplest form which anyone
could understand" and that in return he got "answers communi-
cated through Mrs. Wilson so confused that no one could interpret
them."

Eventually the First Lady took to receiving Cabinet members
in her sitting room next to the President's room. She would tell the
visiting Secretary what the President wanted done about a given
problem, the verbal instructions being, she assured her caller, completely representative of her husband's wishes. She was certain she
had it right, she would point out, because she had had early train-
ing in getting details down correctly: as a child she had learned to
explain things very carefully so as to keep a crippled grandmother
in touch with the doings of the town outside the grandmother's
room. Sometimes, however, the Secretary would feel the instructions were not comprehensive enough and would ask for amplifica-
tion. In response to such requests the First Lady would upon occasion excuse herself, go alone into the President's room for a few
minutes (closing the door behind her) and return with new details
on what she said the President said. But actually she did this very
rarely. She was far more likely to refuse to disturb the President

and would either expound some more on her own as to what the instructions meant or simply leave the Secretary to make his own way with whatever his problem was.

None of the Cabinet men saw the President, none saw a word in his writing save for the handful of frighteningly unfamiliar-looking signatures, and there was nothing beyond the glimpse of him on the South Portico to actually prove that the President even lived. In her life before meeting the President the First Lady had been a completely unpolitical person unknown to anyone who moved in diplomatic or political sets, and it seemed impossible to Washington that she was really taking it upon herself to administer the government of the most powerful state in the world. Secretary of Agriculture Houston, playing billiards with a friend two days after seeing the President on the portico, said that he thought it must be Tumulty and William McAdoo who were running the government. Senator Lodge wrote Theodore Roosevelt's old Secretary of State, Elihu Root, that "a regency of Tumulty and Barney Baruch was not contemplated by the Constitution." But Houston and Lodge were wrong. McAdoo and Baruch might send memorandums offering advice, but they were not running anything.

As for Tumulty, day by day he was becoming less important. The First Lady had always disliked him personally anyway, and his memos and requests were largely ignored, although he valiantly tried to keep up appearances to most outsiders. Tumulty industriously sent up advice on how to make common cause with various Senators so that in the new session of the Congress the League might yet be made a reality for America, but as a powerful force in the White House he was finished. Extremely anxious to see things worked out with the Mild Reservationists, Tumulty wrote the President that "I know you will believe me sincere when I tell you that in my opinion we cannot longer adhere to the position we have taken in the matter of the treaty; the people of the country have the impression that you will not consent to the dotting of an 'i' or the crossing of a 't.'" The memo was ignored. He might write the draft of a letter he wanted the President to send Senator Hitchcock suggesting compromise, he might send his letter up to the First Lady, and it would be ignored. He sent up Secretary Houston's endorsement of his plan; there was no response from upstairs. He asked the First Lady to read to the President an eloquent newspaper editorial calling for compromise; she wrote back, "I would not be willing." This last outright refusal seemed finally to put the quietus on Tumulty and for weeks he sent nothing at all up to the sickroom. Before falling silent, however, he sent up a long memorandum summing up what was being left undone.

"Dear Mrs. Wilson: Please don't think I am trying to crowd you or to urge immediate action by the President, but I thought it would help you if you could have before you a list of matters that at intervals the President might wish to have presented to him for discussion and settlement. I might submit such a list, as follows."

He went on to mention that the railways taken over during the war still awaited return to their owners, that the Costa Rican recognition matter was still up in the air, that a commission to deal with the mining strike situation should be appointed, that the Secretaries of the Treasury and the Interior and the Assistant Secretary of Agriculture needed replacements as the present holders of the jobs would shortly be leaving their posts, that there were vacancies in the Civil Service Commission, Federal Trade Commission, Interstate Commerce Commission, Shipping Board, Tariff Committee, War Finance Corporation, Waterways Commission (seven vacancies), Rent Commission (three), that diplomatic appointments were needed for, in alphabetical order, Bulgaria, China, Costa Rica (if recognized), Italy, the Netherlands, Salvador, Siam, Switzerland. He added, "When you get a chance to talk with the President, will you please tell him that Senator Hitchcock sent for me yesterday and wanted to know whether the President would look with favor upon any effort on his part to make an adjustment with the Mild Reservationists by which to soften the Lodge Reservations and thus avoid splitting the Democratic Party."

The diplomatic vacancies were causing trouble at home and abroad. Secretary Lansing simply accepted resignations—*someone* had to open the envelopes—but appointments could be made only by the President.° The Netherlands appointment, for instance, was

---

° Foreign diplomats sent to the United States, formally without status until they presented their credentials to the President in person, were told they could take up their posts and that the government would consider them "Appointed" Ambassadors with all the status of actual Ambassadors.

sought by the capable William Phillips. Lansing recommended him for the job, but the First Lady sent word the President would await full recovery before naming the Netherlands man. This placed Phillips in a difficult situation. His wife's mother was ill in London and Phillips and his wife were sailing to be with her. Before leaving he wanted to know that the Netherlands appointment was his so that while in Europe he might make all arrangements about getting a home and finding schools for his children. Phillips asked Breckinridge Long, the Third Assistant Secretary of State at whose home the Belgians had stayed, if Long would not talk to Tumulty about getting the appointment made. Long did, and Tumulty said he would try to have an answer within twenty-four hours. When the period had passed, Tumulty said he had no answer and was sorry, but he had done all that he could. Phillips then wrote directly to the President to beg for quick action. There was no reply. Phillips shifted back to Breckinridge Long and asked him to talk to Grayson. Long did so. Nothing happened.

In later years it was said that the First Lady was the first woman President of the United States and that, ruling with an iron hand, she disposed of House and Tumulty because they stood in the way of her power, but it was not so. She did not try to change anything and amend the ways business was done in the past; she made no startling changes beyond the change that faced those who dealt with the White House. It was rather that the White House staggered along as best it could while she ignored all minor things and many large ones. Phillips was a tiny thing to the First Lady. What did it matter who went to the Netherlands? Did it really matter much? Hardly. What mattered was that the President be protected from irritation, from the people asking of him what he could no longer give, from Joe Tumulty saying we must compromise, Governor; from Daniels with his midshipmen and their immoral diseases; from Burleson and his fifteen-hundred-a-year Post Office appointments; from everybody; from the world. As it turned out, Edith Bolling Wilson's operation was a success. The patient lived.

Vice President Marshall went lecturing. He paid a call at the White House with some vague idea of meeting with the President (of which there was no more chance than of his flying to the moon) and was granted a few minutes' talk with the First Lady, who sent him off after saying if there was anything she could think of for him to do she would send for him. Senator "Doc" Moses, speaking in the name of the Senate Republican majority (or so Moses said), was after Marshall to declare himself the President, but Marshall refused to do anything of the sort. However, Marshall's secretary, Mark Thistlethwaite, thought that some consideration must be given to what would be done if one day the Secret Service men or the reporters came and told Marshall he was now the President. Thistlethwaite insisted some plans should be made, but Marshall told him he even hated to think about it.

Finally, before leaving on tour, Marshall reluctantly consented to go over the ground. The first thing, Thistlethwaite said, was that Marshall ought to keep handy a prepared statement on the President's death which would embody the idea that he would carry on the President's policies. Marshall said he would never say any such thing because he would as President have new policies.° "All right," said Thistlethwaite, "change later, but first announce a continuation of the previous policies." Marshall said he wouldn't do it. Thistlethwaite went on to another subject: would Marshall take office if the Congress declared the President incapable of holding office? "No," said Marshall. Such a move would be illegal unless the President assented to it or until it had a two-thirds vote, "and a two-thirds vote is impossible." Would Marshall assume office if the Supreme Court declared the President incapacitated? Well, there was no need to discuss the matter because the Court would never do it. Thistlethwaite finally asked just what Marshall would need to take over. Marshall's answer was, A Congressional resolution approved in writing by Cary Grayson and the First Lady. "I could throw this country into civil war," Marshall summed up, "but I won't." Thistlethwaite wanted something more concrete from his chief, but Marshall refused even to listen to any more talk. "I am not going to seize the place," he said, "and then have Wilson, recovered, come around and say, 'Get off, you usurper!'" Marshall then went off on his tour. (His expenses in giving a posh dinner for the Belgians had never been refunded to him out of the

° Marshall privately told several persons that he thought the Lodge reservations should be accepted.

President's government funds for such purposes, and good lecture dates were available.)

On November 23, Marshall spoke under the auspices of the Moose of Atlanta in the civic auditorium. He was engaged in paying tribute to the memories of Washington and Lincoln when an Atlanta policeman came running up the aisle. The policeman talked with a prominent Atlantan sitting on the platform and told him that word had just been received over the telephone that the President was dead. The Atlantan stepped up to Marshall, asked him to halt his speech, and whispered what the policeman had said. Marshall staggered a few steps and held up his hands. After a moment he steadied himself and said to the audience, "I cannot continue my speech. I must leave at once to take up my duties as Chief Executive of this great nation." He asked the people to pray for him and then, as the organist played "Nearer, My God, to Thee," he went to his hotel surrounded by a hastily materialized police escort. At the hotel, calls to the Associated Press and the White House brought about the realization that the telephoned report was a practical joke. "A most cruel hoax," said Marshall. It was the most awful hour of his life, he later told people. The Governor of Georgia put up a one-hundred-dollar reward for apprehension of the person who made the telephone call, but the jokester was never found. Marshall went on his way, minus the police escort and the fanfare attending it. He was never, save for a brief moment just prior to the inaugural ceremonies of the President's successor, to see the President again.

On December 2, Congress would again convene. Always before, the President had appeared in person to read a message to the legislators, but now it would be impossible for him to do so. It would also be impossible for him to write the message.° Instead, Joe Tumulty asked each of the Cabinet men to submit a report and some recommendations, gathered the papers together, and tossed them on the desk of Charles Swem. "You know how the Chief writes," Tumulty said to the stenographer, "you can put them together." Swem did so and the finished product was sent

---

° It should be said that, unlike many of his successors, this President had never employed speech writers. Every word he had uttered was written by one man—himself.

up to the First Lady, who penciled in some corrections which she said the President wished made.

The message, concerning itself with the need for a simplified tax program, a budget system, the problems of unemployment among ex-servicemen, Federal aid for the road-building program and forest conservation, protection for the chemical and dyestuff industries, and a readjusted tariff, made no mention of the League of Nations. The most pressing problem was left out, perhaps to answer critics who said the President had since 1917 concerned himself too much with foreign policy and too little with domestic problems, perhaps because the First Lady forbade any mention of a subject which, put upon the table for discussion, would excite the President and destroy the quiet atmosphere she was so desperately maintaining. In any event, the Congress received the message with scorn and indifference, many Senators allowing themselves to be quoted as saying the President did not write, knew nothing of, had no connection with, the whole business.

One such Senator was Albert B. Fall of New Mexico. A long drooping mustache adorned Senator Fall's face, his frame was clothed in Western-type rancher's apparel complete with ten-gallon hat, and in time, after serving as Secretary of the Interior, he was going to become the only United States Cabinet officer ever to go to jail, the penalty being one of the results of the sorry Teapot Dome oil scandals. "I wonder when he wrote it," Fall sarcastically said of the message, and intensified his already active efforts to get the President proved either insane, mindless, unconscious, paralyzed, or a prisoner.

The device Fall presently hit upon to achieve this end found its origins in the country's perennial troubles with Mexico, which at the time was a whipping boy for, among other things, the radicals, the high cost of living, the wave of strikes, racial tension and—most important of all to a Senator who even then was so involved with oil investments that his colleagues addressed him as "Petroleum" Fall—the difficulties of American oil concessionaires south of the border. There was a good deal of agitation for a war against Mexico which would, as Secretary Lansing said, "settle our difficulties here," and the agitation speeded up when a United States consular agent, William Jenkins, was kidnaped at Puebla, Mexico.

As soon as word of the kidnaping was received, the Senate

Foreign Relations Committee met to consider what to do about
Mexico. Secretary Lansing came before the group and said that he
had sent down a very strong protest. (In actual fact his protest was
practically a threat to go to war.) Had the Secretary consulted with
the President about the protest? the committee inquired. No. Had
he consulted with the President on *anything* in recent months? No.
At this the Republicans on the committee passed a resolution
appointing a representative of the committee to call upon the
President in order to get his views on Mexico. It is certain that Senator Fall, who introduced the resolution calling for a visit to the
President and offered himself as a visitor, never expected that the
President would receive the delegation. If the President wasn't
even consulting with his Secretary of State, Fall reasoned, he
would hardly receive one of Senator Lodge's outstanding supporters. That refusal could be the lever by which the President would
be pried out of the White House.

The chairman of the committee, Senator Lodge, after solemnly
naming Fall and a reluctant Senator Hitchcock (to represent the
Democrats) as a two-man delegation, called Joe Tumulty and asked
for the men to be received. Lodge, the lending of whose name to
the enterprise would make it even less palatable to the White
House, was astonished when Tumulty, after consulting with the
First Lady, said the two visitors might come that very day—December 4.

The meeting was set for two-thirty in the afternoon. Before lunch
Robert Woolley, head of the Democratic Party publicity organization, went to the White House in response to an urgent call from
Tumulty. Tumulty said Fall would have to be received—otherwise
impeachment proceedings might be begun—and asked Woolley's
help in staging a "dress rehearsal" that would prepare the President for the visit. The two decided to place a copy of a Senate
report on the Mexican situation on a table to the right of the President's bed so that it could be dramatically picked up by the President's one good hand. Apart from the right arm, the President
would be covered with blankets up to his chin so that the paralyzed
left hand would not show. As for the President's ability to concentrate on what Fall would say, and parry his thrusts, they would
have to trust to luck and the presence of Grayson, the First Lady
and Hitchcock as allies.

Promptly on time, the two Senators appeared in the afternoon. By then the impending visit had been headlined in the newspapers, which correctly labeled it as having nothing at all to do with Mexico. The "actual purpose," said the New York *World*, was to force a "disclosure of the President's condition." Reporters anticipating a post-visit interview with Fall swarmed to the White House. There were more than one hundred of them to see the arriving Fall preen himself in the spotlight while Hitchcock, frightened of what might be about to happen, kept in the background. The two men were shown up to the President's bedroom. Grayson stood outside the door. Fall asked if there would be a time limit and Grayson said, "No, not within reason, Senator."

They went in and the President shocked Fall by marshaling all his strength for a firm handshake and a wave to the nearby chair selected for the Senator in the dress rehearsal. "Well, Senator, how are your Mexican investments getting along?" breezily asked the President. Fall, certain the warped Presidential signatures sent from the White House were the work of a forger, and certain the President was not in his right mind, blanched at this use of hand and tongue. "If agreeable, I wish Mrs. Wilson to remain," said the President, and Fall said that would be all right. At once the First Lady began to write down every word Fall said. (She had previously provided herself with a pencil and pad, which, occupying her as they did, allowed her to avoid shaking hands with the Senator.)

"You seem very much engaged, madam," Fall said to her. "I thought it wise to record this interview so there may be no misunderstandings or misstatements made," she grimly answered. Doubtless shaken by the cold look, Fall turned back to the President and asked if he had seen the Foreign Relations report on Mexico. "I have a copy right here," said the President, and reached over to where it was, pointedly waving it in the air. "You see," he went on, "despite the stories going the rounds, I can still use my right hand." He mentioned the medical opinions hawked by "Doc" Moses. "I hope the Senator will now be reassured," he said to Fall, "but he may be disappointed."

Fall desperately started talking about Mexico and the kidnaping of the consular agent. As he spoke, Grayson was called from the room, returning in a few minutes to announce in practically bad-melodrama fashion that word had just been received that the consular agent had been released by the Mexicans. This was the crowning blow to Fall, rendering his mission totally farcical. He got up, defeated. By then the First Lady was out of paper and she picked up a large brown franked envelope of Fall's and continued her note-taking upon it. She was thus able to take down the words of parting between the two men as Fall, apparently trying to salvage some shred of dignity from the meeting, bent over the President and took his right hand. "Mr. President, I am praying for you," Fall said. "Which way, Senator?" asked the President with a chuckle. Fall fled.

Jubilant, Grayson saw Fall down to the door. As they went down, Grayson solicitously asked after Fall's health. The Senator numbly said that he had been working hard and getting little sleep lately. "You have just left a man suffering a breakdown due to overwork and concentration," Grayson said. He added tenderly, "You had better be careful." Then he mercilessly threw Fall to the reporters outside. There were no questions about Mexico; instead it was how is the President, can he talk, is he paralyzed, what is his mental condition? Fall had to give the answers that spelled the end of the campaign to oust the President from his post and insured his continued residence in the White House for the remaining fifteen months of his term. The President had gathered all of his strength and, running in good luck, he had pulled the trick off. The people around him, knowing how it might have turned out, were ecstatic with joy. They knew how lucky he had been.

9   In the mornings he awoke at eight and his valet lifted him into his chair so that, sitting up, he might eat breakfast and have the First Lady read the headlines from the papers. Sometimes, not often, he asked for an entire story to be read out. Then while he rested she went below to tend to the domestic affairs of the White House. When she came back up they sat together for an hour or so and she told him the official business with which she thought he should deal. He was very quiet, rarely speaking, but sometimes he would say a few broken words about what he wanted done. Even as he got the thoughts out he would forget himself in the middle of a sentence and falter into a silence that lasted until, motionless, eyes gazing out into space, he was brought up by her repeating of the last words he had uttered. Then he would come to himself and begin again, but after a few moments the weak voice would drift away so that they sat silently in the quiet which surrounded and inundated a building whose gates were closed, some literally padlocked, to the public and almost all the world. Together they worked on the pardon pleas and departmental reports and sometimes he tried to dictate for a while; but it was no good. In the middle of a sentence he would slide off again into his unmoving silence from which only her gentle prodding removed him. Margaret would often come in to talk with him and he would try to smile for her and want to know about the children of Jessie and Nellie. He would say Margaret should send them his love.

Below, the great state rooms constructed to hold hundreds of people were completely empty. The curtains were drawn and in some the rugs were taken up so that it would be easier for his wheel chair to move over the floor. When the servants went walking through the Red Room, the State Dining Room, the East Room, their footsteps echoed. The Executive Wing was likewise dreary, vacant, quiet, and the reporters in the press room played cards. Ike Hoover's official White House diary, which in other days had listed ten visitors in two hours, drifted away into a series of single-line notations that "Dr. Grayson spent the night." In late November the diary simply petered out.

Before lunch he would be slowly wheeled down the hall to the elevator and then out onto the South Portico looking out over the grounds, empty save for the sheep chomping at the grass. Sometimes one of the two women or Grayson or Ike Hoover pushed the wheel chair along the veranda until they reached the window of Joe Tumulty's office. Someone would tap on the glass so that Tumulty might come to it and say a few words carefully chosen to put in the best light the possibility that the Senate would in the new session pass the League as the President wanted it. Then they would go into the elevator in slow procession and the President and First Lady would take lunch in his study. Afterward he slept while she walked in the grounds. At four in the afternoon he would be propped up in bed and if he seemed strong enough to her she worked for an hour or so with him. After dinner he went to sleep. It would be seven-thirty or eight by then. Sometimes before he dozed off she read aloud to him from mystery novels—which she detested but he seemed to enjoy—but suddenly, in the midst of a passage with no emotional significance, he would begin to cry. His hair was whitened and his face thin and haggard and seared, and he would sit shaking while she took his head into her arms and whispered "Darling, darling" until the sobbing ended.

December drew out and Christmas came and the girls were with him. On Christmas evening after he went to bed the girls and the First Lady and some of her relatives watched a movie run off in the East Room by Robert E. Long, the manager of a Washington theater, on a projector that was a gift of Douglas Fairbanks. The next day the First Lady told the President about it, and he said he would like to see it also, and so Ike Hoover called Long and asked if he would come again. Long again set up the projector and the screen, which was an enormous Lincoln bed sheet. Into the room then came the President in his wheel chair, his head bent forward and down, and Long was shocked to see him so. Before, at Long's theater, he had often seen the President and had thought him the personification of disciplined energy and power. Long and his assistant looked at each other in horror. They could hardly believe this bent figure unable to sit up straight was the same man. The flickering of the light on the bed sheet illuminated dimly the empty East Room with the giant crystal chandeliers and the classic cornicing and the gigantic mirrors and, across the uncovered hardwood floor, hanging on a wall, a gift of the French Government to the First Lady: a Gobelin tapestry depicting the marriage of Psyche. Alone in the midst of all this sat a few huddled figures watching *In Old Kentucky*. But when the climactic horse-race scene began, the excitement was too much and the First Lady told Long to stop. They wheeled the trembling President out and put him to bed and asked Long to come back the next day to finish.

Long did so, and every day thereafter he came again, each day carrying a new film. At ten-thirty he would arrive and set up the machine and a few minutes later the elevator would bring the President down to be wheeled through the empty rooms, one after the other. "My tour of inspection," he said to the servants who saw him, and he would try to smile, his face twisting as he did so. The maids felt something breaking inside them as they watched his attempt to be cheery, and after tremulously returning his smile they would bob their heads and hurry by. At eleven the films would begin, many of them not destined for general release until months in the future.

Hoover and Long had to scour the country to find suitable productions, enlisting the aid of the Hollywood studios. The President did not want to see the risqué comedies and the vamps and sirens, but instead wanted outdoor films, William S. Hart, Tom Mix, William Farnum, horses and the Western deserts and mountains. He would each day nod and try to smile for Long and, the room practically noiseless save for the slight hum of the machine, they would sit and watch—the President, the First Lady, Grayson. Sometimes a few servants would gather behind them, and so in the silent gloom perhaps a dozen persons would be where Abraham Lincoln each New Year's Day greeted thousands. Long asked if the President would like some musical accompaniment to the films, but the President said he would prefer not, which pleased Grayson's desire for quiet around the patient. Now and again the President would ask about a film mentioned in a movie magazine the First Lady read him, and Long would telegraph the movie company involved and get a copy.

The First Lady's eyes rarely left him for a minute; Long noticed how in the dim flickering light she was constantly glancing away from the screen to look at her husband. But one day when she was quietly talking with someone Long noticed the President's head gradually falling forward. As everyone else watched the action on the screen, Long saw the President's head slowly come down so that his chin rested upon his chest. He was utterly unmoving, and the horrified Long was certain that he had just seen the President die. He frantically looked at the First Lady, but she was still talking and had not seen. Long miserably let the film run on, thinking that if he stopped it and the President was not dead it would constitute a shock to him that the film suddenly halted. So for two terrible minutes Long wondered what to do. Then the First Lady looked over and broke off her talk and went to her husband and, oblivious of the people, raised his head and let it rest on her breast while she mothered him and kissed him and gently whispered. The film ended. The next day there was another.

Winter took hold upon Washington and a great dullness fell upon the closed and silent White House. Outside in the city Vice President Marshall was receiving a splatter of letters asking his intervention in the cases of soldiers in trouble and for his aid in getting pardons for Federal prisoners, and now and then a foreign diplomat took it as a duty to call upon him. (Although he would explain he could in no way act for the President, Marshall always had a welcome for the guest—"Glad to see you just the same.") On Capitol Hill they argued about the League, and somehow the Cabinet members went about their duties, Attorney General Palmer doing the most dramatic work, arresting people right and left and nursemaiding the country into what would later be called the Great Red Scare. Just before sailing home, Lord Grey spent Christmas

with the family of Assistant Secretary of the Navy Roosevelt,* and
the fact enraged the First Lady, who remembered Lord Grey's
aide, Crauturd-Stuart.

Into the White House came greeting cards and some of them
the First Lady read aloud to the President. One was from a little
girl, Fairlie Amistead, who said she was sorry about the President
being sick but thought he could recover best if he would come to
her Alabama home, where he could have "milk and butter and
sausages and spareribs and a good time." The First Lady answered
her that "I know the President would like to be well enough to see
some of his little Southern friends who, like you, are interested in
his recovery." Sitting in bed, the President tried to read a little but
found it difficult because his nose glasses would slip, so a Philadelphia eye specialist was called in to prescribe spectacles. "I want to
look at your pupils," the doctor said as he bent over the patient,
and the ex-professor in the bed got off a weak pun: "You'll have
a long job. I've had a great number of them."

At night when he was asleep the First Lady sat long hours working on official papers and once she pointed to a pile of newspapers
and said to a maid, "I don't know how much more criticism I can
take." In fact the White House staff itself was free with criticism
of her, some of the servants saying that now that the descendant of
Pocahontas was in charge they were being forced to work for "an
Indian." Their rumors had it that her reluctance to urge his resignation stemmed from fear that this would destroy his will to live. She
herself rarely smiled save when she was with him, and the strain
told upon the people around her. Edith Benham, her secretary, had
a complete nervous breakdown and had to give up her job, and
Margaret also broke down and went South to try to recover.

In January there would be a Jackson Day dinner in Washington,
and a Presidential letter was expected. Following the Cabinet meeting of January 6, Tumulty said to Secretary of Agriculture Houston
that the letter was all prepared and that the Secretary's opinion
of it was wanted. The letter spoke of the United States' failure to
ratify the peace treaty and go into the League and warned that
because of this Germany was able to defy the rulings of the Allies

* Before the invitation was tendered, Lord Grey was warned that Jimmy Roosevelt had measles, but said this did not worry him as "he did not think he was subject
to childish diseases."

and go on the rampage as she had in 1914. Houston read it and pointed out that there was a treaty and a League ratified by almost every other nation in the world and that the German Army was largely disbanded and the Navy either on the bottom of the ocean or in Allied hands. He did not say so to Tumulty, but he did not for a minute believe the President had anything to do with the letter—"I could not understand how he could." To a friend he said that the President was so ill that "something ought to be done about it."

The letter as sent tempered down the questionable statements, but it was a shock to those who heard it read out. For it repeated that the President would not accept any reservations: "Personally I do not accept the action of the United States Senate as the decision of the nation . . . We cannot rewrite this treaty. We must take it without changes which alter its meaning, or leave it." And the letter said something that frightened the Democrats and hardened the will to resist of the Republicans. For it seemed the President was saying he would want a third term: "If there is any doubt as to what the people of the country think on this vital matter the clear and simple way is to submit it for determination at the next election to the voters of the nation, to give the next election the form of a great and solemn referendum."

It seemed the President had given the final blow to compromise. But still the White House was besieged with appeals that the reservations be accepted, that anything be accepted that would put the country into the League and make the war worth having been fought. Ray Stannard Baker, the President's press liaison man at Paris, went to the White House to plead with the First Lady, but found her ungiving on the issue and resentful of the criticism of the President. "They think him stubborn," she said accusingly; Baker replied, "So much hangs on this issue." "He believes the people are with him," she answered, and Baker left, thinking, This sick man, with such enormous power, closed in from the world and yet acting so influentially upon events! He wrote a letter to the First Lady: "People in the future will forget the minor disagreements if the thing itself comes into being."

Baker had been traveling through all of the country and was sure he was right in saying the President must not stand so solidly upon the letter of what he had brought back from Paris. But the President had other ideas on how to fight. He had the First Lady send Albert Burleson, the typical politican made Postmaster General, a list of some thirty-five Senators with the request that Burleson indicate whether it might be said that these were the men most against ratification. Burleson wrote back indicating which men should perhaps be omitted from the classification and which others should perhaps be added, and the President and First Lady took up the list and wrote a statement to go with it: "I challenge the following named gentlemen, members of the Senate of the United States, to resign their seats in that body and take immediate steps to seek re-election to it on the basis of their several records with regards to the ratification of the treaty. For myself, I promise and engage if all of them or a majority of them are re-elected, I will resign the Presidency." With difficulty the President was persuaded not to make public the statement.

In Europe there was growing apprehension that the United States would not come into the League. One of the most prominent Europeans was fearful that this might come to pass and wrote a letter to the London *Times* saying the reservations attached to American entry would not mean much one way or the other, that they were relatively innocuous and really not terribly objectionable. The writer of the letter was Lord Grey and he ended it by saying the important thing was for the United States to come in on whatever terms were necessary. Only let the Americans come in! When word of the letter reached America the First Lady went to the President's room and came out with a cold statement she had written in her childish scrawl upon blue-lined notebook paper: "Had Lord Grey ventured upon any such utterance when he was still at Washington as Ambassador, his Government would have been promptly asked to withdraw him."

February began. It had been four months since the President fell in the bathroom, and in that time the Cabinet continued to meet on a regular basis. As ranking minister, Secretary of State Lansing each week issued a call for the meeting, and after each one the newspapers duly reported what subjects had been discussed. Two Secretaries had resigned and been replaced by men asked to

take the vacant posts by the First Lady,° and so each department
had its head who offered his opinion at the meetings. Now and
then Grayson or Tumulty sat in, the latter often pointing to the
conferences as indicative that the business of the country was going
on smoothly. More than a score of the Cabinet meetings had been
held when on February 7 Lansing received a signed letter from the
President:

"My dear Mr. Secretary: Is it true, as I have been told, that during my illness, you have frequently called the heads of the executive departments of the government into conference?"

One can imagine Lansing's astonishment at being asked such
a question. He replied, "It is true. . . . Shortly after you were
taken ill in October, certain members of the Cabinet, of which
I was one, felt that in view of the fact that we were denied communication with you, it was wise for us to confer informally together." The President wrote back, "I am very much disappointed
by your letter . . . I find nothing in your letter which justifies your
assumption of Presidential authority in such a matter . . . I must
say that it would relieve me of embarrassment, Mr. Secretary, if
you would give your present office up." Lansing at once sent in
his resignation, saying, however, that he could not permit to "pass
unchallenged the imputation" that he sought to "usurp" Presidential authority and that he still felt the conferences were in the best
interests of the Administration and the country. The President answered that the resignation was accepted.

Lansing then released the exchange of letters to the newspapers
and at once a storm of criticism of the President poured forth.
The President had not forgotten Lansing's doubts about the League
and Lansing's questioning of whether Vice President Marshall
should not take over the White House, but nothing of this was
said in the letters. Instead the President had asked if it was true,
"as I have been told," that something known to all the world was
taking place a few hundred feet from his sickroom. The New York
Evening Post said the question was incredible: "We have been re-

___

° Over teacups, the First Lady asked Secretary of Agriculture Houston to take the
Treasury Department; Houston was replaced in Agriculture by Edward Meredith.
In a personal interview she also asked Judge John Barton Payne to leave the Shipping
Board for the Department of the Interior. Neither Houston, Meredith nor Payne
saw the President.

peatedly assured by those surrounding the President during his illness that Mr. Wilson at all times has been in perfect mental condition and in touch with what was going on in the land. If this is so, is it at all conceivable that Mr. Wilson never stopped to inquire how the business of the country was being carried on during his illness? Was he ignorant of Cabinet meetings at which coal strikes and Mexican complications were discussed? The indignation at a sudden discovery implied in Mr. Wilson's letter is incomprehensible."

Other papers said that if the country had been lied to about how the President was keeping in touch with things, as evidently it had, how could the country trust those who now said the President was in full possession of his mental faculties? "It is unthinkable that a sane man would offer any objection to the department heads getting together," said the Worcester *Evening Gazette*. The President was, said the New York *Tribune*, like the Sleeping Princess, "alive, yet of suspended animation" and desiring "all around him likewise frozen into lifelessness." Why did he not demand that Congress cease operating also, so as to have a complete shutdown? WILSON'S LAST MAD ACT, headlined the Los Angeles *Times*.

The men up on Capitol Hill had their opinions to add. Senator George Norris of Nebraska told reporters the letters showed two things: "First, the President was incapacitated and it was necessary for someone to look after the Government; second, that the mental expert that has been employed at the White House has been discharged too soon."° Representative George Holden Tinkham of Massachusetts was even blunter: "Whom the Gods would destroy they first make mad." The Baltimore *Sun* voiced what many Senators and Representatives were thinking: "They ask in stage whispers at the Capitol whether this is not the work of the enigmatical villain of the play, the dark and mysterious Mr. Tumulty, or, more sinister still, must we look for the woman in the case?"

Actually Tumulty desperately fought against the firing of Lansing, but the President told him "disloyalty" must be "spiked." The First Lady's reaction was different. "I hate Lansing," she said, her bitterness shocking to Secretary Daniels, who found equally frightening her violent anger at Franklin Roosevelt because of his

° The "mental expert" was presumably Dr. Francis Dercum.

Christmas spent with Lord Grey. Daniels was baffled; all of the President's friends were baffled. The wife of Charles Sumner Hamlin of the Federal Reserve Board asked Secretary Houston's wife how it could have come about that the President would do such a thing, and Mrs. Houston said, "There is only one explanation—he is not in his right mind." The journalist Raymond Clapper, before noting in his diary that he and his wife had both had wisdom teeth removed, wrote of what he had heard the day the letters were printed in the papers: "Many believe he is on the verge of insanity. No one can understand it." Even the friendly New York *World* the next day reinforced this impression of its description of how, when Tumulty appeared bearing newspapers with "glaring headlines" about the firing, the President "with the glee of a boy reached out his cane, grasped a railing, and swung his wheel chair in circles, at the same time admonishing Mr. Tumulty to 'see how strong I am!'"

As Tumulty remembered it later, the President said that the whole thing would blow over and nothing would be recalled save the "disloyalty" of Lansing. But the *World* was right in thinking the President was growing stronger, for within a short time, on a warm day in March, Grayson judged the patient capable of withstanding the strain of an auto ride. A platform was put up at the south entrance of the White House so that the wheel chair could be rolled to a position level with the waiting car, and three or four Secret Service men lifted the President to his feet and held him in their arms and put him into the car's rear right-hand corner—the right side in order that the paralyzed left side of his face would not show to the people in the street—and braced him up so that he might not topple to the floor when the car started, and adjusted his cape (he could not wear a coat; it was too difficult to get the inert left arm into a sleeve) and set his hat square on his head. And so he was driven through Washington, his face devoid of all color, grayish white, thin, waxlike, a bright-eyed old man trying to smile, the lips revealing the teeth only on the right side, the eyes protuberant, a thin face on a thin neck ducked down so as to hide the paralyzed side.

There was to him something cruel and terrifying in the faces of the people who looked at him as the car went by; they did not cheer, but stared as if to see if it was all true what they had heard: that the car held a madman. When they came back to the White House policemen were waiting, and when the car pulled up to a remote rear gate all traffic was halted and they drove quickly into the grounds. As they went in, a small group of people by the gate threw into the thin March sunshine a faint cheer. They were backstairs White House workers whose faces the President would not know, and friends and relatives of Secret Service men, and they had been recruited just for this reason: so that on his ride there might be for him one bit of applause. When the car stopped and the men went to lift him out and carry him to the wheel chair there were tears in his eyes and he was saying, "You see, they still love me." The First Lady left him for a moment and went to stand by herself so that he would not see that she wept.

But he was strange on the succeeding drives. He got it into his mind that any car that passed his own was going dangerously fast, although at his orders the chauffeur rarely went faster than fifteen or twenty miles an hour. Whenever a car went by he would order that the Secret Service vehicle overtake it and bring back the driver for questioning. Miserably trying to give him the impression that his instructions were perfectly logical, the Secret Service car would chase after the offending auto, always to return with the excuse that the speeder was going too fast to be overhauled. He brooded over this and wrote to Attorney General Palmer asking if the Presidency carried with it the powers of a justice of the peace; if it did, he told his people, he was going to make sure the speeders were caught and himself try their cases there by the roadside. (The Secret Service men desperately killed the plan by saying to him that the idea was beneath his dignity.)

Even the First Lady fell afoul of him when she arranged for him to go on a ride in a Secret Service Cadillac when his own favorite Pierce-Arrow was sent to a garage for repair work. He said he would not have it that he not be consulted on the matter and declared he would not ride in the Secret Service car. Instead he would use a horse-drawn carriage until his own car was ready for use. He was the President and those were his orders, so he went forth in an open victoria. The offending Cadillac idled along behind him, out of sight but ready at hand if it should be needed.

Meanwhile there were no Cabinet meetings and no Secretary of State. Tumulty sent up the names of some veteran State Department men as nominees, but his suggestions were ignored and he was ordered to telephone Bainbridge Colby, a New York lawyer working on the Shipping Board, and tell him to come to the White House. "What's up now, Joe?" asked Colby; Tumulty said he could not say, but Colby must come to Washington at once. At the White House he was taken to the President, who sat wrapped in blankets on the South Portico. Initially shocked by the President's waxen and deathlike appearance, Colby was completely astonished when he, a man utterly inexperienced in foreign affairs, was offered the job of Secretary of State. It seemed incredible to him—and would seem even more so to official Washington when the announcement of his appointment was made. "Say you will accept," said the President, and Colby thus became Lansing's successor.

The choice was so widely criticized after the first wave of astonishment passed over Washington, and the President so completely damned, that one Senator, Kenneth McKellar of Tennessee, felt impelled to rise in the Senate and make answer. He summed up what had been said about the President on the Senate floor: he was despot, tyrant, madman. Then he spoke of another President who on the same floor had been called uncontrollable, irresponsible, "monster usurper . . . felon . . . weak and imbecile." After reading from Senate speeches of 1861-65, he said, "I stop here long enough to wonder whether the distinguished Senator from New Hampshire° who was assailing the President for alleged physical and mental disabilities the other day did not copy in substance some of the language here used about Abraham Lincoln. It sounds very much like him." Joe Tumulty brought word of the speech to the President and tears rolled down the invalid's cheeks.

But the McKellars were very few, and day by day Tumulty and others saw that the League was in terrible danger unless the President yielded on the reservations. Ray Stannard Baker came again to plead compromise and this time was allowed to talk with the President in person. Buried in blankets, a fur muff at his feet, the President listened while Baker spoke. But the argument had no

° "Doc" Moses

effect. He would accept no reservations. "If I accept them, these Senators will merely offer new ones, even more humiliating," he said. He paused. Baker was silent—there was nothing more he could add. "These evil men intend to destroy the League," the President said. Baker left.

William McAdoo came and made a plea, but the President cut him off by saying, "I am willing to compromise on anything but the Ten Commandments." Senator Carter Glass, a loyal supporter, wrote that ex-President Taft had written up some reservations differing from the Lodge ones—would the President take them?— and the First Lady wrote back questioning Taft's "good faith" and saying the President felt "absolute inaction" was better than "mistaken initiative." Postmaster General Burleson came to talk about using "good tactics" in the fight for ratification, but the President said, "I will not play for position. This is not a time for tactics. It is a time to stand square. I can stand defeat; I cannot stand retreat from conscientious duty." He refused to consider it even possible that the Senate would actually kill the American entry into the League which was the hope of mankind—"The thing is too preposterous to talk about"—but sometimes it must have come to him that perhaps the unthinkable could happen, for once when Tumulty came to him on the South Portico and said, "Governor, you are looking very well today," he turned his head away and burst into tears and said, "I am very well for a man who awaits disaster." The First Lady worried about him terribly; she wrote Jessie, "As the normal strength returns I will be less and less necessary—but now I never leave except for an hour in the afternoon and at mealtimes. For he gets nervous if alone and allowed to think—so I stay every minute of the day. . . . There have been so many things in the conduct of affairs to worry him that I try not to let him have time to think of them."

On March 19, 1920, the entrance of the United States into the League of Nations under the special conditions outlined by the Lodge reservations was voted down in the Senate. The count was 49 in favor and 35 against.

Of the 35 Senators who voted "nay," one dozen were Republicans. The other 23 were Democrats loyal to the command of their

President. Had but seven of those men defied that command, the required two-thirds vote would have been met and the United States would have been in the League.

There would never be another vote taken on the issue. The League was "as dead as Hector," said Senator James Reed of Missouri. "As dead as Marley's ghost," said Henry Cabot Lodge of Massachusetts.

It was Tumulty who came to tell him that it was all over. Tumulty must have known—would have to have known—that it was going to end in this way, and he came prepared. He had with him a book. He would read to the President from it, but first he smiled —loyal Tumulty, he managed a smile!—and then he said, "Governor, only the Senate has defeated you. The People will vindicate your course. You may rely upon that." Then he said, "Governor, I want to read a chapter from the third volume of your 'History of the American People' if it will not tire you." So they sat together and Tumulty read out the words the President had written many years ago as a college professor no one had heard of: "'Slowly the storm blew off . . . But in the meantime things had been said which could not be forgotten. Washington had been assailed with unbridled license as an enemy and a traitor to the country.

"'The country knew its real mind about him when the end of his term came and it was about to lose him.'" Tumulty ceased reading. The President said in the voice that once had been so clear and pure but now was husky and whispering as it came out of his tortured, twisted mouth in the white face above the thin and ravished neck which once, a long time ago, the dead Ellen had massaged and called her daughters to look at so that they might see there were no hollows there—he said to Tumulty that he thanked him for putting him into such company.

That night he could not sleep. Grayson stayed in the White House, going into the President's room every hour or so. The President was very quiet, hardly talking, but about three in the morning he said, "Doctor, the devil is a busy man." After that for a very long time he was silent. But awake. Then he said, "Doctor, please get the Bible there and read from Second Corinthians, Chapter 4, Verses 8 and 9." Grayson went for it and opened it and read out into the room where they were alone, the light visible to anyone who cared to walk along Executive Avenue just as dawn was about to come up and know that the President of the United States lay sleepless: "'We are troubled on every side, yet not distressed; we are perplexed, but not in despair; persecuted, but not forsaken; cast down, but not destroyed. . .'"

The President lay in the bed that Abraham Lincoln slept in, in the House to which once Cousin Florence came in the little hot-dog wagon, in the capital city of the nation which often he said had saved the world and would lead it forward, and in time fell asleep. But a few days later when George Creel, head of the war-time Committee on Public Information, came to see him, he had in Creel's eyes the pallor of very death itself. It came from his heart unguarded against the blow, Creel thought. "I sat with him, miserably fumbling for words of comfort, but it was as though I had not been in the room. All the while his bloodless lips moved continuously, as if framing arguments and forming new appeals. Only as I was leaving did he look at me seeingly, his eyes filled with an anguish such as I trust never to see again. 'If only I were not helpless,' he whispered."

Alice Roosevelt Longworth, daughter of T.R., wife of a Republican leader of the House of Representatives, contemptuously dismissed the invalid in the White House with a thought about what his enemies said of him. "Some of the comments," she remarked, "were noticeably lacking in the Greek quality of Aidos—the quality that deters one from defiling the body of a dead enemy."

He could not stand the staring eyes—so the auto rides were discontinued.

10

Spring came to Washington and to the country, the first spring of the nineteen-twenties, of the bootlegger and speakeasy and hip flask, of the Golden Age of Sports, the Bull Market, the Florida land boom, Al Capone, Bobby Jones, Fatty Arbuckle, Scott Fitzgerald, the flappers, jazz, the Stutz Bearcat, the short dress, the high back, the accepted "Goddamn" in polite conversation. In another spring he had gone through light misty rain to ask for a war to end war and make the world safe for democracy; in another spring he had been the great man of Paris' great men. Now in this spring he sat in the closed and stilled White House grounds and watched the two-year-old son of Cary Grayson and the former Altrude Gordon go for a ride in a cart drawn by a gentle pony. At eleven each morning a glass of milk and a cracker or cookie were brought to him, and with it a cookie for the tiny Gordon Grayson. He would hold back Gordon's snack and then they all smiled when there was a childish whisper from the babyish mouth: "Didn't anybody bring a tookie out here for me?" They went in then for the movie, Gordon riding along on the footrest of the wheel chair or running ahead to get in his kiddie car and race around the East Room.

That the United States and the League were dead one to the other haunted the President, but he tried to fight the terrible depression which settled upon him with the weapons of his religion

and faith. For forty years he had never had the slightest doubt of
the existence of a divine God; Ellen had wondered and doubted,
the girls had their skeptical moments, but he never let go for an
instant. "If I were not a Christian, I think I should go mad," he
said to Grayson when the League died in the Senate. Still it could
not be that he was able completely to throw off his shock and
horror over what had happened. "Good morning, it is a beautiful spring day and warm," Grayson greeted him one day; he replied, "I don't know whether it is warm or cold. I feel so weak and
useless. I feel that I would like to go back to bed and stay there
until I either get well or die." To George Creel it seemed as though
he were consumed by a vast inner loneliness, the loneliness of one
who had marched at the very head of the procession that was the
world's desire for peace and security, but who now was the shattered evangel of a shattered cause. From the Senate came back the
actual physical copy of the treaty he had submitted to them and
they had refused to pass—Ray Stannard Baker thought the dispatch of the document was the work of Senator Lodge, "for it
was like him"—and the President in his agony said that it would
have been better, far better, for the country and for himself had
he died in the train going from the Western prairie to Washington,
or in the bathroom of the White House.

In the early hours of one April morning, sleepless, he spoke to
Grayson of resigning: "My personal pride must not be allowed to
stand in the way of my duty to the country. If I am only half effi-
cient I should turn the office over to the Vice President. If it is
going to take much time for me to recover my health and strength,
the country cannot afford to wait for me. What do you think?" The
doctor reviewed how his patient was keeping in touch with things
and writing more notes every day, and suggested a Cabinet meeting, which would perhaps reassure him of his ability to handle the
job he held. The President acquiesced in the idea of the meeting,
but he could not cease brooding over the death of the League. "I
have had nothing but discouragement from those who should support me and should cooperate with me and stand for the principles
for which I stand," he said, his mouth inert on the left side and the
words coming through the thin lips as from a faraway and muffled
place. "I have stood for principles and not personalities," he said,

an old man bent in a wheel chair, the white hair thin and wispy above the tortured face. "Many have failed me in this crucial time." The husky soft voice murmured on in the night: betrayal, betrayal. But the great fighting spirit and the will for victory were still there in the crumpled and broken body even if physically it could be seen only in the undulled eyes. "If I were well and strong I would gladly and eagerly fight for the cause stronger than ever," he said. There was something in him of the Southerners who loved their Lost Cause and who surrounded him in his boy's days in Georgia and South Carolina. The cause, the cause.

The Cabinet meeting was called for April 14, the first meeting since the final one held by the fired Lansing, the first one the President had attended since August, eight months earlier. The meeting was in his study near his bedroom, not in the Cabinet Room of the Executive Wing. Before the Cabinet members came he was put into a chair and propped up at the end of a desk. When each man came in Ike Hoover formally announced his name and title in a very loud, clear voice, making a horrified Secretary Daniels think to himself that the President must be blind. (But the announcing was only an extra precaution and was not done again in later meetings.) Secretary Houston looked at his chief and thought to himself that it was enough to make you weep to see him, he was so old, so worn and haggard. In repose his face looked somewhat as it had, but when Houston shook his hand and he said hello the Secretary saw how the jaw dropped on one side. The voice uttering greetings was weak and strained.

When all the men were seated, the President convened the meeting with a weak joke: "I thought it would be well that we put our heads together, but not like the Chicago aldermen who wanted to form a solid surface." The Cabinet men sent a chuckle over the desk to him, but then a silence fell. For several moments they sat thus in embarrassed quiet, it seeming that he had nothing additional to say, no more to contribute. At length someone brought up the subject of the nationalized railroads. The President seemed to have difficulty in keeping his mind on the discussion. A debate began between Secretary of Labor William Wilson and Attorney General Palmer about the deportations of suspected anarchists, Palmer saying more deportations would have ended the mining strike and Secretary Wilson saying it would only have aggravated matters.

The President roused himself and said to Palmer, "Do not let the country see Red."

There was some talk of complaints about the Post Office Department and he said of the Postmaster General, "This seems to be an open season for criticizing Burleson." On matters that took place before his illness he seemed clear enough, but on everything else he wished to postpone discussion. Several times in the course of the meeting Grayson appeared in the doorway to look closely at the patient, and after an hour's dragging talk the doctor came in with the First Lady, who with anxiety written all over her features suggested that the men should go. "Holding this Cabinet meeting is an experiment, you know," the President said, "and I ought not to stay long." So they filed out.

The later irregularly held meetings were painful for the Cabinet men, for he would repeat himself to them, telling the same stories, the same jokes. From his seat he waved vaguely and said the last resting place of the League was nearby and every morning he put fresh flowers on the grave. The men continued to run their departments as they saw best, conferring with the First Lady now and again and the President occasionally, and attempting to fit into their work the instructions which reached them in his short notes. But the notes were generally of a bitter nature and it seemed he was lashing out at all the world. The French and British, avaricious nations, were out to take advantage of the other Europeans, and the State Department should "keep on their track"; the French Marshal Ferdinand Foch had a "touch of insubordination" about him and could not be trusted; the Princeton Endowment Fund would receive nothing from Princeton's most illustrious graduate because that graduate did not "believe at all in the present administration of the University"; the American Ambassador to Mexico was, like his predecessors, derelict in his duty: "I wonder if there is something in an assignment to Mexico which makes a man a quitter."

Eugene V. Debs, the Socialist, was still in prison because of his seditious activities during the war, and a nation rushing pell-mell into the Jazz Age was inclined to let bygones be bygones and free him, but the President, still thinking of the dead boys back in France, would not have it so. "I will never consent to the pardon of this man," he said to Tumulty, who thought Debs should be freed. "Were I to consent to it I should never be able to look into the faces of the mothers of this country who sent their boys to the other side. This man was a traitor to his country and he will never be pardoned during my Administration." For this the liberals of the country rose against him, Norman Thomas saying that "his point blank refusal to pardon Gene Debs would, if Mr. Wilson were a well man, put the final seal of vindictive animosity upon the career of a man who at the last proved recreant to every high principle of liberalism which he once professed." Debs himself said the President was the "most pathetic figure in the world," that no other public figure was ever "so scathingly rebuked, so overwhelmingly impeached and repudiated."

In the bitterness which was his that spring he could even get angry at those who served him best; when Grayson said he wanted to take his wife and family to the seashore for a couple of weeks in the approaching summer, the President replied with an invalid's frustration and cruelty that it would be like Grayson to do that, to desert him. "I suppose Tumulty will be going next," he said. "Everyone is leaving me." The doctor stayed, and little Gordon Grayson stayed also, to sit with the President on the wheel chair when in May the first circus of the season came to Washington. The Secret Service men arranged for the circus parade to leave Pennsylvania Avenue at the south end of the Treasury and come north on East Executive Avenue so that the President might see the clowns perform a few tricks in the street. Gordon wanted a balloon and Edmund Starling went and got him one. The child popped it in a few minutes. Starling got him another and, holding it, he sat with the President, a little boy, an old man, and together they looked at the elephants and heard the circus music and received the waved salutes of the painted funnymen cavorting before them.

Almost from the beginning of his illness the President wanted to try to walk—"I want to try my legs"—and now Grayson allowed him to work at it. With two men holding him up, one at each side, he gripped a blackthorn stick in his one good hand and tottered along. The teeth were set and he tried to hold up his head, and he said he was going to walk, he was going to walk. With assistance he was able to go a few steps, the useless left leg being lifted up and put down by a servant bending at his side. One of the rugs in the living quarters was an old one from Princeton days with famous landmarks of the country woven into it, and he joked about going over Niagara Falls—"not a bad stunt for a lame fellow."

There was nothing else for the reporters in the press room to write about but whether or not he could walk, and they worked to find out the situation, but no news was given to them beyond the bare statement that he was well on his way to complete recovery. The First Lady continued with her long hours of work, but as time went on there was less for the White House to do; somehow the various departments ran by themselves.° Sometimes people—ill-advised people—tried to flatter her by saying she was doing a good job of governing the country, but the answer was a flaring "Do you call that a compliment?" For many months, ever since the tea for the reporters after the Western trip, there had been no White House entertaining, but on April 5 she had in the Cabinet wives for lunch along with some of her women relatives and Altrude Gordon Grayson. In the evenings the two of them sat in his room before an open fire—he was always cold—and he played Canfield while she kept the score of each game.

It seemed he was getting a little stronger, enough to be out of bed for several hours each day, but still the question of resignation was in his mind and he said to Grayson that if the time came when he felt he did not have the strength to fill the office he would summon Congress in special session and have Grayson arrange for him to be wheeled into the House of Representatives. "I shall have my address of resignation prepared and shall try to read it myself, but if my voice is not strong enough I shall ask the Speaker of the House to read it. At its conclusion I shall be wheeled out of the room."

The day did not come, and by mid-May he felt strong enough to receive two of the many foreign diplomats waiting to present their credentials to him. Third Assistant Secretary of State Breckinridge Long came with Secretary Colby to present the Belgian Ambassador and the Minister from Uruguay. Long wrote in his diary that night that he was shocked at the way the President looked,

---

° With what success is another question. Joseph C. Grew found his work as Minister to Denmark difficult because of the State Department's lack of interest in what he was doing and the paucity of orders about what he should do. All questions and appeals to Washington were left unanswered. "The only constructive criticism I received was: 'Don't send in too much stuff.'"

at the face that had lost "many of its heavy lines and all of its ruddy color," at the flesh that was no longer of "firm appearance." The men were received in the President's study off his bedroom; he sat in an armchair by a table, his back to the window. He smiled, but it was not the smile Long had known before. His left arm hung listlessly at his side; his right hand held a document pertaining to the Uruguayan. It could not be said the paper was gripped in the hand, Long thought; it was rather only resting in the fingers. Normally the President would have stood to listen to the remarks of the Minister, receive from the Minister's hands his credentials, and then read a reply. All of this was dispensed with. His mouth had a strange tendency to remain open after he spoke. In a soft and husky voice he told of "smiling across the table" at a colleague of the Minister in Paris, not realizing that the Minister was in fact the man at whom he had smiled. The Minister did not call his attention to the mistake.

Before they went in, just prior to reaching the White House, Long had told the Uruguayan in strong terms that he expected, that the State Department expected, that the Minister would be "just as generous in talking of the President's condition as possible," and that if the Minister was going to find this difficult to do it would perhaps be wise for him to refrain from all comment. But when they came out and the reporters gathered around, the Minister followed Long's instructions and said he had "found the President doing well, bright of mind and very gracious." Afterward the Belgian Ambassador went in. Long wrote in his diary, "Of course each of these men will report to their Government their real impressions but it will not be known for some years—too late to hurt." Three days later Long brought in the Minister of Poland and thought to himself that now the President did not look so bad. Perhaps it was because the President was not as self-conscious as the first time, Long thought, or maybe it was that he himself "knew what to expect and the sight was no longer a shock." The President was very gracious to the Polish diplomat, saying he had been happy to help bring about the re-establishment of Poland during the Paris Peace Conference.

The newspapers wrote of the receptions of the diplomats as best they could, treating warily the remarks of the foreigners about his health and mentioning that Washington still teemed with rumors about the President's condition. "It has been difficult to make any clear statement concerning these rumors," said the New York *Times*, "as those acquainted with his condition have shown an indisposition to go into details about his illness. They continue to assert that he is steadily improving." The article went on to wonder if the President could walk.

The auto rides were begun again, and he started seeing more guests. Generally they were brought to him on the South Portico. The First Lady was always there, always quick to do what was necessary, to touch a napkin to his lips after he drank his milk, to put her hand on his when he grew too excited or emotional. On May 31 the important Democrat Homer Cummings came and found him too weary to talk much, with his right fingers picking at the motionless ones of his left hand. Cummings would be giving the keynote address at the forthcoming Democratic National Convention, and he talked to the President about it, saying he would refer to the President as one who had been at the point of death. The President interrupted to say that this was not true, he had never been that badly off. Behind him the First Lady shook her head at Cummings as if to say, "He doesn't know," but Cummings agreed to tone down the remark in his speech.

Other Democrats came to see him and one by one, talking with him on the portico, each learned to his horror what Grayson and Tumulty were also coming to know: he wanted to be President again. Loyal to his chief and loyal to that chief's place in history, Tumulty fought against the idea with all the power of love he felt. He asked the President to say publicly that he would not run again; the President refused. Tumulty wrote the First Lady that the President should speak out and say he would not be eligible for a nomination; the First Lady ignored the note. Tumulty took into his confidence a trusted newspaper friend, Louis Seibold of the New York *World*, and they planned that Seibold should ask for an interview with the President. The request was granted and the date for the reporter's visit was set for mid-June. Together Tumulty and Seibold worked out questions which would draw the President into saying he would not run again. But the First Lady circumvented their efforts and sent Tumulty a note saying there would be no comment during the interview about the forthcoming election. The subject of running again was not to be raised, she dictated. Tumulty took her note and put it in his private files, but before doing so he wrote across it that for what she was doing the First Lady could go straight to hell.

Seibold came and breezily joshed the President, saying that he, Seibold, would soon be running a foot race with him; how much money did the President want to bet on the outcome? The published interview was largely interpreted as meaning the President indeed sought renomination. The day after it appeared in print son-in-law William G. McAdoo, a leading potential candidate for the Presidency, announced he would not wish a nomination for himself. Wall Street sources let it be known the President was the betting favorite to secure the Democratic nomination.

Cabinet members and Democrats close to the Administration came one after the other to indicate tactfully to the President that he should step aside, but he would not respond to their hints. Postmaster General Burleson went very far and boldly said that the contest was between the President and his son-in-law; there were no other choices. The President was silent after Burleson finished speaking. Carter Glass, who had left the Secretaryship of the Treasury to take up the post of United States Senator from Virginia, came for tea on the South Portico and began talking candidates. He mentioned A. Mitchell Palmer as a possibility and the President said it would be "futile" to run Palmer. Glass spoke of Governor James Cox of Ohio and the President interrupted him: "Oh, you know Cox's nomination would be a joke."

Grayson talked with Glass privately and said to him bluntly that the President was determined to run and win and then get the country into the League, but that the campaign would kill him. He ended by begging Glass, who would be going to the San Francisco convention as chairman of the platform committee, to fight against a renomination with all his strength.

Grayson also tried to talk with the President himself about speaking out, but the President said it would be "presumptuous" and "in bad taste" for him to "decline something that had not been offered." He added that in addition it was possible that the convention might get into a hopeless tie-up and that there might ensue a demand for someone to lead the delegates out of the wilderness and that that someone might be himself. "In such circumstances I would feel obliged to accept the nomination." Grayson kept still, not offering an opinion for fear of the reaction if he freely said it would be utterly impossible for the President to conduct a campaign.

But the doctor went to see Robert W. Woolley, the Democratic publicist who had helped set the scene for the sickroom visit of Senator Fall, and said to him that he, Grayson, had been attached to the White House during the terms of three Presidents and had yet to see one who wanted to give up the job. "Get me?" he asked.

"I do," Woolley said. "It is true that Mr. Wilson desires a third term?"

"Correct," said Grayson. "He fervently believes it is still possible to have the United States join the League of Nations. But it is out of the question—he just must not be nominated. No matter what others may tell you, no matter what you may read about the President being on the road to recovery, I tell you that he is permanently ill physically, is gradually weakening mentally and can't recover. He couldn't possibly survive the campaign. Only the urgency of the situation justifies me in coming to you and making such a statement even in confidence. At times the President, whose grit and determination are marvelous, seems to show a slight improvement, is in good spirits for several days, even a week or ten days, transacts business with Tumulty—and then suffers a relapse, or I should say, becomes very morose. At such times it is distressing to be in the same room with him. I repeat, he is definitely becoming more feeble."

Woolley said, "Cary, the name of the President will receive many an ovation, his desires as to the platform will prevail, in other ways will he be honored, but his ambition to succeed himself is definitely hopeless." "We must not take any chances," Grayson said.

As Washington grew warmer and June went into its last days the Democrats began leaving for San Francisco and the convention. Carter Glass called upon the President just before going to catch a train west and after the visit Grayson and Tumulty drove with Glass to Union Station, both urging Glass to fight a renomination. Grayson walked with Glass to his sleeper and remained with him until the train began to move. Glass went to the convention carrying the memory of Grayson's parting words: "If anything comes up, save the life and fame of this man from the juggling of false friends."

San Francisco was alive with lighted portraits of the President and marching bands of men shouting out his name. The convention opened with blaring bands and a file of U.S. marines carrying in the colors. A giant American flag hung in the front of the jammed auditorium, and when the delegates grew silent as they waited for the proceedings to begin, the flag was slowly rolled up to disclose a tremendous picture of the President. He was the leader who had won two elections for the Democrats, and the delegates went wild with applause, marching up and down the aisles and shouting above the noise of the pounding drums and swelling music. State standards went dancing up and down above the heads of the celebrants as men carried the flagstaffs into the aisles, every state standard but one—that of the State of New York, which was motionless among the seated and silent members of the New York delegation.

Then a young and athletic New Yorker went yelling into the delegation and grabbed at the flagstaff. There was a scuffle all around him and curses and perhaps even a few blows before he wrenched it away and, yelling in triumph, rushed it out into the aisle. But the great demonstration only strengthened the will of the President's friends to save him from what might happen. Homer Cummings spoke with Senator Joseph T. Robinson of Arkansas, Glass, Daniels, Burleson, Secretary of War Baker, and found them all agreed that it was "impossible and unthinkable," it would be a "tragic mistake" to name the President as candidate.

But one man at San Francisco was working for that nomination. He was Secretary of State Colby, who had seen the President before heading west and had absorbed his ideas and those of the First Lady. And now Colby was biding his time, waiting for the right moment to present the name of the President for renomination. "The outstanding characteristic of the convention is the unanimity and fervor of feeling for you," Colby wired the White House in code. "Convention seizes every opportunity for demonstration which is most impressive. . . . I propose, unless otherwise definitely instructed, to take advantage of first moment to move suspension of rules and place your name in nomination." Tumulty saw the wire and frantically begged the First Lady to wire Colby that this thing not be done. She refused. A stream of other wires asking the President's endorsement of McAdoo (a candidate despite his earlier disavowals), Homer Cummings, James Cox, Palmer —all were left unanswered also. Frightened of what the convention might be about to do, terrified of a renomination for his chief, Tumulty asked the First Lady to hold Colby back until the convention deadlocked. Away from her and the President, Tumulty prayed there would be no deadlock at all and that someone else would be named.

The balloting began and McAdoo showed the greatest strength. Burleson telegraphed a request that the President endorse his son-in-law, and the wire threw the President into a rage. He wired Cummings an order to bar Burleson from all inner councils at San Francisco and said he would fire Burleson for this. Meanwhile word of what Colby was going to do leaked out in San Francisco and precipitated an immediate tense meeting of the President's friends in a hotel room. They ordered Colby to come to them, and when he arrived they bitterly fell upon him in such a fashion that Secretary Daniels was moved to think that never in any small gathering had he seen more indignation and resentment. "You had no right to send such a message," Daniels raged at Colby; the other men blasted him for his "cruel" and "fantastic" plan and told him that were the President well enough to run, Colby's aid would not have been needed to get him nominated—it would have been seen to by the men in the room. They forced Colby to send a stalling telegram to the President saying the time was not yet ripe for presentation of his name.

At the White House the President hung upon the reports coming in from the west. Ballot after ballot failed to secure enough votes for any of the potential candidates. All wires begging endorsements were ignored, but finally on the forty-fourth ballot, after McAdoo and Palmer were hopelessly deadlocked, the convention nominated Governor Cox, the compromise candidate. When the news reached Washington, the President, who could literally go for years without using a stronger term than "damn" or "hell," burst into a stream of profanities and obscenities. For Vice President the convention nominated the young man who had grabbed the New York State banner—Franklin D. Roosevelt.

It became a question of importance as to whether Cox would call upon the President. That McAdoo and Palmer had gone down to defeat was construed by many as a repudiation of the President, and many of Cox's people did not want their candidate, who was not closely identified with the Administration, to tie himself to the Administration's leader. But Cox saw it otherwise, saying that he would reproach himself forever should the President die without having had a courtesy call from the Democrat who hoped to succeed him. So on a warm day in that summer of 1920 Cox went with Franklin Roosevelt to see the President.

Roosevelt was in a dark coat and gleaming white pants and shoes. Boyish and bright, he ushered Cox into Tumulty's office, where they waited fifteen minutes while the President was wheeled out onto the South Portico. They walked over to him where he sat with a shawl draped across his shoulders, covering the left arm but not concealing the wasted look. "He is a very sick man," Cox murmured to Roosevelt as they walked up. They greeted him warmly and he looked up and in what seemed to Roosevelt a very weak, low voice said, "Thank you for coming. I am very glad you came." The President's utter weariness was startling to Roosevelt, and tears came into Cox's eyes as he looked down. "Mr. President," Cox said, "I have always admired the fight you made for the League." "Mr. Cox," the President said, "that fight can still be won."

They talked a few minutes more, the President saying he was sure Cox would enjoy living at the White House, and then Cox said, "Mr. President, we are going to be a million per cent with you and your Administration, and that means the League of Nations." The President looked up. "I am very grateful," he said. His voice was scarcely audible. "I am very grateful," he repeated. They left him and went to a room in the Executive Wing and Cox sat down at a desk—Franklin Roosevelt would use that desk again, one day—and wrote out a statement committing the candidates to making the League the paramount issue of the campaign.

They got up to go, Cox saying to Tumulty that seeing the President as now he was had touched him more deeply than any other experience of his life. They drove away. They left behind a man working at trying to walk and succeeding to the extent that soon, on the arm of an attendant, he would be able to make his slow and painful way to the library, where each night in a dinner jacket he dined alone with the First Lady. The room had rose hangings and upholstery and small colored vases with a single different-color rose in each, and the two sat there alone, he using only his right hand, an almost noiseless figure eating his food so slowly and quietly in the hot summer evening.

11

There were old canal streams in the country-side only fifteen miles out of Washington, and honeysuckle and scattered pines. Along the Conduit Road running toward Great Falls there were reservoirs and hills thick with trees. Rural Virginia was beautiful in the summer, and along the roads country children waited for his slow-moving car; when it came into sight they ran up flags and yelled. One curly-headed little boy, hardly more than a toddler, always had the same greeting: a tiny hand held up in salute and a piping "Hi, Wilson!" For long hours that summer he was driven in the solitary hills and along the Potomac, and always in almost complete silence. He rarely spoke; he was almost totally mute. He did not display interest in the campaign being fought to determine whether Cox or Senator Warren G. Harding of Ohio was to be his successor, and when Tumulty suggested he make some effort to aid Cox, he replied that he would do it in his own time and in his own way. He ended by letting months go by before he did anything at all.

But who he was and what he was dominated the forthcoming election. "The issue which the American people are going to vote upon," said ex-President Taft, "no matter what Mr. Cox wishes, Mr. Wilson wishes, Mr. Lodge wishes, or Mr. Harding wishes, is whether they approve the Administration of Mr. Wilson." Harding expressed it perfectly, had it just right, when he said that what the

United States wanted was no more parades, no heroics—"return to 'normalcy.'" °

It was obvious to all the world that the Republicans were going to win this election, that the country was going to throw out the Democrats with their taxes and war and crusading for the world's good, but the President could not see that this was so. Secretary Daniels remarked that "of course" Cox had no chance, and the President incredulously asked, "Do you mean it is possible that the American people would elect Harding?" "It is not only possible," Daniels said, "but they are going to do it." The President flared out, "Daniels, you haven't enough faith in the people!" Postmaster General Burleson ventured to predict that Cox would take the worst beating in years, and the President cried, "Burleson, shut up! You are a pessimist!" Stockton Axson, Ellen's brother, tried to raise the subject of possible defeat several times, but the President would not listen. "You don't understand the American people," he said, a sick old man intoning through white lips that it was out of the question that the nation would turn down the candidate who stood for the League of Nations, for the Right, for Truth.

Axson told Grayson he was worried about the effect of defeat upon the President and that something should be done to ready him for the shock that seemed to be coming. But no one could change the President's opinion that his country would opt for the League. In another summer, that of 1919, presenting the League to the Senate of the United States, he said it had come about "by no plan of our conceiving but by the hand of God who has led us into this way." He had said, "We cannot turn back. We can only go forward, with lifted eyes and freshened spirit, to follow the vision. It was of this that we dreamed at our birth. America shall in truth show the way." It was still true in his mind and in his soul where down beneath the pain and helplessness there lived utter faith, belief, devotion. "I am sure," he said to Tumulty, "that the hearts of the people are right on this great issue and that we can confidently look forward to triumph."

All through those hot months of 1920's summer, he continued to say that victory was certain. That vindicating triumph became the raft to which he clung—Cox would be his monument—but he

° The First Lady took the word as a personal insult to herself, saying that she had done her best to keep things normal.

ignored all appeals to do something to help the candidate until October came. On the twenty-seventh day of that month, with Election Day a week off, he received a handful of pro-League Republicans in the Green Room. He sat hunched over in his wheel chair under a portrait of Abraham Lincoln and did not rise when they came in. "I must apologize for receiving you like this," he said. "It is unavoidable and I guess you all understand."

They remained standing grouped about him as he began to read a statement. Although they numbered little more than a dozen persons, the tone of his remarks was that of an address made to a great multitude. "My fellow countrymen: it is to be feared that the supreme issue presented for your consideration in the present campaign is growing more obscure rather than clearer . . ." His voice began strong with each paragraph of this his first speech, his first public appearance, since Pueblo, but it gradually grew weaker, particularly if the paragraph was long, until at the end he would be whispering. Mrs. Schuyler N. Warren of New York saw tears in the eyes of many of the listening men and herself felt crushed and broken to see the President as he was, converted in her eyes from the comparatively young person she had seen some time before into an old, old man. She thought to herself that he in his chair was tragic and glorious—it was tragic that he suffered so; glorious that America had produced such a man.

". . . The nation was never called upon to make a more solemn determination than it must now make. The whole future moral force of Right in the world depends upon the United States." His whispering voice, like that of a man praying to himself, lent the air of a religious ceremony to the scene. It did not seem he would be able to finish and the Reverend Arthur J. Brown thought to himself that this was in the nature of a farewell address, that before them was a dying man speaking his last wishes.

". . . I suggest that the candidacy of every candidate for whatever office be tested by this question: Shall we or shall we not redeem the great moral obligations of the United States?" He had finished. Haggard, breathing with difficulty, eyes closed, trembling, he was wheeled away. Once upon a time when he spoke he leaned forward with eyes narrowed and muscles taut, his fingers closed into a tight fist, and reminded those who saw him of a man about to begin a race.

On November 2 there was a Cabinet meeting. One of the men said he was apprehensive about Cox's chances, but the President interrupted. "You need not worry," he said. "The American people will not turn Cox down and elect Harding. A great moral issue is involved. The people can and will see it." Harding that day scored the most one-sided electoral triumph since the election of James Monroe just one hundred years before. He carried every state in the Union save those of the former Confederacy. "We have torn up Wilsonism by the roots," exulted Senator Henry Cabot Lodge.

During that day, Election Day, as the people went to the polls, the President labored to climb a series of two or three steps Grayson had constructed for him, but he simply could not lift his left leg. In the early evening Tumulty tried to find a few bright reports in the election picture, but there were none to be found. The President had planned to stay up two hours past his nine o'clock bedtime in order to hear the results, but by nine it was clear that Cox was to lose, and so he went to sleep.

In the morning when he awoke the scope of the debacle was clear and also the meaning of that debacle. When the Senate turned down the League it had been in the President's eyes the work of politicians, of the Lodges and Falls—of the Warren G. Hardings. Now it was the people, the people, the people themselves. They had turned on him and he was alone. He made no public comments, issued no statements, but, hurt and bewildered, sank into a terrible isolation from his country and its mood and even perhaps its ultimate meaning. Once he had thought there was an almost magical relationship between himself and the American people he believed the most generous, the best, the most idealistic of all the world, and that in that relationship it had been given to him to speak the deepest thoughts of that people. He had known that people. They were his; he theirs. Now they had thrown him out. He was alone. Or almost alone. The Secret Service man Edmund Starling came to him with a message from a friend of Starling's whom the President had met a few times: "Mr. Barker wants you to know that he is still with you and he will follow you anywhere you want to go." The President turned away to try to hide his quick tears, and blinked them back and looked at Starling and said, "Tell Barker I thank him, but there is nowhere now to go."

For what was Barker's support when the electoral vote was 404 to 127? Those close to him tried to help—but it was useless. Nothing could help. They tried. Nellie wrote: "Darling, darling Father—I just want to send a line to tell you that I *know* this is not a repudiation of the League. . . . Nothing can destroy what you have done—nothing in the whole wide world. I love you so much and I want so much to see you—can I go down soon, darling? With all my love to you both, Your adoring daughter." Jessie wrote: "On election night when I couldn't sleep I picked up a life of Joan of Arc and read it through. It comforted me just a little because though they burned her, and her life seemed stultified and frittered away by intrigues and politicians, it went on inevitably for she had made it alive. With a heart overflowing with love, Your adoring daughter." Secretary Colby: "You have spoken the truth. You have battled for it. You have suffered for it. Your crown will be one of glory, and the heathen who have imagined vain things will some day creep penitently to touch the hem of your garments." Alfred S. Niles of Baltimore: "My dear Wilson: It is impossible for me, as your classmate of '79, to refrain from telling you that some of us (including myself) are now, in the time of the apparent defeat of the principles for which you have stood, more proud than ever of you and your record."

A few days later when he went driving with George Creel along as passenger, he shrank back from a handful of sightseers standing by the White House gate, ducking like a man avoiding a blow. "Why, what is the matter, Mr. President?" asked Creel. "Didn't you see them?" whispered the President. "Of course, sir. But what about it? I saw only respect and devotion." "No. Just curiosity."

One day Ray Stannard Baker was invited for lunch, and the First Lady suggested he come early so as to see the morning's film. Baker came and waited in a parlor where the servants lifted and put aside a heavy red rug so that the President might walk with greater ease upon the bare floor. He came shuffling along slowly, heavily, his left arm hanging straight down. Very few people had seen him walk at that time, and it was a terrible shock to Baker to see the leaden steps in place of the alert and active movements of former days. Baker felt a surge of intense compassion, but it gave way to admiration when he saw the President's determination to persevere shine from the gleaming eyes. The handshake was a mustered-up

show of strength. Baker thought to himself, The will is uncon-
querable; the life untamable. They went slowly down the hall into the East Room empty of all save for a few chairs grouped in the
middle. The room was unlighted and their steps echoed. They took
seats, Baker, the President, the First Lady, a niece of hers, Grayson. The projector clicked and sputtered and the film began. They
were having a pre-release showing of a film on the President's visit
to Europe. By magic, Baker remembered later, "we were in another world; a resplendent world, full of wonderful and glorious
events. There we were, sailing grandly into the harbor at Brest,
the ships beflagged, the soldiers marshalled upon the quay, and
planes skimming through the air. There was the President himself,
smiling upon the bridge, very erect, very tall, lifting his hat to
shouting crowds.

"By magic we were transported to Paris. There he was again,
this time with the President of France, driving down the most famous avenue in the world, bowing right and left. In the distance
we saw the Arc de Triomphe, symbol too of this latest triumph, and
caught a glimpse of the great Napoleon guarding its dimmed glory."

The President bent forward, looking at 1918 in the great empty
East Room in 1920. He was absolutely silent. The film showed the
trip to England, the warships in the Channel, London. "Were there
ever such marching regiments of men, such bowing dignitaries, so
many lords and their ladies! And there was the President, riding
behind magnificent horses with outriders flying pennants, and people shouting in the streets, coming down from Buckingham Palace
with the King of England." It was over. "It was only a film. All
that glory had faded away with a click and a sputter." They sat for
a moment in the dark room and Baker looked over at a stooped,
seated figure: the President, immobile. Someone came out of the
darkness and put a foot against the President's foot so that he might
not slip as he rose from the chair, and he got up and turned slowly
and shuffled out of the room without looking aside and without
speaking. In later years Baker found his memory of that moment
to be an intolerable thing.

He would have four more months as President, and he tried to
pull himself together to get them done with. Writing a Thanks-
giving Day proclamation with the result of the election fresh in his

mind was too much for him and he asked Colby to do it—"though I have no resentment in my heart." He worked to walk and began to take meals regularly downstairs and to receive frequent visitors. But they saw a timidity in him, an apologetic cast to the slipping smile, the request to be excused from rising, the very manner of speaking: "You will pardon me if I put on my hat. I like to keep my hat on." Sewing by his side or with her hand on his, a quick "my darling" for him upon her lips, the First Lady seemed to offer a contrasting cheeriness mixed with an attitude that made visitors feel she was now the captain of their destiny, hers and her husband's. Stockton Axson, Ellen's brother, thought to himself it was well that this First Lady, and not the preceding one, was there to meet the crisis—this one was a far better warrior.

Almost every morning now the First Lady went house-hunting in the District or in Virginia. They had decided to live in the Washington area after long discussions of possible other sites, and had made up a chart listing the ratings of five cities according to Climate, Friends, Opportunities, Amusements, Libraries and Freedom. (New York got the highest rating in Climate and Amusements, tying with Boston and Baltimore in Opportunities; Richmond and Baltimore tied in Friends; and although Washington got the lowest score for Freedom, the Library of Congress and the fact that it was the First Lady's real home carried the day.) Their finances, merged when they married, totaled something like $250,000, and they felt he would be able to make money by writing books and articles. In fact he began the book on government which for decades he had said he was going to write. He did so by typing with his one good hand the first page:

A Dedication.
To
E. B. W.

I dedicate this book because it is a book in which I have tried to interpret life, the life of a nation, and she has shown me the full meaning of life. Her heart is not only true but wise; her thoughts are not only free but touched with vision; she teaches and guides by being what she is; her unconscious interpretation of faith and duty makes all the way clear; her power to comprehend makes work and thought alike easier and more near to what it seeks.

It was the first and the last page.

The cold weather came and in December he was awarded the Nobel Peace Prize, the American Minister to Norway representing him at the ceremonies. In December, President-elect Harding came to Washington and the First Lady sent a note to Mrs. Harding asking her to call. Mrs. Harding wrote back on the stationery of Mrs. Evalyn Walsh McLean—she of Hope Diamond fame—accepting the invitation and asking if Mrs. McLean might not accompany her. The First Lady answered that as the Washington *Post*, owned by Mrs. McLean's husband, had opposed the President, Mrs. McLean would not be welcome. On her husband's United States Senate stationery Mrs. Harding wrote that she would come alone. She wore a dark dress and a hat with blue feathers and a black mesh veil fastened tightly over her face. (The First Lady noted, however, that her successor-to-be wore rouge upon her cheeks.) The First Lady also found her too nervously talkative, too pushy, too effusive. But it was not likely she would approve of any woman whose husband had so decisively destroyed the hope of a happy end to her own husband's work.

They took tea together alone and after half an hour the First Lady managed to "stem the torrent of words" (so she put it) in order to introduce Mrs. Jaffray, the housekeeper, who would show Mrs. Harding the White House, every room save for one in which the President was resting. Mrs. Harding put on a pair of eyeglasses over the mesh veil, did not shake hands with Mrs. Jaffray, and went off with her for the tour. The First Lady said good-by and went out on an errand, returning some hours later. She found Mrs. Harding still there, down in the kitchen talking with the cook. It was not until after eight o'clock that she finally left.

At Christmas they held a little family dinner party and got together small gifts for the children along the country roads. They at first considered building a home, and the President spent much time looking through architectural magazines, but as time grew short they gave up the idea and sought an already-constructed one. They looked very seriously at a house near Alexandria and at one in Massachusetts Avenue Park, and at one situated upon twenty-six wooded acres through which a quiet stream ran, but the plans for purchase did not work out. One morning she went to see two possible places in S Street—one of them would shortly be purchased by Herbert Hoover—but neither met their needs. She was about to leave S Street, which in Washington in 1920 was the point at which country began to take over from city, when the agent with her asked if she would not look at a third house on the block, Number 2340. She did so and decided the house was perfect. She returned to the White House and told the President that she thought this was the place. That afternoon she went to a concert by the touring New York Philharmonic and when she returned he was in the Oval Room with the deed to the house in his hand.° The President had not seen the house at all, but the next day they went to it together. At the door the President's valet, at his instruction, dug out a small piece of sod and with a key to the door gave the earth to the First Lady; it was an old Scottish custom.

The house, four years old, with thick walls and fine high ceilings, was of Georgian design. The front door opened upon a formal hallway with a floor of black and white marble. A small room was on each side. From there one mounted three marble steps to the main hall, behind which were the kitchen, the servants' dining room, and a billiard room. On the second floor were the front drawing room, whose windows opened upon S Street and the wooded terraces across the way; the library in the rear facing the semiformal garden surrounded by a brick wall; and the dining room and a solarium with glass doors, both looking out upon the garden. On the third floor were five bedrooms and five bathrooms. The fourth floor contained the servants' rooms and the laundry. They arranged for the installation of an electric elevator, the construction of a brick garage with a tiled sun terrace upon its top, and for enough built-in bookshelves to hold his library of eight thousand volumes.

New Year's came and January went. On February 1, with no public announcement, he went to the theater, his first visit in a year and a half. He entered through a rear-alley door and before the curtain was raised he was taken across the stage, Starling and Ike Hoover aiding him as he took his slow, hesitant steps, the First Lady going on ahead to screen him from the eyes of the people in the cast. They went up into a box, the men awkwardly half carry-

---

° The purchase price was in the vicinity of $150,000, an extremely large sum by 1920 standards. The President was aided in the purchase by ten friends who contributed $10,000 each to assure him a proper residence. One of the ten, Bernard Baruch, seeking to insure privacy for him, also bought the lot next door and allowed Nature to have her way with it, which resulted in an attractive woods-like setting.

ing him and then lowering him into his seat. The play was John Drinkwater's *Abraham Lincoln* and it must have seemed strange to one who had been Mr. President for nearly eight years to see the actor Frank McGlynn addressed by that title. *"To be President of this people,"* McGlynn said on the stage, *"that's a searching thing. Bitterness, and scorn, and wrestling often with men I shall despise, and perhaps nothing truly done at the end."* McGlynn wore a Lincoln beard; he had a shawl and tall stovepipe hat. There came a scene when the actor knelt at a table and in an agony of horror about war and being President buried his face in his hands. The watcher in the box above had done that also.

"I've a heart that's near to breaking every day." Harding would be President. There would be no American entry into the League.

When the curtain fell for the end of the first act and the lights in the theater came up, the audience for the first time knew the President was there. He was so changed that many of the people were not sure it was he, but enough of them decided that it was indeed the President and they broke into applause. He remained seated, his hands nervously fingering his steel-banded cane and seeking his watch. Soon the whole theater joined in the hand-clapping as people pointed to him and craned their necks upward, and a look of surprise came over his features. The First Lady looked as if she were astonished at the cheering. With great difficulty he struggled to his feet and bowed. At the end of the performance they cheered him again. The reporter Louis Seibold, harking back to the offer of a foot race between the two of them, wired when news of the theater visit was printed: JUDGING FROM YOUR PRESENT FORM YOU'LL HAVE TO INCREASE THE HANDICAP YOU OFFERED SOME TIME AGO IF I'M TO RACE YOU. CONGRATULATIONS TO YOUR GENTLE TRAINER.

Two weeks later he went for the first time in seventeen months to the Executive Wing of the White House for a Cabinet meeting, a walk of six hundred yards. He moved very slowly but with little assistance, the right foot going forward first and then, dragging, the left. He allowed the newspaper photographers two pictures and then held up a hand: "That will be enough." It was now a matter of weeks until it would all be over and he would be a private citizen in S Street. Jessie wrote: "Just one more month now! Isn't it fine— and we shall have you all to ourselves again as in the old days!" But he was still the President, still able to check on prospective appointees to government jobs to find if they were acceptable to anti-League Senators—and to disallow them if they were. He had time now for purely personal matters also—inquiries about the price of installing a safe in S Street, about the location of a woodshed.

George Creel had gone to work for a typical Roaring Twenties mental-improvement mail-order firm and the President asked for a copy of the outfit's printed application form and laboriously filled it out on his typewriter. "Pelmanism," said the form, "can get more out of life for you. . . . Ask yourself the cause of failure. Look about you and see the reason why men and women do not get ahead. . . . Now consider the qualities that have made our most successful men; analyze the characteristics of such men as Edison, Schwab, Hoover, McAdoo, Pershing." ("Our most successful men." His name was absent.) "You have within you the same qualities that these men have. . . . Pelmanism teaches you how to develop ORIGINALITY—how to develop PERSONALITY—how to build CHARACTER—how to strengthen INDIVIDUALITY. HOW TO SUCCEED! . . . All replies absolutely confidential. Is your power of concentration strong or weak?" He typed, "Just about medium, I should say." "Is your memory good or poor?" "Rather good." "Do you lack confidence in yourself?" "No." "Do you suffer much from self-consciousness or shyness?" "A good deal from shyness." "What is the general condition of your health at the present time?" "I am suffering from nervous exhaustion." The form explained the Special Enrollment Terms, one calling for $35 in cash to pay for the course, the other calling for installment payments—five dollars down and seven further payments at 30-day intervals. Below was room for indicating name, address, occupation, age. He typed in his age, 64, but it would have been too fantastic to put down his occupation as President of the United States and his address as 1600 Pennsylvania Avenue, and he put the application away.

February was his last complete month in office; he invited his Cabinet members to come for lunch one by one. Houston came and asked what he thought of President-elect Harding's nominees for Cabinet posts. "Who, exactly?" asked the President, and Houston mentioned Senator Fall, who would be Secretary of the Interior. The President spoke about Fall's sickroom visit to the White House—"the smelling committee" which "I think discovered that I was very much all here"—and told of Fall's remark that he was praying for the President. "If I could have got out of bed," the President told Houston, "I would have hit the man. Why did he want to put me in bad with the Almighty? He must have known that God would take the opposite view from him on any subject." He walked to the elevator with Houston and put his hand on the Secretary's and said, "Old man, God bless you," and Houston went out. It was the first evidence of personal affection or emotion Houston had seen in the eight years of their relationship.

Secretary Colby came and asked the First Lady if she would like to visit the State Department to see the Declaration of Independence and other historic documents. She said she would come the next day. When Colby rose to go he said that now that the end was coming he wanted the President to know what an honor it had been to work under him. The President thanked him for his words and asked, "Well, Colby, what are you going to do?" Colby stretched out his arms and said, "Oh, I suppose I shall return to New York and open a musty law office again, which, after this experience, will be a dreary business. But I must make a living." The President said, "Well, I, too, must make a living. As I was once a lawyer"—three and a half decades had gone by since then —"why not open an office together here?" Colby leaped forward and leaned across the desk. "Do you really mean that, Mr. President?" "Yes," said the President, "I can't face a life of idleness." Colby later talked with the First Lady and Grayson, both of whom thought it was a good idea, and then began to make plans for a partnership in which the President would not have to do too much. The other Cabinet members were all amazed when they learned of the plan, and one of them said to Daniels, "Bainbridge has vamped Wilson." But that was not the case at all—as they would find out.

Margaret was with them now, and every day she practiced her singing in a room across the hall from his. One day as she sang Ray Stannard Baker came in and saw a man with a bird cage and some family pictures going out to a moving van parked before the White House and for the first time actually realized that the long years as President were really coming to their conclusion. Furniture stored in Princeton was being shipped down, and the First Lady was getting her things out of warehouses, and they were working together to determine just what gifts should be given members of the White House staff. (Each person got a U.S. Bond of from $50 to $500, and many were also given personal mementos —paintings and such.) Ellen's brother, Stockton Axson, sent the First Lady a graceful letter: "Dearest Edith: This is just a little 'Goodbye' note to you and the President as you leave the White House. I think the uppermost feeling in your mind will be relief, but there must be a touch of sadness too. I think it was Dr. Johnson (no sentimentalist) who said there is always sadness in doing anything the last time. So much has happened in the White House years that it will not be possible to leave the place indifferently. But, quoting Browning, 'The best is yet to be'—happy, happy years in S Street."

On March 1, with three days to go, he held his last Cabinet meeting. It was in the White House Executive Wing. Secretary Houston arrived early and as he waited saw the President painfully making his way to the Cabinet Room: it was in Houston's eyes a brave sight and a tragic sight. He did not want the President to know that his straining walk was being witnessed, and so he turned away and went into a room nearby and waited there so that the President might take his seat. Then Houston went in with the others. The President remarked that, come what might, he was going to take part in the inauguration despite his weakness and lameness. There was a brief pause. One of the men asked how he would pass his time out of office. Would he write a history of his Administration? The President said he would not, that he was too near the events and too closely associated personally. One of the men said, "But you must do something! What will you do?" The President thought a moment and said, "I am going to try to teach ex-Presidents how to behave. There will be one very difficult thing for me to stand, however, and that is Mr. Harding's English!"

Again there was silence for a moment. Colby said, "Mr. President, if I may presume to voice the sentiments of my colleagues, I have the honor of saying . . ." He talked about the inspiring example the President had given them, of how they loved and admired him. "We shall keep watch of your progress toward better health with affectionate interest and shall pray that your recovery may be rapid." When Colby finished, Houston started to say how much he himself endorsed these remarks, but held up when he saw that the President was trying to control himself and stop his lips from trembling. But it did not work; he could not stop the tears from rolling down his lined cheeks past the quivering mouth. "Gentlemen," he got out brokenly, weakly, "it is one of the handicaps of my physical condition that I cannot control myself as I have been accustomed to do. God bless you all." Houston thought to himself that this must be the greatest trial that could come to a Scotch Presbyterian whose whole philosophy was one of self-control. The men got up and each shook his hand. "Good-by, Mr. President. Good-by, Mr. President." They left and he walked away, trembling and with the marks of moisture still on his face. Joe Tumulty stood watching from his office window and thought, There goes the real hope of the world. "The President finished strong," said Secretary Baker to Secretary Burleson, and Burleson said that George Washington also cried at his final Cabinet meeting. The Cabinet members got together and wrote him a letter:

Mr. President:
The final moments of the Cabinet on Tuesday found us quite unable to express the poignant feelings with which we realized that the hour of leave-taking and official dispersal had arrived.
Will you permit us to say to you now, and as simply as we can, how great a place you occupy in our honor, love, and esteem?
. . . History will acclaim your great qualities. We who have known you so intimately bear witness to them now.
We fervently wish you, dear Mr. President, long life and the happiness that you so richly deserve and have so abundantly earned.

Two days later, March 3, his last full day, the telegrams came in. There were 124 of them, and by order of the President they were all answered by Joe Tumulty. THE DEMOCRATIC CITY CLUB OF BERLIN NEW HAMPSHIRE SEND GREETINGS TO OUR RETIRING CHIEF. WE WISH YOU HEALTH AND HAPPINESS. WE ASSURE YOU OF OUR LOVE AND LOYALTY AND PLEDGE OURSELVES TO CARRY ON . . . The Rotary of Durant, Oklahoma, the Methodist Church of Woodland, Georgia . . . HISTORY WILL VINDICATE YOU AND ESTABLISH THAT FOR WHICH YOU FOUGHT—THE LEAGUE OF NATIONS. AUTOMOTIVE ASSOCIATION OF CHARLOTTE, NORTH CAROLINA . . . Five hundred Boy Scouts of Springfield, Illinois . . . WE REJOICE THAT YOU MAY NOW HAVE A WELL DESERVED REST AND TRUST YOU MAY LIVE TO KNOW THE LOVE AND GRATITUDE OF THE WHOLE WORLD WHICH IS CERTAIN TO BE YOURS. MR AND MRS HOWARD J BAILEY OMAHA NEBRASKA . . . THE TWO HUNDRED AND FIFTY MEMBERS OF THE COME-

BACK CLUB OF COLUMBIA UNIVERSITY DISABLED EXSERVICEMEN TENDER
YOU HONORARY MEMBERSHIP AND WISH GODSPEED AND QUICK RECOVERY
. . . Aerie 85 of the Fraternal Order of Eagles, Dennison, Ohio . . .
THE DENVILLE VIRGINIA YOUNG MEN'S CHRISTIAN ASSOCIATION
UNITES IN PRAYER THANKING GOD FOR SERVICES AND ASKING GODS RICH-
EST BLESSINGS . . . The Protective Board of the Brotherhood of
Railway Carmen of America . . . Scores of Sweet Briar College
Girls. . . TODAY YOU STEP DOWN TO GLORY J J RYAN ZANESVILLE OHIO.

That day also President-elect Harding came with his wife for
the customary pre-inauguration visit. Tea was served to the two
couples in the Red Room. Mrs. Harding wore the same hat she
had worn when she earlier visited the First Lady. Conversation
was strained and difficult. The President-elect sat in an armchair
with one leg thrown over the arm.

Inauguration Day dawned clear and but slightly windy. The
President took breakfast as usual in his room at eight-thirty and
then dressed in morning coat and gray trousers. All along he had
insisted that he would play his full part in the ceremonies despite
a report from the Secret Service man Richard Jervis, who traced
out the walking he would have to do and found he would have to
go 190 steps from an elevator in the Capitol to the President's Room
in the Senate wing, 270 steps from there out through the rotunda
to the top of the steps leading down to the temporary stand where
the inaugural would be conducted, and down 16 steep stone steps
and then 50 steps to his seat—"All in full view of probably 50,000
people and hundreds of motion picture cameras." The walking,
particularly the going down the steps, was completely beyond his
strength, but not until after breakfast did he accede to Grayson's
pleas and agree to forgo it.

Tumulty came in to see him when Grayson had gone, and together, alone, the two sat in the President's study. Now that it
was all ending—the war, the months of difficulty after the fall in
the bathroom, the failure of the League—now that it was all ended,
really, Tumulty asked the President if he remembered March 4,
1917, the second of his own inauguration days, and how on that
day the President had said it would be "great to be free" when
once March 4, 1921, came. The President said he remembered

well. Now that day had come. They had been together eleven years, ever since New Jersey and the statehouse in Trenton, and the President said, "Well, Joe!" "Well, Governor!" "Well, Joe, you've served me faithfully through it all." "Well, Governor, I'm glad to hear you say so." And Tumulty said he was glad as a Roman Catholic to have shown he could work with a Scotch Presbyterian, and maybe it would open a few people's eyes to things.

Then he mentioned a case in which he was interested, that of an aged Nebraska man who had been convicted of a Federal crime. The old man had asked Tumulty to aid him in getting a pardon from the President, and now Tumulty held out the pardon papers he had made up. The old man had a son and a crippled daughter who idolized him, and he reminded Tumulty of his own father, and Tumulty gave the papers to the President. "Governor," he said, "let the curtain go down on an act of mercy—the last act an act of mercy. And I know, some way, when you need mercy the last act will be remembered for you." The President looked at the paper and shook his head and said, "No, Tumulty, no. That case has been reviewed." Tumulty said, "But it's an act of mercy and your last act, Governor, and there is something in the balance of things." The President said, "No, Joe, the country needs to see the law vindicated. The country needs the spectacle of a stable, just, and righteous Government more than that old man needs a pardon or I need an act of mercy." He took a pen and wrote DISAPPROVED across the paper in the strongest hand he had written in months.

A moment later the First Lady came in to say that Warren G. Harding, whose term was to be filled with graft, thievery, misappropriation of government funds, Veterans Bureau scandal, Teapot Dome, waited below. It was ten-thirty in the morning. The President and First Lady went down in the elevator to the Blue Room, where the Hardings and the members of the Congressional Inauguration Committee were.

The cars were outside—for his first inauguration he had ridden in a horse-drawn vehicle with William Howard Taft at his side—and there were also fifty policemen to make sure no pictures were taken until he was seated and ready. The men and the two women, the First Lady and Florence Harding, headed for the door. Harding gave the President his arm and he leaned upon it heavily, his blackthorn stick in his good hand sounding on the White House floor he was walking over for the last time and would never see again. Just before they came to the door the President released Harding's arm and indicated that in front of the people outside it would be improper for him to be thus served by anyone save government employees—his valet, the Secret Service men. Grayson stepped up and gave him a strong drink of whisky.

They went out, he trying to stand as straight as possible. The policemen looked to the photographers as he was all but picked up and bodily lifted into the car. He took off his high hat and held it in his gloved hand until the President-elect had walked around the car and gotten in and seated himself; then the hat went back on his head. Harding sat by him; Senator Philander C. Knox and Representative "Uncle Joe" Cannon of the Congressional Committee sat on the open limousine's jump seats. Behind them in the next car, Mrs. Harding was waving to the reporters. "My boys!" she said to the First Lady, whose once-dark hair had in the months of sickness and ruin developed gray streaks, and whose skin had an unhealthy pallor and whose very flesh seemed to sag on her chin and neck.

They got under way and went out of the White House grounds and into Pennsylvania Avenue to the bands and the troopers with white gloves holding aloft red-and-white guidons; to the cavalry horses, the soldiers in puttees; to soup-bowl helmets, pounding drums, sounding bugles, the sailors, the Legionnaires. Down the Avenue on the other side of the Capitol the American flag, at half staff for the death of Representative Champ Clark two days before, went up to the top of the staff and a transmitter played music above the sounds of the bands tuning up. In front of the Capitol a heavy Negro with a broom came along and swept the spot where Harding would be as he delivered his inaugural address, and youthful pages from the Congress hung wreaths along the front of the stand. Disabled soldiers in wheel chairs sat in the front lines. A flutter of excitement went through the massed thousands at the word that they were coming.

In the car the men in their top hats sat in silence as the first cheers of the people lining the street came rolling to them. Harding took off his hat and waved and smiled his handsome smile, but the President's hat remained on and he looked straight ahead.

They were moving very slowly, no faster than the troops marched, and the Secret Service man Starling could hear the comments of the people on the curb: "Doesn't the new President look fine and healthy? Poor President Wilson—this will kill him!"

Between waves and smiles Harding began a discussion of White House pets, mentioning his Airedale, Laddie Boy. He went on to remark that he had always wanted to own an elephant and the President said, "I hope it won't turn out to be a white elephant!" Harding smiled his big and generous politician's smile and, grateful for finding a subject of conversation, launched into discussing an experience of his sister, a former missionary in the Orient, who knew of a dying elephant that moaned piteously for his native keeper. When the keeper came the elephant wound his trunk around the man and pressed and hugged him and so peacefully passed away, happy that his friend was with him. When Harding finished the story he looked over at the President and saw to his horror that the President was crying, great tears rolling down his face. They were approaching the Capitol and in a moment the car would be halted and people would be gathering around, and Harding wondered if he ought to wipe away the President's tears. He was actually still in doubt when the President got hold of himself and took out a handkerchief and did the job himself.

They stopped in front of the Capitol. It had been arranged for the President to enter the building through a little-used freight entrance in the Senate wing; Harding got out and vigorously walked up the steps, waving his hat. The car drove the short space to the door the President would use and there it stopped. While cavalry mounts screened him off, the President was lifted out of the car. Without assistance, head bent down, cane tapping, he went in and took an elevator up to the President's Room. Senators, Cabinet members and friends stood waiting for him there. They gathered around him and took off his coat. Slipping his right arm out of the sleeve, he was for a moment deprived of the support of the cane which he had hooked into an upper pocket of the coat, and former Mayor John Fitzgerald of Boston° held him and steadied him. The President limply sat down at a desk and for a moment

---

° Whose daughter Rose Kennedy had four years earlier given birth to a boy named for her father.

fidgeted with his hands and looked aimlessly about before setting out to sign the last bills of the Congress which would in a few minutes be adjourning. The first measure he signed authorized more money for hospitalization facilities for wounded soldiers.

Every now and then he interrupted his work to greet people who came in to shake his hand. "Excuse me, General, for not rising," he said to Pershing. He signed bills relating to appropriations for fortifications, water power, agricultural needs. Senator Knox stepped in and asked if he would come into the Senate Chamber to see the swearing-in of Vice-President-elect Coolidge. Referring to the three stone steps leading to the Chamber, the President said that perhaps he had better not do it: "The Senate has thrown me down, but I don't want to fall down."

Colby, Burleson, Baker, Daniels, the others—all stood by and there was quiet chatter in the room, each man wishing. him luck, he saying "Thank you" and calling each man by name. He said, "Well, I think I had better scoot now," but at that moment a complete hush fell upon the room. Someone touched him on the arm to indicate that the committee from both Houses of Congress had arrived to ask permission to adjourn. "This committee begs to inform you that the two Houses have completed their work and are prepared to receive any further communications from you," said a sharp, dry voice, that of the head of the committee.

The voice was that of Senator Henry Cabot Lodge.

For a moment Joe Tumulty thought the President was going to say something violent, something terrible, but the President's face appeared to be about to fall into a bitter lopsided smile and then it froze and he said, "I have no further communication. I would be glad if you would inform both Houses and thank them for their courtesy." He turned his head and looked off into thin air. "Good morning, sir." Senator Lodge silently bowed and went out.

The people in the room started moving out to the stand where Harding would soon be making his inaugural address. Harding himself came in and bent over the seated President in a kindly way—for he was, above all things, a kindly man—and said that he would in no way regard it as a discourtesy if the President did not come out, that the President must do nothing to tax his strength. "I guess I had better not try it," the President said. "I'm afraid I shall have to beg off." Harding said he thoroughly understood. "All the luck in the world," the President said, and Harding went out.

The Capitol clocks were being put back so that, officially, it was not yet twelve noon, but in the President's Room a big clock in the corner started to toll out the hour. Joe Tumulty counted under his breath, One, two, three, four, five, six, seven, eight, nine, ten, eleven, twelve. The clock fell silent. The man at the desk reached for his throat and took off a scarf pin with the Seal of the President of the United States on it. It was made from the same gold nugget which the State of California had given him and his bride upon the occasion of their marriage in 1915. From the nugget also came their wedding rings. Outside, faintly, there was heard the sound of the U.S. Marine Band playing "Hail to the Chief" for Harding. There were very few people in the President's Room now, only a handful. He got up on his feet and struggled into his coat and went to the elevator, the stick tapping on the flagstone, the few people in the hall who saw him murmuring at the slow, slow pace.

He emerged from the building to where the car was, head bent down but eyes up, trying to smile into the sunshine, and more feeble, weaker, than he had been when he got out of the car, he stood before it while Starling got in first and pulled him up into it. Very few people saw him; everyone was watching Warren Harding begin his inaugural speech. The car went about three lengths before it was noticed at all, and then a feeble cheer rose in its wake. Chauffeur Francis Robinson drove down Pennsylvania Avenue, which on this day was as empty and deserted as it would be on a Sunday morning. There was no escort for him who had known escorts for eight years of his life. They drove in absolute silence, he and his wife, Grayson, Tumulty, Starling, the valet Arthur Brooks. Grayson wondered if he was thinking of the crowds and the noise and glamour of his ride with Harding to the Capitol, or of the roaring mobs in Paris, London and Rome, of the banners HAIL THE CRUSADER FOR HUMANITY, WELCOME TO THE GOD OF PEACE. They went into Jackson Place and for a moment the wife turned her head and looked back at the White House. Her husband looked away, off at Lafayette Park and the statue there.

They went up New Hampshire Avenue, into Massachusetts Avenue, and to S Street. To their surprise there were people gathered before the house, and they burst into applause for him. He was taken out of the car, put into the waiting wheel chair, wheeled into his home. Edmund Starling and the valet and the chauffeur saw him to the elevator and he thanked them for their services. Starling turned to go to the car and saw the wife and she shook his hand. Margaret came up to Starling, weeping, and put her young arms around him, and her lips sought his cheek. Starling got into the car and sat in front with the chauffeur and they went back to the Capitol and parked at the head of the procession, waiting upon the man speaking from the stand on the Capitol steps.

In S Street, Joe Tumulty told several White House reporters that they might come in and greet the man whose activities they had covered. They came in and took his hand as he stood, absolutely mute, at the head of the stairs of his home. He did not say one word. They went out, and the people in the street raised a cheer for the house's occupant. He came to a window of the second-floor drawing room and waved his good hand. They wanted him to speak to them, but he pointed to his throat as if to say that he was too choked up to get the words out. He stepped back behind a curtain, but the cheers—perhaps two thousand voices cried for him—drew him back, and once again he mutely pointed to his throat.

Secretary Daniels came in his car and had to get out a block from the house. The car could not possibly get through the people. Daniels walked up to the door and it opened for him and some others—Carter Glass, Cordell Hull, James F. Byrnes—and they went in to talk with him for a few minutes. As they spoke, wishing him well and admiring the flowers which people had sent, some women outside began to sing, "Onward, Christian Soldiers." Once more he went to the window. Then lunch was served. When it was over, Cary Grayson began to say that he thought it would be best if his patient went to bed now, but the doctor got out only two words before he was interrupted: "Mr. President——" "Just Woodrow Wilson."

PART THREE

S Street

That we shall prevail

12 First there were the Presbyterian manses in the South and Tommy and then school and Thomas W. Wilson, T. W. Wilson and, finally, Woodrow Wilson, and then there was Attorney-at-Law and Dr. and Professor Wilson, and Governor, and at the end Mr. President. With it all went the small houses and the little girls growing up, and Prospect, the home of the president of Princeton University, and the White House.

Now came S Street.

There had been 1912 and his election, and 1916 and his election—he thinking the day after that he had been defeated, Margaret coming to the door of his bathroom and calling in that the New York *Times* said the result was in doubt, he yelling back, "Tell it to the Marines!"—and then came the war and the Armistice. He went to Europe, and in Europe they hailed him as a god and he took off his hat to the crowds, waved to the crowds, ended by throwing kisses to the crowds. When he came back New York's streets were filled with people waiting for him and Margaret threw her arms around him and cried, "Oh, darling, wasn't it wonderful? All those thousands of people crying, waving their hats in the air, yelling—all for you! There never was such a triumph, such a homecoming!" And he looked at her and said—and she would never forget the look on his face—he said, "Wait until they turn."

And they did turn—the Senate, the People. The Senate wanted a part in determining what the peace would be about, and the

League, but he upon his sickbed would not, could not, compromise. The People wanted cars, money, liquor from the bootlegger, higher skirt lines, forgetfulness from glory and the marching men and the war to end war. The League went down because he could not meet the Senate's terms; Democratic candidate Cox went down because the People were tired, sick and tired, of their President.

Now came S Street. In S Street's dining room his servant Isaac Scott held him up on his feet, and his lips moved and almost soundlessly he said grace. In S Street's bedroom he lay upon a duplicate of the Lincoln bed of the White House. Above him hung a large picture of the American flag. An old mahogany desk from Princeton days was in the corner with a secret drawer made to look like a book, *The Life of Washington*. On the mantel above the fireplace was a tarnished brass shell casing that once held the first shell fired by the American artillery against the enemy in 1917. There was a Hobart Nichols painting of a wood cutter working by a snow-covered road in the forest, a thermometer, pictures of the girls and the grandchildren, a vase of coconut trimmed with silver. He did not like the dark and so he rarely spent the night without having at least one light turned on, and on a little stand by his bed was an electric spotlight. He could play it on the mantel's clock; with it he could hold off the dark. His old worn Bible was with him and each day he read from it—the Old Testament, the Psalms, the Book of Job.

In S Street's library was a giant old oak table brought down from Princeton; in S Street's library were pictures: the President of the United States and Mrs. Woodrow Wilson standing with the King and Queen of England. In the drawing room there hung upon one wall the Gobelin tapestry that had been the gift of the French people in 1918 to the First Lady of America. It was so large that its bottom half was rolled up and lying on the floor. In the garage was a Pierce-Arrow berline, once the favorite car of the President of the United States, which now, purchased from the government and with the President's Seal painted over, served every afternoon to take S Street's owner for a drive. A tiny Princeton tiger sat on the car's radiator.

His routine was this: He ate breakfast in his bedroom with his wife, or in the second-floor solarium between the library and dining room. Both bedroom and solarium faced south and on sunny days were lighted and alive with the sounds of the garden birds.

Over the trees could be seen the tip of the Washington Monument. When breakfast was over he went in robe and slippers to the Otis electric push-button elevator and down to the first floor, where in one of the rooms facing the street John Randolph Bolling, his brother-in-law and his secretary, told him of the day's mail and received instructions on how the letters were to be answered. He took a walk back and forth across the hall and went upstairs and slowly shaved himself with his good hand. Lunch was usually taken in his room and sometimes there would be a guest to sit with him while he ate. But often he was alone with Edith, she literally feeding him although she could have just as well left that work to Scott. After he ate she went below to the dining room and took her own lunch while he slept. In the afternoon there might be a guest if there had not been one for lunch—Grayson said there must be only one guest a day, and the visit must not exceed half an hour— and then he went for the ride. Dinner was generally off a tray by the library fire, he again in gown and slippers with his wife reading to him. Sometimes after he finished they would have a film, using a windowshade-like roller for the screen. By nine it was time for his male nurse to give him a massage and then he got into bed. She sat with him, the two of them playing Canfield, or she reading aloud, until he slept.

She was with him, in fact, at all times, her few social engagements or errands rigorously limited to the hour or so he spent with John Randolph Bolling and the mail. When she had guests in for dinner it was understood that she must leave as soon as she finished in order to go upstairs and read to him or simply be with him until he felt ready to sleep. Then she would rejoin the guests for cards or billiards. There was no housekeeper. She ran the house herself. She seemed to those who saw her to be happy and younger-looking than she had been in the White House. Never had she seemed so beautiful, and often as she walked around the house she whistled like a boy. Ray Stannard Baker came for lunch one day and the invalid looked up at his wife and then at Baker and said, "You see how well I am cared for!" She smiled and patted her husband on the head.

They had not been in S Street one day when a flood of mail began. Some of the letters were from friends such as Cleveland Dodge, a classmate of the Class of '79, who wrote that now for the first time in eight years he would not begin with "My dear Mr. President" but would go back to "My dear Woodrow"—and it felt "rather funny." Others were in the uncertain writing of very old persons and the salutation would be "My dear Tommy." (But there were not many left who called him that.) There were also, of course, the hate letters: "Hello, you syphilitic old son of a bitch . . . To the Valet of His Britannic Majesty, Dear Judas: The Lord has stricken you for your wickedness. . . ." But mostly the letters were from people who wanted something. A man wrote saying his father had disappeared when he was a boy. Could Mr. Wilson help him find his father? Bolling, new then to his job, wrote back saying Mr. Wilson knew of no way to aid the man's search. (Later such letters would be faithfully filed away but not answered.) Old students of decades in the past would want job references. (They would not get them.) People offered country homes for sale. (There was not to be any purchase.) A man wanted an introduction to the President of Czechoslovakia. (He must go elsewhere for it.) A home economics expert compiling a list of favorite recipes of great men asked about Mr. Wilson's favorite food. ("Mr. Wilson directs me to say that as he doesn't know of any recipe which he regards as his favorite, he is unable to comply with the suggestion contained in your letter of yesterday. Yours very truly, John Randolph Bolling, Secretary.") Would Mr. Wilson receive this high school civics class, Boy Scout troop, women's group, visiting South American delegation, these friends of that Senator? ("Mr. Wilson regrets that the state of his health and the circumstances surrounding his convalescence at present make it unwise for him to see large groups of people.") Then the business suggestions—requests that he write book reviews, prefaces, forewords, a history of the peace negotiations in Paris (for a fee of $150,000), a newspaper column, a series of monthly articles for the *Ladies' Home Journal* ($5,000 per article), a life of Jesus Christ. Would he be interested in a series of speaking engagements? Always the answer was that Mr. Wilson was not engaging in any such work at the present time.°

° Writing the letters of refusal was Bolling's job, but occasionally the ex-President dictated one in his own words and name. To a publisher asking if he would write an autobiography he replied: "There ain't going to be none." Asked for a statement on the virtues of grinning—this by the promoters of National Smile Week—he dictated: "I have no message to send on such a silly subject."

Requests for expressions of opinion constantly came in. Would he please make known his views on whether the United States should join the World Court? Does Mr. Wilson think there has been a growth of sentiment in favor of American entry into the League? What does Mr. Wilson think of the use of the pictorial chart as a teaching aid? How can the world best work to keep the peace? What can be done to aid the American Indians? What are the responsibilities of the country to Armenia? "Dear Mr. Wilson, If you were Santa Claus and could put into the world's stocking what it most needs this Christmas, what would you give it?" Will Mr. Wilson express a view on the necessity for better railroad safety measures to be made use of by the Association for Grade Crossings? Will he offer a statement upon the anniversary of the birth of Patrick Henry that can be used by the Richmond Historical Pageant? What does Mr. Wilson think of the government bond purchase campaign as it applies to the salaried man? How can crime be prevented? Prohibition enforced? What is the best method of educating the orphaned boy? Should there be motion picture censorship? What is the Secret of Success? Is Mr. Wilson in favor of a Federal anti-lynching law? A bonus for the ex-soldiers? To all these requests, all without exception, the answer was that Mr. Wilson had nothing to say. ". . . He does not think it opportune nor proper that he should express his views on your question . . . does not care to contribute an opinion on this matter . . . Mr. Wilson prefers to reserve anything he may have to say on this subject until a later time . . . does not feel he is sufficiently well acquainted with the subject to which you refer to warrant him in expressing an opinion concerning it . . . prefers not to enter into a discussion of the matter to which you refer . . . the program of complete rest which he is now taking will not permit him to prepare a statement such as you request. . . . Mr. Wilson asks me to reply to your letter and say that he is not making any statements for publication on any subject at this time."

To private requests from old acquaintances for his evaluation of political figures, however, he had answers in plenty: Senator Reed was "thoroughly false, entirely impossible, one of the most despicable men in public life, a blackguard"; Lord Birkenhead was an "egregious ass" characterized by "quite absurd vanity and empty-headedness"; President Poincaré of France was a "tricky skunk."

But such remarks were never for publication. For the public at large there was to be nothing of him; he would give not a bit of himself. His withdrawal extended also to those, or most of those, who asked for his autograph. Bolling had a printed form: "During Mr. Wilson's illness he was excused by thousands from sending them his autograph and from autographing books, photographs, etc. In view of this he does not feel he can in conscience begin the practice again, and therefore hopes that you will excuse him from complying with your request." America had turned him out—he was the living embodiment of Finley Peter Dunne's remark that the Americans should build their triumphal arches of bricks that could easily be pulled loose and flung at the hero—and it was not for him to court the favor of any American.

But sometimes something in a letter would reach through the aloofness. Ex-soldiers who wrote of wounds or disabilities often got answers from him signed "Very truly yours, Your War Comrade." (Had he not sent them overseas and brought them pain and blood on the misty April evening he went down Pennsylvania Avenue and asked America to save democracy?) People who sent him gifts for no reason but that they wanted to also got answers. The gifts, of negligible financial value, usually took the form of something the donor had grown or made by his own efforts. A Virginia farmer sent eggs produced by his prize hen; a Chesapeake Bay barber sent a dozen clams plucked from the mud during an afternoon's outing; a turkey farmer sent a giant specimen of his flock. Tomatoes came, and figs and pecans, some flowers grown by a suburban woman who wanted him to have them, a brace of ducks shot out of season by a man who wrote he would not mind having to pay the game warden's fine if Mr. Wilson enjoyed the results. A Potomac River trawler regularly sent over part of the day's catch. And all these people touched him very deeply and he wrote and told them so: "Please accept for yourself and your sisters assurances of sincere gratitude not only for the apples but for the generous words which accompany them. It is just such words that keep a man in good heart." It was not easy for him to frame such letters, for he had not been in the past a man who wanted or accepted the gifts of others. Now the newspapers called him the Lame Lion of S Street and it was not in his power to get the things he wanted and do the things he wanted to do, and he must find it in him to be crippled and old and beaten and to thank those few who cared that he had lived and lived still.

Children also got answers to their letters. For they were the innocent ones. "Dear Mr. Wilson: No doubt you will be surprised to receive a letter from a small girl whom you don't even know, but I feel as though I know you. I am the girl who you saw on Wednesday last, a little before you reached Union Station, Alexandria, who was all dolled up in kaki riding breeches, white sweater and a bright red scarf and tam, and pulling a sled. Last summer do you remember seeing a little girl playing tennis on a court in Rosemond who everytime you went past would throw her racquet in the air and wave at you? I am the girl. I am a great admirer of you and your lovely wife and take the opportunity to write to you. I appreciate so much your waving at me. Yours Very Truly, Virginia Dare, 14 years." She was no relation "to the original Virginia Dare," but was a sophomore at Alexandria High School and had a brother at the University of Virginia. He was a member of the Ravens there. The ex-President wrote back, "My dear Little Friend, It was a pleasure to receive your letter and to know more about the little girl whose greetings have given us pleasure as we passed along the road in our afternoon drives. I am interested in all you tell me about yourself and hope that every happy fortune will be yours as you grow older. Mrs. Wilson joins me in cordial good wishes. With warmest greetings, Faithfully yours."

He refused to join hundreds of organizations that wanted to make use of his name, but to the Washington Order of the Merry Men he wrote that he would accept membership. The letter asking him to join explained that the Merry Men stood for "the protection of public property, particularly the woods around Mount Pleasant, and roam the woods collecting plants and rocks and taking notes of animals, insects and birds." The dues consisted of five cents a month from regular members. The Honorary Member—Woodrow Wilson—would not be required to pay the dues. The constitution of the Merry Men explained that if any member misbehaved at an Official Meeting he was given a demerit. "Upon receiving five demerits he will be put through the paddle." A picture of the Order's flag was sent him and his attention was drawn to the Chinese letters on it: "A Chinaman offered to interpret our name into his language, and on the spur of the moment we accepted," explained the Merry Men's constitution, "and it was embroidered on our flag by my mother, so now we cannot change." He wrote the boys he was proud to be their Honorary Member. "I wish that I could wander about the woods with you."

The summer of 1921 passed. In the White House open liquor bottles stood on upstairs tables; the President explained to callers that he considered the lower rooms the property of the people of the United States and perhaps Prohibition should not be violated there, but upstairs was his home, where his personal preferences could be followed. Spittoons were under the poker table used three times a week, and men with cigars in their mouths called the First Lady "Ma," "Boss" or, imitating the President, "Duchess." The President played golf several times each week. He made love to his mistress in a White House closet. The people had elected him President, but, said Charles Willis Thompson, "they did not vote for anybody; they voted against somebody; and the somebody they voted against was not a candidate; it was Woodrow Wilson." That Woodrow Wilson, said Mark Sullivan, was to a nation tired of heroics the "symbol of the exaltation that had turned sour, personification of the rapture that had now become gall." And in fact it was with a certain justification, a certain very considerable justification, that America in 1921 could ask what in hell the war had been all about, anyway. But now it was over and Warren Harding was President and he believed in live and let live and keeping everybody happy and giving your pals a job. The pals looted every department of the government he let them into—and he let them in everywhere. Sometimes they went too far, and then a visitor coming into the Red Room might see, as one man did, the President of the United States standing with his hands around the throat of the Director of the Veterans Bureau, choking him while he shouted, "You yellow rat! You double-crossing bastard!" But not too many people saw such things. Those who did usually had their fingers in the pie anyhow. The rest of America saw and appreciated the informality of a President who called everybody by his first name and a First Lady who came running downstairs to shake hands with the tourists being shown through. "Aren't things different now?" delightedly asked the wife of Senator Pomerene when she came to a lavish White House garden party and saw the red uniforms of the bandsmen and the bright-colored hats and parasols of the women. Now when Woodrow Wilson and his wife drove on West Executive Avenue in the afternoon they could see, as they did just one week after leaving office, photographers dispersing after taking pictures of Henry Cabot Lodge when the Senator paid a call on the President.

Mostly, however, the rides were not city ones, but rather country trips. He took with him an old cape bought years ago in Scotland and even on warm days wore it around his shoulders beneath the long thin face. A cap was always on his head. He lived but did not live in the America of 1921; he was like some apparition from the past, from Yesterday, coming along the road in his big old open car with two small W's painted where once the Seal of the President had been. Motionless and silent, he roused himself only at the sight of a soldier or an American flag. For the soldier there would be a slow salute with the good hand. For the flag he would lift his hat and take it off and hold it over his heart. Always. Atop the government buildings and in the parks a fluttering banner would catch his eye, and his arm would come up and for a moment as his car glided by he would be bareheaded, the face seemingly even more stark now that it could be seen that only a thin fringe of longish hair came back from his forehead to run down to his collar in back.

But it was possible to live in the Washington of that day and never know that he lived there also, so rarely was he seen. He belonged to no organizations of note; his wife was patroness of no dinners or women's affairs and was not seen in the shops. For the first month in S Street they had retained the services of a guard, but then they let him go. There was no need for the guard, for Washington and the world did not, save for the letters, bother with the ex-President any more than with the widow of General Philip Sheridan, a neighbor. The world did not seem to care that he was there, an ex-President and aged figure with an expression of infinite sadness upon that ravaged face, a look of questioning also, a wondering request of God and Fate to know what had happened, where did it all go, was this what life was—ruin and a terrible loneliness?

On November 10, 1921, there came a letter written in pencil upon the stationery of Louis Miller, Cut-Rate Dealer in Hardware, Paints, Oils, Kitchen Supplies and Sporting Goods, Floyd Avenue, Richmond, Va.

"To my Hero," it began. "Dear Mr. Wilson, Tomorrow we celebrate Armistice Day and my Daddy says its to honor the Brave Boys who made peace possible. I think the biggest honor is you. I take my hat way off to you. I pray God will let you live and be happy and healthy. From David H. Miller seven years old."

He wrote back, "My dear Little Friend, Your delightful letter gave me a good deal of pleasure. I send you, besides my warm thanks, my most cordial good wishes, and am glad to call myself your friend."

On that Armistice Day the body of the Unknown Soldier would be going to its grave in Arlington and on that day the former Commander in Chief would be in the funeral parade. In the days preceding the burial, when the plans were made, the former Commander in Chief's presence had not been expected, so no arrangements for his participation were made. A letter to President Harding, however, brought forth an invitation. The other mourners would be marching on foot behind the coffin, but it would be impossible for this mourner, and so, early on Armistice Day morning, in black, wearing a tall black hat, he came out to where a rented horse carriage waited before his house. His man Scott lifted his left leg to the carriage's step, and the coachman held the horses, a bay and a black, and with difficulty he was gotten up onto the seat. His wife sat by him, she also in black. A poppy was in his lapel and one at her breast. He held a cane in his good hand. The Secretary of War had asked that by eight twenty-five he be at the east entrance of the Capitol, where an Army officer would take him into his place for the funeral procession down Pennsylvania Avenue to the White House. There he would drop out of the procession in compliance with the Secretary's request—only military contingents would march all the way to Arlington.

With Scott beside him on the victoria's box, the coachman drove by way of Massachusetts Avenue and First Street, N.E., in order to avoid the congestion of the many troops that would march. But when they got to the Capitol there was no sign of the officer who would direct them to their place. The crowds and confusion affected the horses and they grew restless, but finally a police sergeant took over and led the carriage to a place in the line. And so the funeral of the Unknown began, and down Pennsylvania Avenue, behind six jet-black horses with black trappings, came the cortege. The hoofs of the artillery horses drawing the great caissons were muffled, and upon muffled drums a slow, rhythmic beat dully sounded. The flags were draped in mourning and lowered, and dirges played. Faded flowers brought from overseas sat atop the draped flag on the casket. A wall of humanity, silent save for an occasional sob, watched as the Unknown went slowly by.

President Harding marched side by side with General Pershing, who wore no decorations but the Victory Medal which every American soldier could wear. The Cabinet walked behind the coffin, and the Senators, and the Representatives, and the Supreme Court Justices, and the soldiers in long regimental formations, and the sailors, the lumbering guns of the artillery, the banners, the generals, the admirals. And the foreigners who would present to him in that coffin their Victoria Crosses and their Croix de Guerres— Marshal Foch, Admiral Lord Beatty, the others. All passed by the people standing on the curb in a great silence, and so did a marching group of Congressional Medal of Honor winners, and then, gripping a cane and leaning on it so that he might sit up the straighter, came Woodrow Wilson.

And the silence of the funeral was broken, for the people were whispering to each other, "It's Wilson; look, President Wilson." A flutter of applause came out to him, and a few low calls of greeting. And more cheers. He had seventeen blocks to go in the procession, and by the time those blocks were traveled the people all around were cheering him. His carriage stopped before the White House, where he would be leaving the procession, and President Harding and his wife took up a position in a box opposite the west gate, and the President looked over toward the halted carriage and bowed to its occupant. Inside the grounds a couple of Negro servants saw who was there, and they came running out to look up at him and say their names and ask if he didn't remember them from before. All around the carriage people were pushing to get closer, and more White House servants came crying their greetings. It was a funeral, and the funeral of the Unknown Soldier at that, but the cheering got louder until it was an ovation. With no smile, seemingly with the greatest reluctance, Woodrow Wilson took off his high black silk hat and held it out to the cheers. His stern face was unrelaxed, and nothing showed, but from that moment on nothing would be for him as it had been before, before he heard those cheers and saw those people crying, "Oh, Mr. Wilson, Mr. Wilson."

The coachman turned the bay and the black and they went to S Street. When they got there they found the pavement covered with people. For a small group of women had gathered at Connecticut and Florida avenues with the aim of marching to his home to stand before him and let him know that they cared. As they marched other people came up to ask, What is it? Where are you going? And when they found out they too joined the double column. In the end the people numbered thousands.

They stood in front of his house, and as the guns were firing in salute to the Unknown in Arlington across the river they shouted, "Three cheers for the greatest soldier of them all!" and gave those cheers. And "Three Cheers for Woodrow Wilson!" and gave those cheers. Bursts of hand-clapping spontaneously broke out after he went inside, and spontaneously also people shouted for him. After a time there was a great roar, for the door opened and, leaning upon his cane, he came out and stood underneath the flag waving from his house because this day was Armistice Day and the soldier who served under him was being laid to rest. Three disabled young men, fellow soldiers in the past to that Unknown, sat in a car before his house, and when he saw them he went down the steps, Scott on one side, his cane holding him up on the other, and shook their hands. Hamilton Holt, long identified as a League supporter, came forward to speak for the people.

"Mr. Wilson," Holt said, his voice carrying to the outermost reaches of the crowd and to the trees brown with November's leaves, "we congratulate you, a wounded soldier of the World War. You have our respect and our affection. Your work will not die."

The people burst into applause, but then those in front turned and beat at that applause with their hands, crying "Hush! Hush! He's going to speak!" Silence fell. He took off his hat and moved forward one step. It had been two years and two months since Pueblo. *I believe that men will see the truth, eye to eye and face to face. There is one thing that the American people always rise to and extend their hand to, and that is the truth of justice and of liberty and of peace. We have accepted that truth and we are going to be led by it, and it is going to lead us, and through us the world, out into pastures of quietness and peace such as the world never dreamed of before.* He said, "I wish . . ." His voice was broken and quavering. His hand was shaking; the high silk hat he held was trembling. "I wish I had the voice to reply . . ." Tears ran down his cheeks to the black coat. ". . . to reply and to thank you for the wonderful tribute . . ." The faces before him were strained as the people leaned toward him as if to lend him strength to go on. ". . . for the wonderful tribute you have paid me. I do thank you from the bottom of my heart. God bless you." He tried to turn away, but the people pushed forward and threw flowers before him. He groped for his wife's hand and found it, and it was wet, for she was crying, crying, Edith Bolling Wilson crying as though she were a little girl back in Virginia long before the nights when he lay in the Lincoln bed and she at her desk worked on the papers and looked across at the lights of the State, War and Navy Building. He waved his hat and at the last kissed his hand to them and then he was gone, the thin shoulders shivering as his wife and his servant took him inside. The people sang "My Country, 'Tis of Thee."

For hours after that the people stayed in the street although police came and asked them to please move on and clear the area. The aged Senator John Sharp Williams of Mississippi sat on the ground on the terrace across the street and tried to hear what the people were saying as they slowly went away, always casting long glances back. But the Senator's hearing was bad and so he relied upon his wife to tell him what they were saying. She gave him the comments she picked up and he thought to himself that it was remarkable, remarkable, that so many people would gather with nothing to be accomplished of any actual use but that tribute be shown to a broken old man in a tall silk hat.

The writer Ida Tarbell saw something else: that the crippled body was as the crippled hopes of the people who went to war with the wish and belief that by so doing they would make the world better, and good, and clean, and right; she saw them as asking if he too had lost his hopes and ideals, his faith and vision, the ability to believe. "They seek him," she wrote. "He means something to them; they don't quite know what. He is a living link with their noblest phase." They wanted to see him, she wrote, to get, if only in a fleeting glimpse, something that would bid them to live again as they did in the great but quickly dead moment of their Great Crusade, the war. She called her article "The Man They Cannot Forget."

13

Joe Tumulty was warm, alive, enthusiastic, a wonderful story-teller. His Negro stories were very good, his German accent was first-rate, and his Irish brogue was perfection itself. Edith Bolling Wilson thought him a cheap political hack from Jersey City. She had never liked him, she told people. In April of 1922, Tumulty asked the ex-President if it would not be a good idea to send a greeting message to the Jefferson Day banquet of the National Democratic Club in New York. "It would hearten and inspire everybody," Tumulty wrote his former chief. The ex-President wrote back to Tumulty at Tumulty's Washington law office, "I do not feel that the occasion is a specially appropriate one for breaking my silence."

Tumulty telephoned S Street and spoke to the lady of the house. "Mrs. Wilson," he said, "can't you get the Governor to send a letter to this dinner in New York?" She said, "Why, Mr. Tumulty, he answered your letter yesterday. Haven't you gotten it?" Tumulty said that he had indeed gotten the letter but still hoped the Governor would change his mind. He asked if he might not call that afternoon. She said he could if he wanted to, and from three to three-thirty Tumulty sat with his former chief in the library.

On April 8, 1922, the dinner was held. A woman speaker read off messages of greetings from persons not able to attend. Among the messages was one typed on yellow paper that looked, to the audience, like a telegraph form: "Say to the Democrats of New York that I am ready to support any man who stands for the salvation of America, and the salvation of America is justice to all classes. Woodrow Wilson." The audience cheered. Immediately afterward, the chief speaker of the evening made an address. The chief speaker was James Cox, the defeated Presidential candidate of 1920 and a potential candidate for 1924. The next day the New York *Times* said, "Cox Boom Launched on Wilson Keynote of Justice for All."

The *Times* headline brought consternation to S Street. At once a letter went out asking the newspaper upon what authority it represented the alleged message as anything but "an absolute fabrication." Another letter went to Tumulty asking his aid in determining how such a message was given to the banquet. The explanation was that Tumulty had typed the message on the yellow paper but had not meant it to be interpreted as the ex-President's endorsement of Cox. The reporters present had misunderstood the import of the words, Tumulty announced to the public. The whole thing came from a "casual conversation with me at Mr. Wilson's home on Friday last when he remarked he would support any candidate who stood for justice for all," he told the *Times*. "He simply gave a casual message to me in a casual manner. It had nothing to do with any individual." The *Times* published Tumulty's explanation and with it reported that members of the National Democratic Club felt the whole thing was a "slight misunderstanding" that would easily be cleared up.

But this was no slight misunderstanding to S Street. Mrs. Wilson was in a fury and her husband was upset and unnerved. Tumulty wrote and apologized profusely and asked if he could not come and explain, but no hearing was granted him. Tumulty was terribly disturbed and frightened of what might be coming and wrote again to say that he hoped his explanation to the *Times* would clear the air, but that if it did not, and further action was to be taken from S Street, it did not matter to him: "I will never engage in a controversy with you. No slight bruise nor public rebuke from you can in any way lessen my devotion and affection."

"Sob stuff," said Edith Bolling Wilson to this, and the next day the *Times* printed a letter to the editor:

My dear Sir:
    I notice in the issue of the *Times* this morning an article headed "Doubt Cast on Wilson Message to the Cox Dinner."
    I write to say there need be no doubt about the matter. I did not send any message whatever to that dinner nor authorize anyone to convey a message.
    I hope that you will be kind enough to publish this letter.
Very truly yours,
Woodrow Wilson

    The ground was completely out from under Tumulty's feet. He had said he bore an informal message to the dinner; Woodrow Wilson had said there was no message. Reporters came to Tumulty. He said, "If Mr. Wilson says the message was unauthorized, then I can only say I deeply regret the misunderstanding which has arisen between us. I certainly would not have given the message if I had not believed it to be authorized."
    Tumulty did something else. He wrote a letter to Edith Bolling Wilson:

    The colloquy between poor Julie and Louise in the play of "Liliom" gives a perfect picture of my feelings in this vital matter. It is as follows:
    Louise: Is it possible for some one to hit you hard like that—real loud and hard—and not hurt you at all?
    Julie: It is possible, dear, that some one whom you love may beat you and beat you and beat you—and not hurt you at all.
    That is the way I feel toward the Governor. I want you to feel, you who have been so wonderful and generous to me in all things, that I shall always be around the corner when you or yours need me.
    I expect no reply to this letter. I shall understand.
    Cordially and sincerely yours,
Joseph P. Tumulty

    Joe Tumulty was right to expect no reply, for none ever came. And when he said he understood, he told the truth. His understanding was shown by the fact that he wrote to Edith Bolling Wilson and not her husband.
    Joe Tumulty never saw Woodrow Wilson again.

    The law offices of Wilson & Colby opened a few months after the two partners left government service. Elaborate suites were maintained in New York and Washington, and stupendous offers of business poured in. Colby was ecstatic at the giant retainers proposed for the services of a former President and a former Secretary of State, but every potential client was turned away by order of the senior partner. For Woodrow Wilson was not going to capitalize upon the position which once he had held. The Government of Ecuador asked if Wilson & Colby would assist in securing a United States loan for $12,000,000, and Colby hopefully wrote his partner that this "would be a very fine piece of business," but the answer was no. An ex-President—or, rather, *this* ex-President— could not be a party to getting money from the government of which he had once been the head. The Western Ukrainian Republic sought Wilson & Colby's help in obtaining recognition from the League of Nations, and the answer was that the senior partner could not make use of his influence with the League to make money for himself. Harry F. Sinclair and E. L. Doheny wanted the firm to act as consultants in the Teapot Dome matter, and Colby wanted to take the case, but Colby was vetoed—a former President's name and authority could not be used to put pressure upon government employees investigating the oil scandal. The retainer suggested by Doheny and Sinclair was $100,000. Another group of men in a different matter offered half a million for representation, but again were turned down by the senior partner. Colby wrote, "To a man who has spent his life in the rough and tumble of the legal profession, as I have done, it makes one a little dizzy at times to turn away business which one's professional brethren are bending every energy and resource to get, but it's a fine game and worth the candle as long as we can hold out." To Mrs. Wilson, Colby said, "Day after day I sit in my office and see a procession walk through—thousands and thousands of dollars—and not one to put in our pockets." But, "It is a sublime position on the part of your husband."

It could not go on, of course. It seemed that in the ex-President's mind there was the picture of a Robin Hood type of operation in which Wilson & Colby helped unfortunate people in trouble and with no other redress. But things did not work that way. The people who came did so because they wanted the twenty-eighth President of the United States to fight corporations for them or do

battle with the government, and always for many thousands of dollars. After a year had passed, the senior partner's fees totaled just
five thousand dollars (most of which was spent to buy his wife a
Rausch & Lamb electric auto) and the junior partner, who insisted
upon paying all expenses, was minus many thousands. There was,
beyond the idealism and rigid concept of duty to the past, something else working against success of the firm. It was that although
S Street's occupant kept saying there was no such thing as brain
fatigue and the more work you did the more you could do, this
was not so. For he could not concentrate on the cases. He went
only once to the office.

Finally, in the fall of 1922, Colby asked if perhaps his partner
wanted to reconsider his participation in the firm. It was not an
easy thing for Colby to do, for he had believed this work would
bring a meaning to the life of his former chief in the government.
And it was not easy for that former chief to admit to Colby that
perhaps it was best that they have done with the brave attempt.
Let it be over, he wrote. Only, say the dissolution did not come
through the dissatisfaction of either partner.

Colby had tried hard to make it work; he had wanted to do
right. He wired: YOU ARE THE DEAREST MAN IN THE WORLD. I WANT TO
COME DOWN AND JUST TAKE YOU BY THE HAND. I LIKE TO FEEL THAT
THERE IS NO HURRY ABOUT THE NEXT MOVE. I FEEL ALL BROKEN UP.

Ten days later Colby got out a statement to the newspapers saying Mr. Wilson's continued progress toward good health, so grati-
fying to his friends, caused him to turn his energies to other important questions, matters the importance of which could not be
overestimated. Therefore he was withdrawing from the firm. His
disciplined powers as a lawyer, his effectiveness as one, had been
a veritable revelation.

The next day Colby got a wistful letter: "I wish that it were all
true."

And so 1922 passed. He was sixty-six that year, an old man trying to walk and asking Grayson when his health would come back.
Cardinals sang in the garden by a red shrub near the wall and
sometimes he sat there in the sun. The movie-theater audiences
cheered when the newsreel would upon occasion show a brief shot

of him going on his ride, and each day the Washington sight-seeing buses paused in S Street and the tour guides pointed out Number 2340. The house itself was always quiet, the servants speaking in low tones so as not to disturb the old man dreaming through the long days or slowly lifting and dropping the cards as he played his game of Canfield. "I suppose and believe that I am getting better," he wrote his son-in-law McAdoo, "but not in a way that would startle you with its rapidity or at all excite you with a sense of haste. Patience has never been my long suit but it now contains evidently all the winning cards, and I must do the best I can to stimulate it." McAdoo knew, of course—they all knew; everyone knew—that there would never be a recovery, never any more good health, but the son-in-law wrote back that it was fine to hear from you, Governor, fine. It was like old times, Governor. Douglas Fairbanks was a friend of McAdoo and Nellie, and they had the actor arrange to make a short film of the two little granddaughters, complete with titles and all.

In Edith's mind there lived every minute of her day the knowledge that her husband could not be more than now he was. But her smile never faltered. He had no real work to do and the girls were gone, Nellie to California, Jessie to Massachusetts with Frank Sayre, Margaret to a series of New York jobs, and he had only Edith, nothing but the lilting sweet buoyant part of her nature she saved for him and him alone. He was dying by degrees, he was an old dying man given to dull spells of noiseless sobbing, but she loved him as few women have ever loved a man, and alone she carried him forward, cheering him with her jokes and her whistling. "She is simply great," wrote Carter Glass, "not divine as we often say in exaggeration, but with human qualities that are nearest akin to the divine." She had been brutal with Tumulty, but she would have been so to anyone who in any way disturbed her man if only for an instant. She did not regret for one moment that Tumulty was hurt, and lonely for Woodrow Wilson. Tumulty had given her man embarrassment with his message to the dinner, Tumulty had upset the quiet of S Street for a few days, and that was enough for S Street's mistress. Tumulty could go to the devil, and James Cox along with him, and so could anyone else who brought an increased trembling to her man's shaking hands. Every day she told John Randolph Bolling, her brother turned secretary, just which letters should be read out loud and which should not. Let one letter contain a word that might bring upset to the man it was addressed to, and that man would never know the letter had been written. Let Tumulty beg to be allowed a visit, let him beg John Randolph and Wilmer, another brother, let him ask Carter Glass to intercede, and Grayson also, but no visit would be allowed. She had had enough of Joe Tumulty. Franklin D. Roosevelt might write asking for an autograph, but Franklin D. Roosevelt's hospitality to Lord Grey was not forgotten, nor was the resentment of the then-President of the United States, nor the possibility that mention of Roosevelt's name might bring emotion now, and so Bolling wrote that Mr. Wilson must beg to be excused from complying with Mr. Roosevelt's request.

So she fought to bring him peace. But in the crushed body and in the tortured mind there yet lived the man Woodrow Wilson. His wife thought of him as a wonderful, beautiful, wounded eagle chained to a rock, and so he seemed to many others. But he was an eagle that longed to fly. For years he had been at the heart of great events, and now simply to sit alone, protected and sheltered, was not enough. He began to work on a paper he called The Statement or The Document. It would embody his ideas on how the country should be run and what the ultimate meaning of America was. Those who surrounded him in the great days were asked to contribute their thoughts and recommendations—Bernard Baruch, ex-Secretary Houston, ex-Secretary Baker, Colby, Justice Louis D. Brandeis, all were asked to give guidance in their various fields of expertise. Central to The Document, of course, was that America must enter the League; the other economic and agricultural plans surrounded this. It was never established just how The Document would one day be used, but perhaps it would be given to all Democratic candidates for office, they to subscribe to its provisions or face the denunciation of the former titular leader of the party. Or perhaps it would be given to newspapers as a guideline for the entire country. There was something else The Document could be used for, also: it could be made the explosive charge that would propel a well man, cured, free, able to walk, himself as once he had been, into one more try for the Presidency. But no one mentioned that. He did not ever say it himself, and of his people there was not a one who could find it to say aloud that he was before their eyes slipping into that grave whose digging began the day in Paris when he fell ill; that his skin was the color of yellowed parchment and drawn down over his temple and cheekbones so that the long sharp nose came into new prominence; that he could never again be anything but this that he was: Yesterday.

Still The Document's fire lighted and warmed him and when he talked about it something rose in him and he put his curse upon his enemies and said that soon, soon, when he was cured, he would smite them and smite them well: "I'm going to get some scalps!"

Visitors who would not disturb this picture were allowed to come, encouraged to come. Sometimes they found him in fine fettle, as he put it, alert and anxious to hear their news, but sometimes they found him blankly looking out into the garden and deep in depression. Ex-Secretary Daniels came one hot day and found him in bed and feeling very low. Edith sat with the two men, and Daniels tried to find something cheery of which to speak. He said, "Mrs. Wilson, did I ever tell you of the near-panic created in the Democratic Party in 1915 when the leaders believed the President was trying to persuade you to become Mrs. Wilson?" Mrs. Wilson had not, and so Daniels in his Southern way told the story. It had seemed a marriage would cost the election of 1916, and after much harried consultation a group of prominent Democrats came to Daniels. Daniels was, they announced, the perfect man to step up to the President of the United States and give him the word that he should not marry. Daniels felt like Caesar declining a crown, he said now, seven years later in the third-floor rear bedroom of 2340 S Street, but he had declined nevertheless. And he had offered the prominent Democrats a little advice in the bargain. The advice came embodied in a story Daniels gave the men. It seemed that once there was a Western Congressman with the largest nose in all Washington. Everywhere the Congressman went people stared at him. One evening in a restaurant the Congressman saw a man looking at the giant nose with a particularly incredulous air. The Congressman went to the man. "Why are you staring at me?" he demanded. The man said, "I beg your pardon, sir." The Congressman said, "Beg my pardon nothing. Why are you staring at me so rudely?" The man protested he meant no harm, but the Congressman cried, "You are looking at my nose and wondering why it is so big!" The man had to admit this was the case. But he had meant no offense. "Of course not," said the Congressman, "but if you really desire to know what made my nose so big, I will tell you. I kept it out of other people's business and gave it a chance to grow!"

The ex-President laughed hugely. That day he had needed laughter, but on other days he could produce it himself. William Gorham Rice came one day and the two men talked about automobiles, the host remarking that some of his afternoon trips covered up to forty miles. "Like flying!" exclaimed Rice, and his host was reminded of a joke. It seemed, he told Rice, that Sandy the Scotsman owned an airplane. A fellow countryman, Donald, asked if Sandy would take Donald and his wife Maggie up in the plane. Sandy said he would do so for five pounds. Donald demurred at this price. The two Scots argued. Finally Sandy said, "I will do this: it will cost ye nothing if ye will not speak a word while we're flying. But if either of ye speak a word it is to be five pounds." Donald and Maggie said the terms were agreeable. They got into the plane and sat behind Sandy while he dipped the craft up and over and flew upside down in an attempt to get them to speak. But nothing was heard from them. Finally, defeated, Sandy flew down and landed the plane. As the wheels touched the ground, Donald tapped Sandy on the shoulder from behind and asked, "May I speak noo?" Sandy said, "Ye may." Donald said, "Maggie fell oot."

A few minutes later Mrs. Wilson came into the room and Rice thought to himself that it was wonderful the way her husband's face lighted up when he saw her. "I have been telling Mr. Rice the story of Sandy and Donald and Maggie," he said. It was beautiful, Rice thought, the way they were with each other.

Other people came. One spring day three young men came. They were the chairman of the Woodrow Wilson Club of Washington's National School of Law° and two of the members. The club had seventy members and had what they called an annual banquet at a dollar a head, and they met after classes in a room of the school and believed that Woodrow Wilson had been meant to be the savior of America and of the world and wrote him saying they wanted to send a delegation to be with him for a little while. The chairman

---

° Now a part of George Washington University.

was Henry P. Thomas and to his note Bolling sent a reply that Mr. Thomas and two others might come for half an hour. When the Bolling invitation came the Woodrow Wilson Club held a two-hour meeting to discuss what the delegation should say. Each of the seventy members had an opinion, but none of the opinions had much in common with one another save for the unanimously held one that the delegation must not use a Yellow Cab Company taxi to go to S Street. For the Yellow Cabs charged too much and tried to take advantage of students. So nothing was decided, but Henry Thomas and the others put on their Sunday suits and on the afternoon of April 14, 1922, they went to find a cab. Many cabs passed, but all were Yellow Cabs. Time grew short and the delegation was in a predicament. They searched for some sort of conveyance, anything but an accursed Yellow, but in the end they had to capitulate. The Yellow Cab took them to S Street and at 3 P.M. Bolling took them up to the library.

Woodrow Wilson shook their hands, three young men—boys, really—and asked where their homes were. Henry Thomas said he was from Virginia, from Leesburg, and their host said, "I was born in Staunton." Thomas thought, As if I didn't know it! and remarked that his late father had been a private in the Confederate Army. Woodrow Wilson said, "Can't you tell me some of his stories?" Thomas talked about how once his father went on a raid to steal Yankee horses and how years later old Confederate soldiers used to visit the father and each one said, I killed two Yankees at Gettysburg, or I killed three Yankees at Chancellorsville, but the father never said anything about killing anyone until one of the other old soldiers said, Well, you know you killed at least one Yankee. And the father said, No, I just knocked him in the head. And the explanation was that on this horse-stealing expedition the Confederates were not out to capture men, not even a general, because they would have had to feed a general, but only horses, which were easier to provision. So they went to a Yankee encampment and held weapons on the Yankee troops and Thomas' father was told to go to the stable and get the horses. When he went in, he saw, standing up, half asleep, a Yankee soldier on guard. The father took a plank of wood and raised it high and conked the Yankee and took the horses and ran. And this was the one Yankee he might have killed, but he never found out.

Their half hour slipped by. Thomas wanted to offer something about how the seventy boys at school in the club were for the League and for Woodrow Wilson, but he could not get it straight in his mind how to say it—nothing had been decided at the damned meeting but that no Yellow Cabs should be used—and finally the time was up and they stood to go. Thomas had one last minute to get it out that the man before them meant something to them that was very big. Something very big. But it was too late. Bolling showed them out. They went into S Street and nothing, really, had been accomplished but that now the man by the library fire knew that some boys in school cared for him enough to organize a club for him. Forty years later it was still all clear in Thomas' mind. "I was born in Staunton. . . . Can't you tell me some of his stories?"

Also in that spring there came a large delegation of ladies attending a Pan-American conference in Washington. They gathered before the house and when he came out for his ride they begged him to give them a few words. He said his voice was not up to it, but he would recite a limerick for them. Leaning on his cane, his "third leg," as he always called it, he gathered himself to say:

> "For beauty I'm not a star
> There are others more handsome by far.
>   But my face, I don't mind it
>   For I am behind it.
> It's the ones out in front that I jar!"

The next day there was a letter:

> Your courage is nobler by far
> Than mere beauty e'en though like a star.
>   And your face? Why, we find it
>   Just right! *You're* behind it.
> So we people in front cry "Hurrah!"

There also came to see him the officers of the Woodrow Wilson Foundation, created to establish annual awards for "meritorious service on behalf of democracy, public welfare, liberal thought and peace through justice." The aim of the Foundation was to raise one million dollars to finance the awards. (Held in Jessie's arms, little Woodrow Wilson Sayre, two and a half years old,

opened the drive to raise $85,000 in Massachusetts by ringing
the bell in Boston's Old State House. He resisted violently when
Jessie made him stop pulling the line that made the bell ring
so delightfully.)

Originally the Foundation was to be called the Woodrow Wilson
Memorial, but during the planning stages Franklin D. Roosevelt,
chairman of the National Committee, received a letter from the
man being honored which pointed out that the word "memorial"
suggested death—"and I hope in the near future to give frequent
evidences I am not dead." The word "endowment" was suggested
in the letter, but Roosevelt wrote back that this might "suggest to
some people that we are endowing you!" Finally "foundation" was
chosen. With the correspondence there came a softening of S
Street's attitude toward Roosevelt, and when in August of 1921
Roosevelt fell ill with that disease which would leave him little better equipped to walk than was Woodrow Wilson, the letters took
on a much warmer tone: "I am indeed delighted to hear you are
getting well so fast and so confidently, and I shall try to be generous enough not to envy you." Word was sent to Roosevelt that it
was now a race between the two invalids to see which one would
play golf first, and when, partially recovered, Roosevelt came to
Washington, Bolling asked him to call at S Street: "If Mrs. Roosevelt is with you Mrs. Wilson would be so happy if she would come
along too—and let them have a little talk while you are with Mr.
Wilson."

On December 28, 1922, his birthday, the officers of the Foundation came to S Street to say the raising of the one million dollars
seemed assured. Hamilton Holt, the executive director, spoke
for the group and told of a check for $100 given to the head of the
North Carolina division of the Foundation, the wife of ex-Secretary
Daniels. Attached to the check, Holt said, was a note: "From the
family of Frank M. Thompson, who died in the World War for
world peace, in gratitude to Woodrow Wilson for the faith he has
kept for the dead." As he sat in the library the quick tears came to
the invalid's eyes. He was unable to speak, and when the people
left he was upset over his silence. He said to his wife, "I wish I
could have controlled my voice so I could really have expressed
what I felt, but I could not control myself lest I break down and
cry like a schoolboy." Days later he was still anxious about it; he

said to her, "I am still worrying over my silence. Please make up
for my omission if you can and let them know why I can't express
myself."

But the Foundation people had understood and so would have
those many people who on that birthday sent him cards of greeting. Grayson came to pay a call and the ex-President showed the
remembrances and said, "I am having quite a card party today!"
But he had a bitter laugh when he discussed a Senate resolution
adopted unanimously that day saying the Senate had heard "with
great pleasure" of the "rapid recovery to good health of former
President Hon. Woodrow Wilson" and wished to "express to Hon.
Woodrow Wilson the pleasure and joy of the Senate of the United
States" at the news. "Think of them passing it and not meaning
it," he said to Grayson.

The Senate, or at least many Senators, may indeed have been
hypocritical, but there were those in the United States in that year
who were something else. Those others were the people who, in
Ida Tarbell's words, more and more sought the man they could
not forget. Few could get to see him at his home, but they stood
in the rain and in the snow and wind each Saturday night to see
him when he went to the vaudeville at Keith's Theatre. "Wilson
Night," it was called—Saturday night after a week in which the
ticket sellers had constantly to say, "This is as near to him as I can
place you." Always he sat in the same seat, U-21. At eight in the
evening a police lieutenant with a squad closed off G Street between 14th and 15th to all vehicular traffic and took up station in
a little alley by the side of the theater. The street filled up with
people—always they were there, no matter what the weather; and
week by week they grew in their numbers—and a little after eight
the big Pierce-Arrow came slowly down the way and halted in the
alley.

The servant Scott, in black suit instead of the white jacket he
wore at home, helped the ex-President out of the car and to the
alley door held open by a member of the theater staff. He was
always in evening clothes. As he came out, behind him there would
be a thrill of excitement in the waiting crowd and a series of audible
whispers: "There he is!" Inside, Edith helped him out of his coat
and took off his hat and put them in a little vestibule, and he
moved to Seat U-21, she preceding him with a guest or two, John

Randolph Bolling, perhaps, or Margaret down for a weekend. The
theater's house detective stood in the aisle to keep people away.
He had always loved the theater and in another day used to put
a record on the victrola that stood in the Oval Room at 1600 Pennsylvania Avenue and dance to it in imitation of the stage hoofers.
Now there could be no dancing for him, but still he could laugh at
the stunts and the jokes. When he missed a line, Edith whispered
it to him, and when he dropped his handkerchief she picked it up.

At the end of the performance people dashed out of the main
entrance and circled back to the alley to see him into his car. Often
a group of performers waited there to hand him a spray of flowers
and say a few words. Cary Grayson remembered a young actress
still in costume and stage make-up offering flowers and speaking
for the other girls with her, saying, "We simply want to tell you
that we love you dearly." Sometimes there might be a card accompanying the bouquet: "The Little Folks of Singer's Midgets Act
wish you good luck and the best of health and thank you for the
opportunity of playing before you."

It was those people in the street at Keith's, and the ones who
came to his house, but mostly it was the people who cheered him
when America buried the Unknown Soldier. And it was what was
within himself—faith, belief, surety that, like his minister-father
and minister-grandfather, he too had been about God's work. For
the people and the faith changed him. He had prayed every night
of his life, and he had said the people would in the end do right,
and now God and the people came to his aid. The terrible bitterness began to drop away, and the hopelessness and the loneliness,
and instead there came a feeling that it had not all been for nothing that he had lived. He said, "If it turn out well or if it turn out
ill, it will turn out right," and then he said, "I would rather fail
in a cause that some day will triumph than to win in a cause that
I know some day will fail." He said, "I am confident that what I
have fought for and stood for is for the benefit of this nation and
of mankind. If this is so I believe that it ultimately will prevail,
and if it is not, I don't want it to prevail." And the visitors went
away, the politically shrewd ones knowing that America would
never enter the League of Nations, but all of them thankful that
now at the last he was coming to terms with life and with his fate.

In the years to come he was to be compared to Samson shorn of his locks, to Apollo blind, to Prometheus bound, to St. Paul, even to Jesus of Nazareth hanging on a cross. But in his own eyes now he was but a tiny figure in God's plan for the Right, an implement, a tool. Nothing more. One day Margaret came to sit with him in a peaceful silence and he slowly began to talk in what she thought was contemplation of the past. It was the great soul that spoke, Margaret thought, not the tired body. He said, "I think it was best after all that the United States did not join the League of Nations." She was startled. "Why, Father darling?" He said, "Because our entrance into the League at the time I returned from Europe might have been only a personal victory. Now, when the American people join the League it will be because they are convinced it is the only right time for them to do it." He was smiling a little. He said, "Perhaps God knew better than I did after all."

After that there was pain for him from the crippled body and from the tortured nerves, but above that pain was exaltation. *He had not failed.* God would make it right. George Creel came to see him and saw religious serenity in the eyes where there had been despair and fear. There was peace in the lines around the mouth which once, when the two drove past the staring crowds outside the White House, had said to George Creel that only menace and curiosity lived in those crowds. "It will come, yes, it will come," he said to George Creel now in S Street. Creel wrote, "I saw glory shining from his face. 'It will come.'"

14

Nineteen twenty-three. His eyes, always weak, became so impaired that he could read only through a magnifying glass held in the good hand. Soon even that was too difficult, and all he could do was look at the pictures in the *National Geographic* and the motion picture magazines, *Film Fun, Screenland, Photoplay*. She read aloud to him—Stevenson, Dickens, O. Henry, Scott, the *Home Book of Verse*, and the mysteries: *Malcolm Sage, Detective; Find the Woman; Twenty-Six Clues*.

He thought about the past. Nellie came in and read to him and when it seemed he had drifted into sleep she put away her book. He opened his eyes. By the bed was a little dwarf pine tree someone had sent him. A light shone upon it. He had dozed off looking at it and now, awake, he smiled. "I was back on the island at Muskoka," he said to Nellie softly. "Do you remember our picnics there, and your mother reading poetry under the pines? I wish I could hear her voice."

He was cold all over now, always cold as his night came on. More and more he spent his time in bed before the fire, but when people came to see him he said to them over and over that he was glad he had broken down in the West in 1919's hot September after the cheering and the speeches and the little boy in Billings handing up the dime and saying, "Give it to him!" It had all been God's will, he said. It was God's way of bringing America to the

League. "As it is coming now," he said, "the American people are thinking their way through, and reaching their own free decision, and that is the better way for it to come." He said, "The thing is right; it is true; it cannot fail. It is right; and right will prevail."

In that spring he decided to try to write something. He began to work on an essay, dictating a sentence at a time to Edith. In the small hours of three, four, five o'clock in the morning, he awoke and, not realizing it was night, rang for Scott and asked that Mrs. Wilson come in. Scott went for her and she took down the few words and went back to her room. Two hours later he might ring again. For weeks they worked on it, and when it was finished it was just more than a thousand words in length, a dozen paragraphs. They sent it to George Creel, who was well connected in the publishing world, and asked Creel's opinion on where the essay might be placed. "The Road Away from Revolution," they titled it.

Creel read it with a horror and a sadness that made difficult the task of offering an opinion. For to Creel the piece was thin, vague, unworthy of the Woodrow Wilson that had been, completely unlike earlier writings and speeches. Creel wrote to Mrs. Wilson that in other circumstances he would advise "instantly and with all my power against its publication." To do that, however, might crush the ex-President, who had for years done no intellectual work save this. But to publish it might bring a depressing critical reaction. "What, then, are we to do?" Creel wrote Mrs. Wilson, and answered his own question by suggesting that perhaps it would be best to get it published with as little fanfare as possible. Perhaps then the public, not expecting too much, would understand. And understanding, perhaps no one would be too unkind. Creel ended: "Surely you can understand how painful it is for me to have to write this letter. It leaves me sick at heart. . . . This letter is for your own eyes, to be torn up instantly, and I enclose herewith another letter for you to show Mr. Wilson." In the second letter Creel told a merciful lie and said the article was fine, first-rate, but that to submit it to a major commercial magazine or to a newspaper syndicate would bring cheap "huckstering" and therefore perhaps it would be wisest to publish the essay in a modest, quiet way.

But Edith was not going to lie to her husband. She went riding with him and with Ellen's brother, Stockton Axson, who was a professor of English, and she plainly said that Creel felt the article would not do, that it lacked body. Her husband flared up and said that Creel had been after him for years to do some writing, and now he had done his best and it would have to stand. Edith said, "Now don't get on your high horse. I am just telling you that what the article needs is expansion, reasoning out the case more." But he sulked with an invalid's impatience and said, "I have done all I can and all I am going to do. I don't want these people bothering me any more." He had wanted "The Road Away from Revolution" to be a high clarion call, it was his first work in so long, he had put so much into it—and she had had to tell him it was a failure.

When they got back to S Street and he was being helped upstairs, Stockton Axson went into Bolling's office for a moment and as he stood there he heard Edith sobbing in the hall. She was to Axson such a strong woman, so strong, and he had never before known her to cry. He went out to her at once. "All I want to do," she said, "is just to help in any way I can. I am not urging him to do things he doesn't want to do. I just want to help and I just don't know how to help. I don't know what to do."

It was so unlike her to break this way, to falter. Axson begged her not to cry and asked if he might see the article. She gave it to him and after reading it he said that perhaps it could be pruned down a little and presented not as an argument but as a challenge. He went upstairs and said so to the essay's author; the answer was, "Why, you see exactly the point. Fix it." Axson drew a line through two or three paragraphs and the article was retyped and sent to the *Atlantic Monthly* with an accompanying note: "My dear Mr. Editor, In former years, whenever I happened to have produced an essay, it used to be my preference and pleasure to send it to the *Atlantic*. . . ." The *Atlantic* accepted the piece for $200 and so it came out, a plea for unselfishness in life, a following of the way of Christ. It could be read in a moment.

That summer another President took a train trip west. Haunted and frightened and muttering to himself and asking what should you do when your friends betray you, President Harding went across the country playing cards twelve, fourteen, sixteen hours a day. Cabinet officers spelled each other at the table. The President said he was off liquor, but he needed it now, and his aides collected bottles from the reporters. Teapot Dome came in on him, Teapot

Dome and the money running through the hands of the old friends
from Ohio. He was distraught, gray, collapsing, trying to fight off
the fear by dealing cards hand after hand. He fell sick and in San
Francisco he was sicker. He died in a room of a hotel where his
predecessor spoke for the League in 1919. Ever after they whispered that his wife poisoned him to save him from the revelations
that were coming. Or perhaps he took the poison himself.

In S Street, Warren Harding was always considered a "fool" and
a "lightweight," but when the newsboys shouting the headlines
brought the news, Harding's predecessor was shocked. No one seeing the two men riding to Harding's inauguration could have pre-
dicted the new President would die first. Edith went up to the
bedroom and together they got out a condolence telegram to Florence Harding.

In San Francisco the casket was placed level with the window
of the funeral car so that mourners by the track, weeping, could
see it. Church bells tolled as the train went by on its way to the
state funeral in Washington, and when it arrived at Union Station
thousands stood by to watch the catafalque going up the Avenue
to the White House. Tears were in the eyes of most of those
people.

The funeral would be held in the White House on August 8. It
would have been very difficult, almost impossible, for Harding's
predecessor to alight from his car and go into the building he had
left in company with the handsome and vigorous man who now
was dead, and so with Cary Grayson and Edith he sat outside while
the services went on. It was a very hot day; several of the marines
standing in formation fainted from the heat. The old Pierce-Arrow
that had spent so many years in government service drove up to
the place where it had done that service at a little past nine-thirty
in the morning. The chauffeur parked by the west side of the North
Portico. White House servants came out to say hello and the troops
saluted. Cary Grayson was in white summer uniform and wearing
a mourning band on his sleeve and the former First Lady in black
crape; her husband wore formal mourning attire with a black cra-
vat. As they sat in the heat a stone's throw from where they had
had their greatest moments, both personal and official, and also
their most terrible ones, a red-faced and perspiring colonel of cavalry came up. The officer said in an excited voice, "Mr. Wilson,

may I ask you a question?" "Certainly, Colonel." "Mr. Wilson, do you know where I can find Senator Lodge?"

Woodrow Wilson looked at the man. "I am not Senator Lodge's keeper," he said evenly. The Colonel saluted and spurred his horse and dashed off. Woodrow Wilson said, "What asylum did that Colonel escape from?"

Edith was tired, weary, all but played out. It had been four years since Pueblo and in that period she had not had a rest of any kind. Grayson said to her that she was ready for a breakdown and must get away. Her husband also worried about her and urged her to take a trip for a few days. So she went to visit her friends Charles Sumner Hamlin° and his wife and daughter, Anna, at the Hamlin summer place in Mattapoisett, Massachusetts. In late August she went to them and every morning took a walk with Anna and the family dog, Moses, a big black spaniel, along the shores of Buzzards Bay. Reporters asked her if her husband's essay in the *Atlantic* signaled an active writing career in the future—"Is his long silence over?"—but she simply smiled and expressed her admiration for Moses, one of the handsomest dogs she had ever seen, who had a "permanent wave" that all Anna's bobbed-hair girl friends envied. For a week she was gone, Grayson staying at S Street twenty-four hours a day to try to make up for her absence, and then she came back. And when she did she looked with new eyes at her husband and saw what before had not been clear because it was so familiar and she had been too close: he was dying. It could not be long now. She gathered herself.

The Hamlins came for dinner and the ex-President ate with them, Edith getting them out of the dining room on the pretext that they come and look at the garden so they might not see how Scott had to lift their host to his feet. He went to bed and the guests played pool below with his wife, who afterward went to dine several times with them. She also played bridge once a week with the Washington hostess Mrs. J. Borden (Daisy) Harriman, never knowing the invitations stemmed from a visit Mrs. Harriman had paid to S Street. Sitting with the guest, who during the war had headed the Red Cross women's motor corps in France, the ex-President

---

° Hamlin was a former head of the Federal Reserve Board.

said, "I want you to do something for me. Don't tell Mrs. Wilson I asked." And he said he would like Edith to go out to play cards; she needed some recreation so much.

In that year, 1923, his last full year, a New Jersey newspaperman, James Kerney, came to call and suggested that he run for the Senate. But he said no, he would not want that, it would just mean getting into rows with "old Lodge," and anyway the Senate didn't mean "a damn"; they hadn't had a thought there in "fifty years." No. There was only one place where he could really exert his influence. When he said that, the newspaperman understood what he meant. Had not Cary Grayson, who knew, said years ago, right before the 1920 convention, that no man who lives at 1600 Pennsylvania Avenue ever wants to leave it?

But thinking of a return to what he had been for eight years did not blank out the gentler parts of his nature, and often the lined face seemed placid, content, very loving. Some of the people who wrote him caught his interest, and wrapped in his shawl in the garden sunshine he listened to his wife reading the letters. Two elderly English spinsters, Cicely and Gertrude Ford, became friendly with him through the mails and it pleased him to hear of their interests, of the farmer down the road from their Heather Cottage at Bournemouth, of how they sat up until midnight reading to each other from *Tom Sawyer* and that despite the extreme lateness of the hour they continued because "we simply could not leave him in the midst of his thrilling adventures in the cave!" In their neat old maids' writing they wrote of working to support the League: they were going to hire a band and hold an open-air meeting in support of international co-operation. "We have been 'hustling about some,' in American phrase," they wrote; and the meeting was a great success. Several hundred people turned out. They were interested, they wrote, "in all things American, from Congress to Clabber—what ever that dainty may be." As the months and then the years passed they wrote to S Street of how they founded a branch of the League of Nations Union in Bournemouth; first they themselves *were* the branch, but then they had two and four and five helpers, and where once a half-filled small room was large enough for their meetings, the time came when the spacious pavilion of the Bournemouth Winter Gardens was not large enough. He in return wrote back that "it makes me very impatient of my present inability to travel when I think of the great pleasure I would otherwise have in visiting Bournemouth and paying my respects in person to my highly valued friends, the Misses Ford." They sent a limerick for him; they had read he loved limericks:

> There was an old man of Khartoum
> Who kept two black sheep in his room.
>   To remind him, he said,
>   Of two friends who were dead.
> But he never would specify whom.

He delighted in the old man of Khartoum and recited it to Lloyd George when the Welshman visited S Street—he replied to Lloyd George's request for an opinion on Calvin Coolidge by quoting Oscar Wilde, who, meeting an individual, adjusted his monocle, sniffed, and asked, "Are you anyone in particular?"—and recited another limerick also. This one had to do with a lawsuit instituted by the aristocratic Cabots of Boston against an immigrant family, the Kabotskis, who sought to take the Cabot name. "The limerick had to be made over," he said gleefully, and recited it:

> "Here's to Massachusetts,
>   The land of the bean and the cod.
>   Where the Lodges can't speak to the Cabots
> Because the Cabots speak Yiddish, by God!"

In that fall Bernard Baruch's daughter, Belle, an active worker for United States entry into the League, came to see him with a friend, Evangeline Johnson, and begged that he go on the radio the night before the fifth anniversary of the Armistice and give an address that would promote interest in the League. He had always disliked the radio, then in its infancy, and fought Edith's attempts to get him interested in the programs, but for such a cause on such a day he would override his antipathy. So again they went to work, the husband and wife, and worked for weeks on a talk that would take less than ten minutes. On the Western tour in 1919 he went to the train without one word of his half a hundred speeches written out; but that was in 1919, a long while ago.

On the afternoon of November 10, a truck bearing the transmission facilities parked in the driveway. Only a microphone attached to a wire would be in the house itself. No photographers.

All day he was in bed with a sickening headache, but he was up on his feet—he had always said he could speak only while standing up—and in the library at eight-thirty when an announcer said, "Mr. Woodrow Wilson will now say a few words."

He began to speak into the device carrying his voice to anyone who on a Saturday night cared to hear what Woodrow Wilson thought about Armistice Day. He had tried to memorize the address but found it impossible, and so he tried to read it from a typed page. But he had great trouble seeing the words and his voice failed him. The first few faltering sentences were almost unintelligible to the listeners all across America gathered in the homes of persons who had radios, headsets and amplifiers. In a Madison Square studio a New York *World* reporter saw a woman turn her head away from the radio speaker. "Oh, he is so ill, so broken," she cried. But he steadied himself and, standing in the library, he managed to get the words out even though between sentences he gasped as a man does when hit by cold water. Now and then he seemed to halt completely until Edith prompted him with the next words. Over most sets it could not be heard that she was doing this, for she stood well away from the microphone, but at New York's Station WOR, a very clear signal came in and her voice was plainly heard.

He said now, five years after the guns of the war stopped all along the fronts: "Memories of that happy time are forever marred and embittered for us by the shameful fact that when the victory was won . . . we withdrew into a sullen and selfish isolation which is manifestly ignoble because manifestly dishonorable.

"The only way in which we can worthily give proof of our appreciation of the high significance of Armistice Day is by resolving to put self-interest away and once more formulate and act upon the highest ideals and purposes of international policy. Thus, and only thus, can we return to the true traditions of America."

He was finished. He stood in S Street's library and said, "That is all, isn't it?" The words came over the speakers of all the radio sets, and in the Madison Square studio a man softly repeated them. "That is all, isn't it?"

But he had spoken to the greatest audience in the history of radio up to that time. Upward of three million persons heard his voice. Dozens of them wrote to the originating station in Washington.

"Dear Sirs, The speech of ex-President Wilson came in fine and I sure did enjoy his speech. I tuned in after he had started his speech and when he finished and they announced who had been speaking, I nearly fell out of my seat. Radio sure is a wonder. I enjoy your other programs. Lawrence Campbell, Jr., Mannington, W. Va." . . . "I have just listened to Woodrow Wilson talk over the radio and wish to tell you we heard every word clear & plain and you would think Mr. Wilson was right in the room. Sure was good. If you get this letter kindly let us know if Mr. Wilson knew how plain his voice was heard in Green Bay. I am sure he would be glad . . ."

The next day, Armistice Day, twenty thousand persons came to S Street. The trolley lines put on extra cars to carry them. They were not the elite of Washington or the government, noted William Allen White, and among them were fewer than a dozen persons whose names a regular newspaper reader would recognize. They were clerks, housewives, some Negroes, young veterans. Joe Tumulty, still barred from Number 2340, hired a little scratch band to lead the people, and a man who used to dress up as Uncle Sam and march in Washington parades was at the head of the musicians. Behind came the people, the largest crowd ever to go to S Street. The New York *Times* the next day frankly called them "pilgrims," and to the writer Mark Sullivan there was indeed something of the religious in the solemn fashion in which they conducted themselves and in the mood that was theirs. They were something like a church congregation, Sullivan thought, holding the meeting out of doors. In the windless air maple leaves dropped upon them as they covered the streets for five blocks in every direction. Many of them carried white chrysanthemums; others had League of Nations banners and American flags.

They began to gather after Sunday lunch, around two o'clock. At three-thirty Senator Carter Glass of Virginia came out of the house, and with him was the servant Scott, and behind them, leaning heavily on his cane but outfitted in morning coat and gray trousers, was Woodrow Wilson. The band played *Over There*. Some ex-soldiers wearing their old uniforms were directly in front of the house, and when during the music and the cheering their old Commander in Chief looked at them he found a smile to give back in exchange for those on their young faces. When the waiting thousands were silent, Glass began to read a prepared address. "We are here," Glass called out, "to renew our faith and to signify the unabated loyalty of millions of Americans to that immutable cause which you, more than any man on earth, so impressively personify." The people burst into a roar. Glass was standing on the lower step of the entrance to the house and the man he was speaking to stood just above him on the upper step, head bent, eyes on Glass's hands. The lips were slightly parted and now and again the bared head nodded up and then down. Glass said, "What might have been accomplished had America given heed to your wise counsel and taken the imposing place which still awaits her coming!" Glass spoke then of how it yet would come, that America would yet join the League, and that when it did all America and all the world would "stand uncovered before him to whom, through the goodness of God, will belong the most enduring honor." Cheer after cheer rose from the people. Glass stepped back.

Woodrow Wilson's eyes were on the ground as the applause slowly quieted. Edith stood behind him in a moleskin cape with sable collar. He moved forward one step and put on his hat so that he might lift his cane and with his good hand hook it into the top pocket of his overcoat. Then he took off his hat again and for perhaps thirty seconds he stood silent, swaying slightly. He raised his bowed head and peered at the ex-soldiers in front and at the people in the street. He moved the right hand holding the high silk hat in a vague gesture and then he began to speak.

"Senator Glass, ladies and gentlemen: I am indeed deeply touched and honored by this extraordinary exhibition of your friendship and confidence; and yet I can say without affection that I wish you would transfer your homage from me to the men who made the Armistice possible. It was possible because our boys had beaten the enemy to a standstill. You know—if you will allow me to be didactic for a moment—'Armistice' merely means 'standstill of arms.' Our late enemies, the Germans, call an Armistice '*Waffenstillstand*,' an armed standstill; and it was the boys who made them stand still." There was laughter and applause. "If they had not, they would not have listened to proposals of armistice. I am proud to remember that I had the honor of being the commander in chief——" Someone yelled, "The best on earth!" "—the commander in chief of the most ideal army ever thrown together——" And his voice broke and his eyes filled for a moment and he said, "Pardon my emotion," and went on: "Of the most ideal army that was ever thrown together, though the real fighting commander in chief was my honored friend Pershing, to whom I gladly hand the laurels of victory. Thank you with all my heart for your kindness."

He turned away and put on his hat. He said, "That's all I can do." Huston Thompson of the Federal Trade Commission, a former student at Princeton, stepped forward to help him back to the house, and as the crowd cheered, the band broke into the hymn *How Firm a Foundation*. But as Thompson took his arm he moved his lips. Above the cheers and the music Thompson could not understand the whispered words; Thompson put his ear to the speaker's lips and faintly heard, "Stop the band. I have something more to say." Thompson waved his arms at the band to quiet them and they stopped playing and again S Street became completely silent.

Before, Woodrow Wilson had spoken in a monotone, and what he said was mild, graceful enough, of no real significance. It was a sick old man's few remarks in front of his house; it meant nothing. But now he was going to speak again for one moment, one paragraph, and he was going to find it in him to speak so that his voice, suddenly strong, would carry to the outermost reaches of the crowd ranging down S Street's hill; to the little boys perched up in the maple trees; to the people on the sloping mud banks across the street. For this moment, this one last instant, that voice was the voice of the Professor Wilson who long ago called to the students at the football games that they should cheer louder for the team; the voice was that of the President in the West crying aloud that there would be a terrible war if the nation did not enter the League. These were the last words he was ever going to say in public. The long crusade was over. This was summation—valedictory. And no tears.

He said:

"Just one word more; I cannot refrain from saying it. I am not one of those that have the least anxiety about the triumph of the principles I have stood for. I have seen fools resist Providence before, and I have seen their destruction, as will come upon these again, utter destruction and contempt. That we shall prevail is as sure as that God reigns. Thank you."

On Christmas Eve they went to Keith's. Helen Bones, who introduced them—(eight years . . . Edith Galt in muddy shoes and the President in tatty golfing suit and Grayson saying he thought the ladies could at least invite the men for tea)—Helen was down from New York for the holiday and so was Margaret. Two strong doormen waited at the alley entrance to the theater and half carried him in to Seat U-21. The headliners that night were the madcaps Olsen and Johnson, the latter playing a maniac version of Santa Claus, and the final set was of a living room with a fireplace. Above the fireplace was a portrait of Woodrow Wilson. The cast came out on the stage for the finale, and the actress Nan Halpern stepped forward and said to the audience in the dark, "Merry Christmas to you and you and you." She turned her back and went to the picture and looked up at it and said, "And to you, an abundance of Yuletide blessings and a bountiful year." The people in the theater were entirely silent then, both those on the stage and those sitting before them, for she was raising herself to the picture and she was holding it in her arms and pressing her lips to it in a long sweet embrace. Down the aisle came showgirls. They carried roses. They went to Row U and handed them over. Onstage the cast began to sing *Auld Lang Syne* and at the first slow familiar notes the audience got up—every last one of them, Olsen noted—and stood and turned toward Seat U-21 and sang along with the orchestra. This was no ordinary singing, Olsen thought. He had never heard such singing. At the end there was a long silence that seemed to Olsen to last and last until one of the girls on the stage stepped forward to the footlights. The brightness illuminated her tears glittering down through the mascara and stage make-up. She said, "Merry Christmas, Mr. President."

Four days later, December 28, they celebrated his birthday. Richard Linthicum, a Democratic Party publicist, sent a limerick:

> On S Street resides a great sage
> Whose name brightens history's page.
>   Is he old? Fiddlesticks!
>   One year past sixty-six!
> A very young age for a sage.

Outside when he went for his afternoon drive at three o'clock there waited a magnificent birthday gift from a group of his old friends and associates. It was a Rolls-Royce, specially constructed to make his entrances and exits easier. It was black with a thin orange stripe—Princeton's colors. On the doors was "W.W."

New Year's came and Helen and Margaret left. Now he was alone with Edith, to whom he had always been My Dear One, My Beloved, My Darling, My Own; to whom he would always be these. Her smiles to cheer him did not stop, but now in this last winter, these last weeks and days, he could hardly see her or the letters he dictated. His pen dragged badly when he tried to sign his name; one letter to the Misses Ford of Bournemouth was filed away with a notation by Bolling: "Not sent on account of bad signature." For days, in fact, he lay too weary and spent to try even to lift his pen. But on January 16 he asked Cordell Hull, chairman of the Democratic National Committee, to bring the members of the committee, in session in Washington, to call. They came in a fleet of taxicabs driving up S Street through a heavy cold rain. They hurried in through the outer doors thrown open for the first time—for this was his first reception—and formed a line to go up the staircase. There were 125 of them. Edith stood at the top of the steps in front of the library, where he sat before a blazing fire. In a green afternoon frock, she shook hands with each visitor, but constantly, every few seconds, she turned her head to look at her husband. The guests went single file into the library to where Hull stood by to say their names quietly. There was no cheering, no music; there were no speeches. There were hardly any words. For each person there was a slow lifting of the right hand no more than six inches in the air, but above the rustling of the moving people and the swish of their damp clothing nothing he might have said in his weak voice could have been heard. His lips moved and there was an almost imperceptible nod of the head; that was all. He grew ever more fatigued as the line kept coming, and his head sagged forward, so that he could no longer look up into the anxious faces of the people gently reaching their hands out to his. After an hour it was over. He had shaken the hand of every man and woman.

Four days later, on January 20, terribly weak, he met for a few minutes with Raymond Fosdick, who, although an American, had served as a League of Nations official in Geneva. Fosdick asked him how he felt, and he said he would reply by quoting something another President said when asked about his health: "John Quincy

Adams is all right, but the house he lives in is dilapidated, and it looks as if he would soon have to move out." But mostly they talked of the League. Constantly he talked about 1914 and the utter wastage of the war. "It must never happen again!" he said. "There is a way of escape if only men will use it." The escape was the League, the authority of law substituted for the authority of force, he said. His voice rose when he spoke of criticisms of the League as a too-idealistic conception. "The world is *run* by its ideals," he said. He grew excited and tears rolled down his face when he said to Fosdick that it was unthinkable that America would permanently stand in the way of human progress; it was unthinkable that America would remain aloof, for America would not thwart the hope of the race. His voice broke and he whispered huskily that America was going to bring her spiritual energy to the liberation of mankind. Mankind would step forward, a mighty step; America could not play the laggard. Fosdick was young, and when Fosdick rose to go he pledged in the name of the younger generation that they would carry through to a finish the uncompleted work. At this the tears flowed unimpeded. Fosdick wrote it all down: "My last impression of him was of a tear-stained face, a set, indomitable jaw, and a faint voice whispering, 'God bless you.' With his white hair and gray, lined face, he seemed like a reincarnated Isaiah, crying to his country: 'Awake, awake, put on thy strength, O Zion; put on thy beautiful garments, O Jerusalem!'"

January in Washington is cold and damp. Cary Grayson wanted to get away for a little while and Bernard Baruch obliged him by offering an invitation for a week's shooting at his South Carolina estate.° On January 26, Saturday, Grayson came to S Street for a few moments before heading for the train south. The doctor was seen to the door by the mistress of the house, who said as they walked down the stairs that she was very worried about her husband, for he seemed so weak. She asked Grayson if he shared this fear, and Grayson said, "No. If I did, I would not leave him, and if you want me to give up the trip, I will. But I think you are mistaken." *

She left Grayson and went up to her husband's room, where he

° Still in Navy service, Grayson had been assigned by President Harding to duty in Washington so that he might be at hand to care for the invalid in S Street. President Coolidge did not change Harding's orders concerning Grayson.

sat with his head bowed. She asked how he felt; he said, "I always feel badly now, little girl. Somehow I hate to have Grayson leave."

She said, "He is still downstairs. Let me run and tell him and he will stay." She made as if to go, but he caught her hand. "No. That would be a selfish thing on my part. He is not well himself and needs the change." But then he said, "It won't be very much longer, and I had hoped he would not desert me. But that I should not say, even to you."

And so Grayson left. On Sunday the invalid went over his mail, but he seemed terribly, terribly tired. On Monday he was even weaker. On Tuesday night the nurse on duty, Lulu Hulett, said to Bolling that she thought her patient was a very sick man. She asked Bolling if Grayson was in Washington. Bolling told her the doctor was in South Carolina. She said, "Oh, I wish he were here." That night, a little after midnight, Edith decided that Grayson, gone four days, must be recalled. She went to her brother's room and woke him to say that she wanted Grayson to be telegraphed. Bolling got up and sent a prearranged code telegram, charging it to the telephone of another brother, Wilmer Bolling, so that no word of the crisis might leak out. The wire did not arrive at Baruch's South Carolina place until morning, and as Grayson was already out shooting, he did not see it until noon. When he did, he telephoned and said he would take the next train north. He would be in Washington on Thursday morning and would come to the house at once.

Grayson arrived at ten on Thursday and examined the patient, who had sent word to Bolling that unless there was something of great importance in the mail he would let all correspondence go for a day. Later on Thursday, in the afternoon, Edith asked Grayson if the girls should be notified. Grayson said perhaps not; doing so would alarm them unnecessarily. But the woman's eye—the wife's —had seen something the doctor had missed. All that night the two of them sat with the patient, and when Bolling arose at eight his sister told him it was time to tell the girls. Grayson came down and said she was right. Margaret was in New York; they telephoned her and she said she would be down on the next train. Nellie was at her home in California; Jessie was in Bangkok, where her husband was acting as adviser to the Government of Siam. The telegrams went out: CONSIDER CONDITION EXTREMELY SERIOUS. Nellie

wired Edith: OUR DEAR LOVE TO YOU BOTH DARLING. WE ARE LEAV-
ING TOMORROW FOR WASHINGTON. SURE EVERYTHING WILL BE ALL
RIGHT. She and McAdoo took reservations on the Santa Fe Railroad's California Limited leaving Los Angeles at 11:30 A.M. Saturday. Nothing was heard from Jessie, but the Siamese Embassy
in Washington offered all aid in expediting messages to and from
Bangkok.

Later that day, Friday, word leaked out and brought a platoon
of reporters to S Street. Grayson went to speak with them. There
was no attempt to minimize the gravity of the situation; Grayson
said frankly that the situation was very bad. That evening every
paper in America told its readers: WOODROW WILSON VERY WEAK. END
IS THOUGHT TO BE VERY NEAR. FAMILY OF EX-PRESIDENT SUMMONED TO
BEDSIDE. As the papers appeared on the streets the reporters were
phoning in a statement by Grayson that it could be only a matter
of time. A rumor spread through Washington that the dying man
was delirious and that in his mind he was back in 1919 where he
still sat in the White House leading the fight for ratification of the
League.°

Other doctors came, H. A. Fowler and Sterling Ruffin, both of
whom attended him in the White House. (Ruffin had had another
professional duty to perform that day. With two other doctors
he went as a Senate-appointed committee to determine if Albert
Fall, who once went to a sickroom to see if the President of the
United States was insane, was too ill to testify before the Senators investigating Teapot Dome. Fall said he was far too sick.
Ruffin and the other doctors did not agree.) When Fowler and Ruffin arrived, Grayson went into the sickroom to say that the two
doctors were coming in to make an examination. When they came
in behind Grayson, there was a tiny smile from the patient, and a
faint whisper: "Too many cooks spoil the broth."

Last jest, thought Grayson.

Grayson stayed when the other doctors left. Late that night, after
the fog came in and covered S Street and the reporters shivering
in front of the dimly lit house and in a flimsy little construction
shack in an empty lot nearby, Grayson said to his patient what
was the truth: that he was dying. Woodrow Wilson listened and

° The rumor was untrue.

breathed, "I am a broken piece of machinery. When the machinery is broken . . ." His voice petered out. There was a moment's silence in the sickroom where hung the original of the most famous Red Cross poster—"The Greatest Mother in the World"— and where he lay in the replica of the White House's Lincoln bed underneath a picture of the American flag and across from the fireplace where stood the casing of the first shell fired at the enemy. Then he said, "I am ready."

Outside, unasked, the morning milk wagons detoured around the block so that there would be no noise. It was barely light and cold February dawn had hardly come when one of the servants came out and busied himself sweeping the steps. The reporters came rushing up to ask for Grayson. The servant said the doctor had spent the entire night with his patient and could not come out now. The reporters became insistent and the servant went inside and closed the door. But shortly he had to open it again and again, for a flood of telegraph boys came bicycling up S Street. They bore messages for Edith: THREE HUNDRED GIRLS OF GALLOWAY WOMENS COLLEGE ARKANSAS SEND THEIR PRAYERS AND DEEPEST SYMPATHY TO YOU IN THIS TIME OF CRISIS AND THEIR LOVE TO THAT TRUEST AMERICAN YOUR HUSBAND . . . The Newport News, Virginia, Young Men's Hebrew Association . . . The Cedar Rapids, Iowa, Greek Association . . . TONIGHTS PAPERS SAY THAT YOUR ILLUSTRIOUS HUSBANDS CONDITION IS SUCH THAT HIS PASSING AWAY IS MOMENTARILY EXPECTED STOP IF THIS IS SO THE GREATEST AMERICAN SINCE LINCOLN IS PASSING STOP LET ME SORROW WITH YOU STOP A FORMER AMERICAN EXPEDITIONARY FORCE CAPTAIN J A LYNCH CRESSON PENNSYLVANIA . . . The American Women's Club of Vancouver, British Columbia . . . Forrest Cavalry of the United Confederate Veterans . . . OUR TENDEREST SYMPATHY GOES OUT TO YOU FROM OVERFLOWING HEARTS. WE LOVED HIM SO DEARLY. MR AND MRS LAWRENCE C WOODS DAYTONA BEACH FLORIDA.

With the breaking day, Saturday, February 2, the people came. They gathered before the house, waiting. The trees stood bare above the lines the police put up to hold them back, and autos inched their way up S Street's hill. Callers stepped from cars to leave their cards in a silver tray Scott held in his hand when he came to the door. Mr. and Mrs. William Howard Taft left their cards, and Mr. and Mrs. Alben W. Barkley, and Daisy Harriman, and Cordell Hull; the French Ambassador, the Italian Ambassador,

Herbert Hoover, Oscar W. Underwood, the widowed Florence
Kling Harding. Anna Hamlin, with whom Edith had walked along
the shores of Buzzards Bay as Moses, the spaniel, played about
them, wrote on her card just: "Dear love——"

Grayson came out, and the reporters lounging in the driveway
against the electric coupé that was the only tangible result of the
firm of Wilson & Colby came running. He said, "Mr. Wilson real-
izes his fight is over. He is making a game effort. It almost breaks
one down. He is very brave. He is just slowly ebbing away. He is
not talking to anyone but he is still conscious." Down the hill toward Massachusetts Avenue, other reporters waited by the telephone in an apartment building for the signal from their colleagues
that it was all over. The telegraph company ran lines to the muddy
slopes of the empty lot across from Number 2340, and operators
waited in the construction shack. The people kept coming to stand
before the house and look up to the third floor where, out of sight,
for his room faced the rear, he was making his fight. With the
people came, steadily, the bikes of the uniformed telegraph boys.
The Polish Fellowship League of Chicago . . . DEEPLY DISTRESSED
AM HOPING FOR THE BEST YOU ARE BOTH CONSTANTLY IN MY THOUGHTS
FRANKLIN D ROOSEVELT JACKSONVILLE FLORIDA . . . American Legion
posts . . . The Virginia Writers Club . . . DEAR NOBLE LADY COURAGE
AND GODS HELP TO YOU BAINBRIDGE COLBY . . . The Acting Governor
of the Territory of Hawaii . . . Evangeline Booth of the Salvation
Army . . . OUR HEARTS ARE WITH YOU IN LOVE AND DEVOTION AND ANX-
IETY MR AND MRS JOSEPHUS DANIELS.

Senator Carter Glass, who made the speech on the last Armistice Day, three months before, came with Bernard Baruch. The
doors opened for them and they took seats in the library, as did
Joseph Wilson, the kind, well-meaning, mild, untalented brother.
Grayson came down and Glass asked if the doctor could say to
the dying man that Carter Glass wanted him to know how much
he loved him. Grayson went up and said, "Senator Glass sends
you his love." Woodrow Wilson tried to smile and his eyes gleamed.
The fingers of his right hand moved slightly. Grayson went downstairs and with lowered eyes said to Glass, "He smiled when I
told him."

At four-thirty in the afternoon Grayson went out with a bulletin
for the death-watch reporters: "Mr. Wilson's general condition is

the same as it was this morning. He grows steadily weaker." The reporters telephoned it in to their city rooms, ready and waiting for a flash to print the extras with black mourning at the edges of the pages. The whole country was hanging on the papers, and in all major cities rumors periodically sprang up that it was all over. Flags went down to half staff and then the rumors were found to be false and the flags went up again.

Always the people outside were noiseless, voiceless; always the same, although the individual men and women came and went, standing for an hour, two hours, and then going away. Joe Tumulty came. It had been twenty-two months. Joe Tumulty slipped in the door and asked for Grayson and said, "It seems to me that ten years' faithful service have earned me the right to go in and look once into his eyes, or maybe just pat his forehead before he goes." It had been very bad for Tumulty, those twenty-two months. Grayson said, "Yes, Joe, you're right, and he will be glad to see you. But he's asleep now." And Grayson promised that Joe could see him before the end. But by the bed, night and day, old-looking, no longer chic, no longer beautiful as she had been in the days when she used to walk with Helen Bones in Rock Creek Park, sat Edith Bolling Wilson. Joe Tumulty did not get to the sickroom.

Saturday wore on: crowds; four soldiers saying, "We served under him in France and we want to be with him until the end"; Edith and Margaret sitting by the bed with the two nurses; Grayson going out to tell the reporters that no nourishment was being taken although Mrs. Wilson had carried in a tray with chicken broth and meat juices, Grayson adding that he was himself present more as a friend than a doctor, for no doctor could do anything now; President Coolidge issuing a statement that he was much disturbed; the papers crying in black headlines ALL HOPE GONE; the letters coming in: "My dear Mrs. Wilson"—this on the stationery of the Woodrow Wilson Club of Minneapolis—"I so much want Mr. Wilson to know how deeply we love him. I know that you have received so many messages of this kind that it is probably not possible to mention them to him, but it would make me happy to feel that he knows of our Club and that it is founded upon a deep and abiding faith in him and the principles which he has advocated. . . . May God bless him and keep him always. Mrs. Genevieve Barton Curtis."

Saturday night: "There has been no radical change in Mr. Wilson's condition during the day, but rather a gradual wearing-away process." The reporters stuffed back into their pockets the handkerchiefs quickly yanked out at the sight of Grayson and intended for use in signaling to the other men by the telephones that the extras could be put on the streets. When it got dark Scott came out and addressed himself to the hushed people standing behind the reporters and the policemen: "Mrs. Wilson asks you please not to remain." The people drifted away, save for one woman, who said she would pray for him.

Saturday night: The Kiwanis Clubs . . . The United Spanish-American War Veterans . . . John W. Wescott, who twice nominated him for the Presidency: WORDS FAIL BUT I SEND WITH BREAKING HEART ALL MY LOVE AND HOPE.

For a moment she went out of the room. It had seemed he was totally unconscious, unmoving, eyes closed, hands limp on the blanket, but he sensed that she was gone. It could not have been that he knew it with his eyes, for he was blind now, nor with his ears, for his hearing was gone now, but he knew that he was alone now, for all that Margaret and Grayson and the nurses were there. The last word he would ever say came from his lips:
"*Edith!*"

Sunday morning, and in the dark the worn and tired and unshaven reporters ruing lost Saturday nights with girls, with families, with theater tickets given to friends, stamped their feet and tried to keep warm. Scott appeared and swept the steps and the street and took in the ice and milk incongruously left on the step despite this coming event monopolizing the world's press. At eight-thirty Grayson, haggard, came out and handed the reporters a typed statement and several carbons: "Mr. Wilson is unconscious and his pulse is very weak." Two hours later Grayson came out again. When the door opened the reporters straightened up and leaped to the steps to take the typed sheets with their free hands. But the handkerchiefs went back into their pockets, for the statement was: "After a quiet night, Mr. Wilson is very low and the end may be expected at any time."

It had been going on for more than seventy hours—three days. He would not die. "I am ready"—but he would not surrender.

Grayson came out and said, the people gathered behind the news-papermen straining to hear him, "He is holding life by a thread so slight that it may break at any moment." Winter sunshine, brilliant, bathed Washington. It was Sunday, although perhaps after the long stint, the endless waiting, the cold and fog, the reporters hardly knew it. Church bells faintly sounded off in the distance toward the center of town. Upstairs, Margaret and Edith now and then whispered to him. There was no answer, no movement of the eyes closed for hours past, no change in the barely perceptible breathing. The shades of the room were drawn to keep the light out.

Mr. and Mrs. Charles Evans Hughes, he the defeated Republican Presidential candidate of 1916, came and left their cards. It was ten-fifteen, ten-thirty, eleven, on this Sunday morning in Washington.

He opened his eyes.

Edith bent forward and took his right hand. Margaret took his left. Cary Grayson looked into the open blue-gray eyes. At the foot of the bed nurse Lulu Hulett and nurse Ruth Powderly stood by. Edith spoke and Margaret spoke. "Woodrow." "Father." But there was no answer, although the eyes, unblinking, stared upward. Grayson felt for a pulse. Seventy-two hours. But the pulse was still there.

Outside, the crowds gathered after church. The street was closed to all traffic by the police and was entirely silent save for occasionally the voice of a child too young to understand why the hundreds stood voiceless. Among them was Mrs. Minnegerode Andrews, who passed out slips of paper upon which was written, "Peace on earth, good will to men." As she moved from person to person she said, "This is not so much for Woodrow Wilson as for the people left to carry on his ideals." When the last of the slips was out of her hand, she stepped off the sidewalk and in her Sunday finery she sank to her knees in the cobblestone gutter underneath the bare maple trees. For a few seconds she was there alone, a kneeling woman among hundreds of standing people, but it was only for a few seconds. All around her men and women went down, the men taking off their hats. The policemen and the reporters in front of the house turned away, unwilling to stare at this. The New York *Times* man gazed off down the hill and there he saw, slowly coming up from Massachusetts Avenue, a crippled girl on crutches. As he watched, the girl saw the people on their knees and tried to get down so that she might be as they were. She shifted her weight to one crutch and used her free hand to try to adjust her braces so that she could kneel. But she could not get it done; the braces held fast. As the reporter watched, she gave up and simply stayed as she was, leaning on one crutch. But she brought her hands together in front of her breast and clasped them as she looked up toward Number 2340. Her lips were moving.

In front of the house, then, it was so quiet that the sound of a dog scurrying in the leaves of an empty lot could plainly be heard.

Upstairs, the blue-gray eyes closed. They had been open for some ten minutes. The wife said, "Woodrow. Woodrow." It was a few minutes past eleven. In the street the people were getting up one by one.

The telegraphers were ready, and the reporters in front of the house and down by the telephones. Edith was still holding the right hand and Margaret the left. Weeping, Nellie was heading east on the California Limited. Jessie was in Siam. Grayson was bending over him, holding his wrist, and the two nurses stood at the foot of the bed. He had been three days dying his long death when, at 11:15 A.M., February 3, 1924, Grayson straightened up and stepped back.

15

Five minutes after Cary Grayson came out for what would be the last time that day, Sammy White went up to the door of 2340 S Street. Sammy was five. He had on a dark sailor suit, stockings, high button shoes. His mother must have loved his blond hair, for he wore it long. He held in his hand a single red rose.

The reporters were gone from the front of the house when Sammy came up. As soon as Grayson had appeared and said, "The end came at eleven-fifteen," the reporters dashed out into the street and jumped up and down so that the waving handkerchiefs could be seen by the men at the phones down the hill. Then they came rushing back to Grayson, who read from a typed slip of paper. "Mr. Wilson died at eleven-fifteen this morning," Grayson began, but the reporters at the outer edges of the circle around him interrupted, yelling, "Louder! Louder!"

Grayson raised his voice. "Mr. Wilson died at eleven-fifteen this morning. His heart action became feebler and feebler and the heart muscle was so fatigued that it refused to act any longer. The end came peacefully." Behind the reporters the people straining forward against the police lines could not hear, but when Grayson wiped his eyes they understood. A reporter asked, "Was Mrs. Wilson in the room when the end came?" Grayson said, "Yes, she was there—right there. Miss Margaret was there also." "Did he smile or give any evidence of consciousness just before he died?" "He died——" Grayson choked and began again and said, "He died peacefully. He just went to sleep. There were no words spoken. It looked to me as though he had just gone to sleep." Grayson blew his nose. The reporters broke and ran, heading down the hill to the telephones, a little covey of runners weaving in and out of groups of women standing with bowed heads, of men one by one taking their hats off.

Then Sammy White, five, came forward with his red rose. It was perhaps eleven-thirty and the thin winter sunshine was as strong as it was going to be that day. Someone asked Sammy what he wanted and he timidly said, "My father bought the flower and my mother told me to bring it over." A newspaper photographer came and told Sammy to stand in front of the house and hold his flower off to one side so that it would not cover his face in the picture. Sammy did as he was told, squinting, a solemn-faced little boy born about the time the President of the United States went to Europe and to the Peace Conference, and then reached up to ring the bell. When Scott came Sammy mutely pushed the red rose forward, and Scott took it. There were no words between the two.

The reporters came back from the phones and were standing in front of the house when the Minister of Uruguay, who had come to leave a card for a dying man, instead became the first person to leave one for a dead man. Minutes after the diplomat left, the first papers were on the streets, the boys who carried them shouting aloud the news. In Washington's First Congregational Church, those shouts penetrated the closed doors and windows and were heard by the minister, who halted the services and asked that the worshipers pray for the man who had just died. President and Mrs. Calvin Coolidge and the rest of the congregation bowed their heads. The shouts of the newsboys also reached the bell-ringer of the McKim Memorial Chimes in the tower of Epiphany Church, and he left off playing peals of welcome to churchgoers and changed to peals of sorrow, to hymns. He played *The Strife Is O'er, the Battle Done, Abide with Me, Lead, Kindly Light*. In the Central Presbyterian Church the pew once reserved for the President of the United States was draped in black crape.

In Princeton the chapel services were just ending. As the students and members of the faculty came out, bells began to toll and flags on the campus sank down to half staff. In New York, Mary Peck, who had once hoped to be the second Mrs. Wilson, listened to a church choir. The voice of one of the male singers rose above those of the others; the man sang, "The heart of the world is dying for just a little love." Mrs. Peck felt a sudden knowledge. He is dead, she thought. Aboard the California Limited speeding in the West, Nellie learned she was too late. Her husband started writing a statement for the press.

At S Street, visitors began to arrive. Stockton Axson came, and Helen Bones, in black, leaning on Altrude Gordon Grayson. A close woman friend of Margaret's came in response to a telephone call. And as soon as the services at the First Congregational Church were over, two White House cars drove up S Street's hill past the police officers standing to block all traffic. It had been less than an hour since the death announcement when Calvin Coolidge stepped out of the car and helped his wife onto the sidewalk. Movie cameramen came rushing for pictures as the Secret Service men took up places around the President. The President was in high silk hat and black overcoat with silk lapels. Grace Coolidge wore a brown velvet suit. They put their cards on Scott's outstretched silver tray. As with Sammy White, not one word was spoken. Soon after, Joe Tumulty drove his car up, the police letting him past the lines. He slowly went through the crowd standing in the street and parked across the street from the house. He got out, took a few steps, and stopped and simply stood there. A reporter asked, "Are you going in?" Tumulty hesitated in an uncertain way and a look of bewilderment came to his face. "My God, I can't make it," he said, and suddenly burst into tears. He staggered and put his hands over his face. The reporter caught him and other reporters came and half carried Tumulty to his car.

Church services were over now, and in many homes Sunday dinner also. In Boston an audience filed into Symphony Hall for a concert by the Negro tenor Roland Hayes. When the singer came out on the stage, there was applause, but he quieted it by solemnly holding up one hand. He spoke of the passing of a great soul and then began a song not listed on the program. It was *Goin' Home*. He sang:

"Goin' home, goin' home,
I'm just goin' home.
It's not far, just close by, through an open door
Work all done, care laid by,
Goin' to fear no more."

Many of the people in the hall did not understand at first, for only a fraction of the audience knew of the death in S Street. When the singer finished his song he stood with bowed head and a few people began to applaud. But the noise of their clapping hands suddenly seemed completely out of place, and in a moment there was silence and no movement either from the seated people or the motionless figure standing with eyes on the floor. In St. Paul the Minneapolis Symphony Orchestra was giving a concert at Minneapolis Auditorium. The first selection on the program was the *Rienzi* Overture, but without any explanatory announcement the orchestra began Chopin's Funeral March. In different sections of the audience people who understood got to their feet. There was whispering all over the auditorium: "It must be for Wilson. Wilson must be dead." When the music ended, there was perfect silence for a moment and then the people sat for the *Rienzi* Overture.

There had been some three or four hundred people standing in S Street when Grayson made his announcement, but when the news spread in Washington the crowd swelled to many times that number. Through the people came the telegraph boys. MOST HEARTFELT SYMPATHY IN THIS HOUR OF SORROW JACOB S LAUL PRESIDENTS CHAUFFER IN PARIS METUCHEN NEW JERSEY . . . Samuel Gompers . . . The Knights of Pythias . . . WOODROW WILSON SANDLER NAMED FOR HIM IN NINETEEN HUNDRED TWELVE NEW YORK CITY . . . The Polish Fellowship League of Chicago . . . WHILE A NATION GRIEVES . . . THIS DARK HOUR . . . HE IS WITH THE PRINCE OF PEACE NOW . . . The Elks, the Rotary, the War Mothers Service Star Legion of Fulton County, Georgia, the Central Conference of American Rabbis. MY WIFE AND I WISH THAT IT WERE IN OUR POWER TO SAY ANYTHING OR DO ANYTHING THAT COULD HELP AND LESSEN YOUR GRIEF BUT WE KNOW WE MUST LEAVE THAT TO GOD AND TIME HIS SERVANT JOHN SHARP WILLIAMS . . . The Improved Order of Red Men of Georgia . . . IT MUST BE A COMFORT TO YOU TO KNOW HIS GREAT SOUL LIVES ON AND WILL FOREVER . . . The Catholic Study Group of Detroit, Michigan

... SINCEREST SYMPATHY I AM A GOLD STAR MOTHER MRS E R DROPHY BIRMINGHAM ALABAMA ... The Bristol, Tennessee, Chapter of the Knights of the Ku Klux Klan ... DEEPEST SYMPATHY OF THE CHILDREN OF PRESIDENT GARFIELD ... Italian-American Protective Association of Portchester, New York ... J R THOMPSON SOLDIER IN CHARGE OF PRIVATE TELEPHONE SYSTEM AT MURAT MANSION PARIS FRANCE DURING MR WILSONS STAY IN PARIS ... The School for the Deaf, Knoxville, Tennessee ... IT WAS A PRIVILEGE TO HAVE LIVED IN HIS GENERATION.

Upon the door Scott hung a wreath of early spring flowers— yellow jonquils, mignonettes and forsythia. John Randolph Bolling filled out the death certificate, which Cary Grayson signed as attending physician. Under "Trade, profession, or particular kind of work," Bolling wrote: "Retired."

Foreign cablegrams began to arrive in addition to the domestic telegrams. PARIS WHO IN THE DAYS FOLLOWING VICTORY WELCOMED PRESIDENT WILSON TO HER HEART AND ACCLAIMED HIM NOW ENTERS INTO YOUR MOURNING MUNICIPAL COUNCIL CITY OF PARIS ... Edward P. ... THE QUEEN AND I EXTEND TO YOU OUR DEEP SYMPATHY IN ASSURING YOU OF THE LASTING MEMORY WE SHALL ALWAYS KEEP OF THE GREAT ONE WHO HAS GONE ALBERT R. ... The President of Liberia ... Chamber of Representatives of Belgium ... The Secretary General of the League of Nations ... WE SHALL NEVER FORGET THE HOURS THAT YOU AND YOUR HUSBAND SPENT AS OUR GUESTS ON YOUR WAY TO THE PEACE CONFERENCE GEORGE R. ... Clemenceau ... Lloyd George ... A PRINCE AMONG THE SONS OF MEN HAS DEPARTED JAN CHRISTIAAN SMUTS.

President Coolidge's secretary came up the hill. He spoke to Bolling and said the President offered the aid of all government departments in funeral arrangements, but he was told the widow would wait until Nellie McAdoo arrived before making plans. That evening electric-light signs in most cities were dimmed, and radio fans twirling their dials and manipulating their headsets found no programs of any kind were going out on the air.

The next day, Monday:

BY THE PRESIDENT OF THE UNITED STATES OF AMERICA:
A PROCLAMATION:
To the People of the United States:
    The death of Woodrow Wilson, President of the United States from

March 4, 1913, to March 4, 1921 . . . deprives the country of a most distinguished citizen and is an event which causes universal and genuine sorrow. . . . In testimony of the respect in which his memory is held by the Government and people of the United States, I do hereby direct that the flags of the White House and of the several Departmental buildings be displayed at half staff for a period of thirty days, and that suitable military and naval honors under orders of the Secretary of War and of the Secretary of the Navy may be rendered on the day of the funeral.

Done at the City of Washington . . . In the year of Our Lord one thousand nine hundred and twenty-four, and of the Independence of the United States of America one hundred and forty-eight.

CALVIN COOLIDGE

In the Senate it was voted that all business, including all committe meetings and investigations—which included the one concerning Teapot Dome—be suspended for three days. A delegation of Senators was appointed to attend the funeral. The Senate adjourned.

One of the Senators named as a member of the funeral delegation did not get home to his residence at 1765 Massachusetts Avenue, N.W., until several hours after the adjournment. He found waiting for him a note delivered by a Postal Telegraph boy. On the envelope was attached a Postal Telegraph sticker requesting an immediate reply. The note was handwritten. It said:

My dear Sir:

I note in the papers that you have been designated by the Senate of the U.S. as one of those to attend Mr. Wilson's funeral.

As the funeral is private and not official and realizing that your presence would be embarrassing to you and unwelcome to me I write to request that you do *not* attend.

Yours truly,
Edith Bolling Wilson

The Senator wrote back in his own hand:

My dear Madam:

I have just received your note, in which you say that the funeral services of Mr. Wilson are to be private and not official and that my presence would be unwelcome to you. When the Senate Committee was appointed I had no idea that the Committee was expected to attend the private services at the home and I had supposed that the services at the church were to be public.

You may rest assured that nothing could be more distasteful to me than to do anything which by any possibility could be embarrassing to you. I have the honor to be

Very truly

yours,

H. C. Lodge

Nellie and McAdoo arrived in Washington, the Rolls-Royce meeting them at the station. The young woman was in constant tears. Just before her father's death, the malodorous E. L. Doheny of Teapot Dome fame had revealed that he, Doheny, had paid McAdoo $250,000 in legal fees over a period of some years. The revelation was working to shatter McAdoo's hopes of ever becoming President, and along with newspaper articles about the death in S Street appeared stories headlined FEAR MC ADOO CANDIDACY DOOMED. Panic-stricken Washington supporters of McAdoo flocked to S Street as soon as he arrived, and in the library one floor beneath the room in which his father-in-law died McAdoo held frightened conferences. Completely undone, he dictated telegrams to all points saying "skunks" and "calumniators" were trying to smear him. This talk of the forthcoming nominating conventions just half a year off, and the elections later in the year, seemed completely sacrilegious to the mistress of the house, and she savagely lashed out at McAdoo and Nellie, saying in a rage that the young woman "cared more about getting her husband elected President than she does about her dead father." The statement was untrue and very unkind, but Edith was far from a responsible person in the grief which flung her into headlong spells of unrestrained weeping. The control she had shown ever since the morning the *Mayflower* halted on the prairie outside Wichita fell from her and the accumulated strain of the long years came pouring out. No one had ever seen her like this. Distraught, she said things that erected a wall between herself and Nellie that would never be torn down. She was also bitter at Margaret's attitude. Margaret, interested in religion all her life, was at the time involved in a study of Christian Science, which led her to wear a smile as she went around the house telling callers that death was really an illusion and that there was hence no reason to grieve for her father.

The funeral plans were completed on Tuesday. They had thought of burial in Staunton, the birthplace, but none of his flesh and blood were there and in fact he had lived there only one year of his life. There was a family plot in Columbia, South Carolina, where his mother and father were; but a few years earlier, when his sister, Aunt Annie Howe, was buried there, Edith remembered that he had said that the sister's body now occupied the last free space. And once on a ride into Virginia he had said that he did not think he would want to lie in Arlington. So they decided interment would be in the crypt of the Cathedral of St. Peter and St. Paul, commonly called Washington Cathedral. Not completed, but an immense and beautiful church, it stood atop Mount Saint Alban, the highest elevation in Washington. Stones from Canterbury were in it, and the Bishop's formal seat was from the ruins of Glastonbury. It was decided there would be a brief service at the house and then the body would be taken to the Cathedral and its Bethlehem Chapel, where there would be room for three hundred invited guests. This would not be a state funeral, and the body would not lie in state. The funeral would be on Wednesday, February 6.

That day was cloudy, wet, cold. The sunshine of Sunday morning was gone, and it was overcoat weather and a time to wear galoshes. At sunrise that morning, by order of the Secretaries of War and Navy, guns began to fire, every half hour on the half hour, at every United States Army post, at every Navy yard or station. They would continue pounding all day at the half-hour intervals, and at sunset forty-eight gun salutes would be discharged. All regimental colors and standards were draped, officers wore mourning bands, and crape was on sword hilts. The foreign embassies and consulates all had their flags at half staff, all save for the German Embassy, where the Ambassador announced that as his government had instructed him to take no official part in this burial of an unofficial person, he would not put the German flag down. Washington seethed at this slight by the recent enemy, and a former U.S. sailor studying at Georgetown University climbed up the Embassy porte-cochere and hung an American flag there. Everyone who saw the flag applauded the gesture, but the police were called by the Embassy and they removed the flag. A policeman took up station in front of the building to guard against any disturbances. But the German attitude drew a violent reaction, and in Wall Street many bankers said that because of the matter they doubted a proposed loan to the Weimar Republic would be made.

A woman member of the German Reichstag, visiting America, made a public appeal that the loan go through, that German children not be forced to suffer because of the faux pas.

At eight in the morning, troops were paraded at all service posts, and the Presidential Proclamation of mourning was read out. In Washington, the President suggested to his Cabinet members that it be made clear to all government employees that although they could not officially be released from their duties for the funeral of an unofficial person, no work would be expected after lunch. The New York Stock Exchange announced trading would end at twelve-thirty. At that hour, too, Washington's school children were released from classes after standing in silence for five minutes.

By noon the Cathedral grounds were jammed with upward of fifty thousand persons. Most of the people had umbrellas, for alternately snow and rain came down from the leaden dark skies, Many sat upon newspapers laid on the soaked grass. Some brought sandwiches and ate lunch in the rain.

A little after noon it was announced that Senator Lodge, suffering from a sore throat, would not be able to attend the funeral. "No alarm is felt over Senator Lodge's illness by members of his family," said a spokesman from the Senator's office.°

During that morning, also, McAdoo telephoned Joe Tumulty°° and learned no invitation to the funeral had been received at the Tumulty home. McAdoo said, "I'm going to see that you're invited," and shortly afterward Altrude Gordon Grayson telephoned Tumulty and said that "of course" Tumulty and his wife would be expected.

Upstairs in S Street, in the bedroom, the body lay upon a couch by the window. Dr. Edward P. Davis of Philadelphia, a college classmate and the man who ten years earlier had the task of telling the President of the United States that the former Miss Elly Lou Axson of Rome, Georgia, was dying, stared down into the face he first had seen when both were boys at Princeton so many years ago.

° Chief Justice William Howard Taft's office also announced that illness would prevent his attendance. However, the decision was made upon the recommendation of Cary Grayson following an examination at Taft's home.

°° Who, it is interesting to know, had years earlier advised McAdoo to have nothing to do with E. L. Doheny.

It was extraordinary, Dr. Davis thought to himself, the way his friend looked. For he looked young now. Young. The hair seemed prematurely gray for such a young face. "The lines of care, of anxiety and weakness had disappeared. The outlines of the face were smooth and beautiful. It was as if a distant sunrise had touched the features."

Below, flowers were ranged all around the library and drawing room, and on the tables there were eight thousand messages of condolence. (Three years earlier, leaving the White House, he had received just 124 telegrams.) The services at the house would be at three; a little before that hour the police admitted through the ropes blocking the street those cars whose occupants bore invitations. Crowds stood in the slow-falling snow for blocks in all directions, and already along Massachusetts Avenue up toward the Cathedral tens of thousands of people were waiting behind lines of infantrymen and marines standing at evenly spaced intervals. At the Grayson house, the doctor came out with Altrude, and a reporter asked, "How do you feel?" Earlier, Grayson had made a formal statement to the press: "In sick days and well, I have never known such singleminded devotion to duty as he saw it against all odds, such patience and forbearance with adversity, and finally such resignation to the inevitable. I once read an inscription in a Southern country church yard. It said: 'He was unseduced by flattery, unawed by opinion, undismayed by disaster. He faced life with antique courage, and death with Christian hope.' These words, better than any words of mine, describe Woodrow Wilson." Now to the reporter asking how he felt, Grayson said, "Oh, I am all right. But I don't mean that exactly. I'm still under the strain of it all. That is keeping me going. But I can't really feel all right when I have lost my closest friend for the past twelve years. The fact that I can't call the nurse up there in the morning or run in there to see him has left an awful emptiness. I miss it now." As he spoke, the batteries at Fort Myer across the Potomac fired. Guns pumped also from Governors Island, and at Gordon, Dix, Carson, Shafter, Upton—all the posts. At sea, the dull thunder of the destroyers and dreadnoughts rolled across the February waves.

At fifteen minutes to three the President and First Lady stepped into their limousine for the short drive to S Street. When they arrived, it was nearly time for the services to begin. The body was in the drawing room in a closed black casket, and the guests were standing in the library and along the stairway. When the President entered the house, the drawing-room doors were opened and the guests filed in and sat down. The shades were drawn on the windows facing the street. It was just three o'clock. In Washington the streetcar motormen and conductors got out of their vehicles and stepped into the streets and took off their hats. Independence Hall's tower bell in Philadelphia began to toll. People in New York's department stores came to silent attention. Church bells sounded in Chicago. Detroit's traffic came to a halt. In the nation's large railroad stations Taps came over the loudspeaker systems. All telegraph service everywhere in the country halted. Outside in S Street the people were unmoving and the motorcycle policemen switched off their noisy engines. In Madison Square Garden both the people inside for a memorial service and the overflow standing in the street outside were motionless. Theaters in every city the country over interrupted performances. In the auditorium of Montana Deaconess School in Helena, a fourteen-year-old boy sounded Taps on his cornet as all the children, the youngest six years old, sang the words. In the front of the room where they would pass by it before their assembly was dismissed, a flag-draped picture of Woodrow Wilson looked out at them.

Once in S Street he had said that he missed the bonging of the White House's many clocks. He had liked that. So Edith had had made for him a magnificent grandfather's clock that would loudly ring every fifteen minutes. It stood at the second-floor stair landing. Now in S Street the last reverberations of the clock ringing the hour sounded throughout the house. The Reverend James Taylor of Central Presbyterian Church said, "'The Lord is my shepherd . . .'" Before the minister, dimly lit by the soft wall lights, a small spray of flowers sat atop the black steel of the casket. Orchids, black orchids, from Edith. On the wall hung a copy of Bouguereau's Madonna, done by Ellen. Behind the seated people, from the stairs, came the sound of Edith sobbing.

The Reverend Sylvester Beach of Princeton University prayed, then, that there would be divine aid to help the world to a realization of the vision of a world at peace that had been seen by this

dead man before them. He asked that there would be consolation
for the family.

Outside, snow mixed with the rain falling upon the thousands
around the house, on the policemen, on the eight servicemen—
soldiers, sailors and marines—who would carry the casket to the
black hearse, on the men and women standing on the muddy slopes
across from the house.

Bishop James Freeman of the Washington Cathedral, holding
in his hand the khaki-bound Bible of the dead man, said, "Now
unto him that is able to keep you from falling, and present you
faultless before the presence of His glory and with exceeding joy;
to the only wise God, our Savior, be glory and majesty, dominion
and power, both now and evermore. Amen." The clock chimed the
quarter hour: three-fifteen.

The three clergymen went down the aisle between the people
seated at right and left and down the stairs through the opened
doors and out into the snow and rain. They took off their hats and
stood in a line. Utter silence attended them. The eight servicemen,
all young, the soldiers in khaki, the sailors in blue jackets, the marines in field green, went up the stairs and took the casket and
came down, passing on both upward and downward journeys the
sobbing widow. As the boys came through the door with their
burden, almost every man in the street except the saluting servicemen joined with the clergymen in standing bareheaded. The spray
of orchids moved up and down with the movement of the black
steel coffin. There was no sound but the clicking of press and movie
cameras.

The hearse driver started his motor and when the casket was
inside moved down the hill a short distance. Another car pulled up
directly in front of Number 2340. The widow came out on the arm
of John Randolph Bolling. She wore a plain black cloth coat with
lynx cuffs and collar. Her mourning veil was square and bordered
by a three-inch band of crape. It completely covered her features.
Behind her came McAdoo with Nellie on one arm and Margaret
on the other, both sisters also wearing heavy black veils. Then
came the guests: the President and First Lady, the honorary pall-
bearers ex-Secretary Daniels, ex-Secretary Baker, ex-Secretary Houston, ex-Secretaries Redfield, Meredith, Gregory, Payne, Senator

Glass, Bernard Baruch, Jesse Jones, General Tasker Bliss, Cleveland Dodge, Dr. Davis and Dr. Hiram Woods—these last three representing the Class of '79—some other old friends. The Cabinet came out, and the Senators, and the household servants, and even two men from Keith's Theatre, doormen who had been kind and understanding. The names of the passengers for the waiting limousines were read out. After the servants and the doormen were assigned their places in the cars, the names of Mr. and Mrs. Joseph Tumulty were spoken.

The procession got under way, a slow rolling line of cumbersome high-roofed black automobiles heading down S Street's hill. By the first car, the hearse, marched servicemen. Other servicemen, the soldiers and marines standing in a two-mile line to the Cathedral, one by one came to a salute as the hearse reached them. For as far as could be seen hands came up and stayed at foreheads for a moment and then dropped. No sidearms of any kind were worn, and there were no muffled kettledrums, no gun caissons, no horse with empty saddle and stirrups reversed, no band to play a dirge. At the junction of S Street and Massachusetts Avenue some young American Legionnaires stood with standards and flags, the only color in the gray afternoon.

They turned up the Avenue and headed northwest, the crawling line of cars going no faster than the slow march of the boys by the hearse, the unbroken line of people under the black dripping umbrellas motionless save for those women—and men, also—who reached under their coats and brought out handkerchiefs. Fort Myer's guns thudded.

In New York, Rabbi Stephen S. Wise spoke to the crowd jamming Madison Square Garden. His words were carried out to the overflow in the street by transmitters. He touched for a bitter moment on those who opposed the League: "May history compassionately embalm in oblivion the names and deeds of those who, to punish your and my leader—the hope-bringer of mankind—struck him down and broke the heart of the world!" He tried to go on, but a terrible roar, a great swelling snarl, reached up to him. "God forgive them!" he shouted, but he could not be heard. Outside in the street the overflow crowd joined in and the frightening sound rolled in to meet that of the people inside. Rabbi Wise shouted again, "God forgive them!" In a soft hat wet with New York's rain a small, slim man looked on: Colonel House, uninvited to the funeral.

Up Massachusetts Avenue wound the silent procession approaching Mount Saint Alban and the towering arches of the Cathedral of St. Peter and St. Paul. The sound of the tolling bells came through the wet air to meet the cars, and when the hearse turned into the spacious grounds the bells played *Nearer, My God, to Thee.*

The tires of the cars whispered through the slush on the winding road leading past the gardens to the church itself. It was maintained by the Protestant Episcopal Cathedral Foundation, but all Christian denominations made use of it, for it had no congregation of its own. It was meant to be, and was, a church of prayer for all groups. Under dripping cedars the fifty thousand who waited pressed forward, their umbrellas making a solid black mass.

The hearse stopped, the other cars halting behind it. The eight boys reached in for the casket and drew it out and took it up and in step marched with it to the door of the Bethlehem Chapel. Over that entrance, in raised stone lettering, was: *The Way to Peace.*

The boys carried their burden down the narrow corridor leading to the chapel sepulchre, passing thousands and thousands of banked flowers, the greatest floral display Washington had ever seen, flowers from the Republic of Armenia, Gouvernement Belge, Embasada Mexico, flowers "with the homage of the President and Government of the French Republic," the People of Poland, the Girl Scouts of America, the King of Siam, and an old woman who lived along Conduit Road to whom a President and a First Lady had once given a set of knitting needles in appreciation for a scarf she had knit and sent to the White House. In front of the entrance to the chapel was a big American flag made of flowers, the tribute of a group of Confederate veterans. Pinned to it was a little silk Stars and Bars.

The eight servicemen went in and put the casket down in the center aisle in front of a beautifully carved altar of the Nativity. Tall waxen candles gleamed and dim light came through the high Gothic windows, each showing in tinted glass a part of the story of the Nativity. The invited guests for whom there had been no room in the house sat in their seats on either side of the aisle; those who had been in S Street filed in and sat down also. The organist, Warren F. Johnson, who had been a White House Executive Office employee, played Chopin's Funeral March. Outside, transmitters brought the sound to the people; radio stations brought it to listeners gathered by their sets in every part of the country and to the now silent throng inside and outside Madison Square Garden. Above the waiting tomb in the very heart of the crypt shone a tri-cornered lamp symbolic of the Trinity.

The choir came down the corridor and entered and stood in the aisle with the casket, some at the head, some at the foot. Bishop Freeman said, "'I am the Resurrection and the life, saith the Lord. He that believeth in me, though he were dead, yet shall he live: and whosoever liveth and believeth in me, shall never die.'" The Reverend Taylor said, "'The days of our age are three score years and ten, and though men be so strong that they come to four score years, yet is their strength then but labor and sorrow; so soon passeth it away and we are gone.'" Outside the church and outside the District of Columbia and many miles away, the prayer was heard; in the Cathedral grounds people sank to their knees in the slush and men took off their hats and prayed even as the dampness of the fading gray day came drifting down in soft snow to wet their heads and drop upon their shoulders.

Bishop Freeman said, "'So when this corruptible shall have put on incorruption, and this mortal shall have put on immortality, then shall be brought to pass the saying that is written, Death is swallowed up in victory. O Death! Where is thy sting? O Grave! Where is thy victory?'"

The organ notes sounded faintly a favorite, favorite hymn. The choir sang:

> "Day is dying in the west,
>   Heaven is touching earth with rest.
> Wait and worship while the night
>   Sets her evening lamps alight."

The singing ended, and in the chapel and through the transmitters outside and the radios came the Apostles' Creed recited by clergymen and mourners.

They recited the Lord's Prayer and Bishop Freeman prayed for the family. Then with raised hand he pronounced the benediction.

Those members of the choir between the altar and the head of the casket moved past the casket and joined the other members at the foot and went down the aisle and out into the corridor. Their chanting grew softer and softer in the distance, so that finally only a gentle hint wound back to the hearing of the people sitting in the chapel with the black coffin and the orchids: "That we may live and sing to Thee, Alleluia," and a far-off final "Amen." It was dusk outside.

The organ played the Recessional softly. President Coolidge arose and walked out and the other mourners followed him. Only the family and Cary Grayson were left with the eight servicemen at attention in the rear of the room and the workmen who would move away the marble slab in the aisle that covered the entrance to the underground cavern where the casket would rest. Those workmen stepped forward and moved the great heavy slab and put it to one side. The boys came and took the casket and put it on the beams that would lower it down many feet into the vault's darkness.

Edith stood at the foot of the casket by the open hole in the floor which the slab had covered and looked up toward the altar. The girls were with her, and McAdoo, and Cary Grayson. Bishop Freeman said, "Man that is born of woman hath but a short time to live, and is full of misery. He cometh up and is cut down like a flower. He fleeth as it were a shadow, and never continueth in one stay. In the midst of life we are in death.'" He recited Tennyson's *Crossing the Bar:*

> "Sunset and evening star,
> And one clear call for me!
>
> Twilight and evening bell,
> And after that the dark."

Slowly the casket began to sink down into the vault, the orchids riding down with it and with the simple plate on it saying Woodrow Wilson Born December 28 1856 Died February 3 1924. Bishop Freeman's hand moved slowly through the dim candlelight. "'Earth to earth, ashes to ashes, dust to dust.'"

Outside, standing by the chapel door, Sergeant Frank Withey of the Third United States Cavalry lifted the bugle with which he had sounded Taps for the Unknown Soldier at Arlington and raised it to his lips to send into the darkness of this day once again the notes he played then.

> Day is done.
> Gone the sun.
> Goeth day, cometh night,
> And a star,
> Leadeth all,
> Speedeth all,
> To their rest.

Edith turned and headed blindly toward the door. McAdoo took her arm and led her out, and the two girls trailed after them. The clergymen went out. The eight boys went out.

Only the workmen stood waiting for the casket to finish its slow trip to the vault so that they might move the great slab back into position, only they and one other: Cary Grayson. *"Please take good care of Woodrow,"* Ellen had said. The casket went down and vanished from view.

Not long afterward, Edith Wilson in her home at S Street came across a little change purse that her husband had always carried in his pocket. She opened it and saw that in a special closed section of the purse there was an object carefully wrapped in tissue paper. She undid the paper and shook it out. Something fell into her hand. At once she knew what it was she held. It was the dime the little boy handed up as the train pulled out of Billings, Montana.

*Acknowledgments,
bibliography, and notes*

About the photographs

If not otherwise credited, all photographs are from the Collections of the Library of Congress.

Acknowledgments

I am indebted to, and want to thank, those who offered me recollections and insights concerning Woodrow Wilson and the people close to him. Those who knew the President include Mrs. Eleanor Wilson McAdoo, Francis B. Sayre, David Lawrence, Mrs. J. Borden Harriman and Henry P. Thomas.

Others giving generous aid include Cary T. Grayson, Jr., Joseph P. Tumulty, Jr., Alden Hatch, and Miss Katherine Brand, who before her retirement was in charge of the Woodrow Wilson Collection of the Library of Congress.

I was extremely fortunate to have steady access to two scholars active in the Wilson field for many years: Drs. John Wells Davidson and David W. Hirst of The Papers of Woodrow Wilson sponsored by the Woodrow Wilson Foundation and Princeton University.

The staff of the Manuscripts Division of the Library of Congress was courtesy itself. I must particularly single out two gentlemen whose interest and assistance made my months in the Library more fruitful than they otherwise might have been. They are Roger Preston and Joseph Sullivan.

I must also express my thanks that there exist the New York Public Library, the Butler Library of Columbia University, and the Ferguson Library of Stamford, Connecticut.

Bibliography

Adams, Samuel Hopkins. *Incredible Era*. Boston: Houghton Mifflin Company, 1939.

Allen, Frederick Lewis. *Only Yesterday: An Informal History of the Nineteen-Twenties*. New York and London: Harper and Brothers, 1931.

Alsop, Em. Bowles (ed.). *The Greatness of Woodrow Wilson*. New York and Toronto: Rinehart & Company, 1956.

Annin, Robert Edwards. *Woodrow Wilson, A Character Study*. New York: Dodd, Mead & Company, 1924.

Anonymous (Clinton Wallace Gilbert). *The Mirrors of Washington*. New York and London: G. P. Putnam's Sons, 1921.

Anonymous (Nellie M. Scanlon). *Boudoir Mirrors of Washington*. Chicago, Philadelphia and Toronto: John C. Winston Company, 1923.

Bailey, Thomas A. *Woodrow Wilson and the Lost Peace*. New York: The Macmillan Company, 1944.

———. *Woodrow Wilson and the Great Betrayal*. New York: The Macmillan Company, 1945.

Baillie, Hugh. *High Tension*. New York: Harper and Brothers, 1959.

Baker, Ray Stannard (ed.). *The Public Papers of Woodrow Wilson: War and Peace*. New York and London: Harper and Brothers, 1927.

———. *American Chronicle*. New York: Charles Scribner's Sons, 1945.

Baruch, Bernard M. *The Public Years*. New York: Holt, Rinehart and Winston, 1960.

Bell, H.C.F. *Woodrow Wilson and the People*. Garden City, N.Y.: Doubleday & Company, Inc., 1945.

Bender, Robert J. *"W.W.": Scattered Impressions of a Reporter Who for Eight Years "Covered" the Activities of Woodrow Wilson*. New York: United Press Associations, 1924.

Blum, John M. *Joe Tumulty and the Wilson Era*. Boston: Houghton Mifflin Company, 1951.

Bolitho, William. *Twelve Against the Gods: The Story of Adventure.* New York: Simon and Schuster, 1929.

Bonsal, Stephen. *Unfinished Business.* Garden City, N.Y.: Doubleday & Company, Inc., 1944.

Bradford, Gamaliel. *The Quick and the Dead.* Boston: Houghton Mifflin Company, 1929.

Butler, Nicholas Murray. *Across the Busy Years.* New York: Charles Scribner's Sons, 1935.

Clapper, Olive Ewing. *Washington Tapestry.* New York and London: Whittlesey House, McGraw-Hill Book Co., Inc., 1946.

Colby, Bainbridge. *The Close of Woodrow Wilson's Administration and the Final Years,* an address delivered before the Missouri Historical Society, St. Louis, Mo., April 28, 1930. New York: M. Kennerley, 1930.

Connally, Tom, as told to Alfred Steinberg. *My Name Is Tom Connally.* New York: Thomas Y. Crowell Company, 1954.

Cox, James M. *Journey Through My Years.* New York: Simon and Schuster, 1946.

Cranston, Ruth. *The Story of Woodrow Wilson.* New York: Simon and Schuster, 1945.

Creel, George. *Rebel at Large: Recollections of Fifty Crowded Years.* New York: G. P. Putnam's Sons, 1947.

Daniels, Jonathan. *The End of Innocence.* Philadelphia and New York: J. B. Lippincott Company, 1954.

Daniels, Josephus. *The Life of Woodrow Wilson.* Chicago, Philadelphia and Toronto: John C. Winston Company, 1924.

———. *The Wilson Era: Years of War and After 1917-23.* Chapel Hill: University of North Carolina Press, 1946.

Dunn, Arthur Wallace. *From Harrison to Harding.* New York: G. P. Putnam's Sons, 1922.

Eaton, William Dunseath, Harry C. Read and Edmund McKenna. *Woodrow Wilson, His Life and Work.* Chicago: J. Thomas, 1924.

Elliott, Margaret Randolph. *My Aunt Louisa and Woodrow Wilson.* Chapel Hill: University of North Carolina Press, 1944.

Garraty, John A. *Woodrow Wilson: A Great Life in Brief.* New York: Alfred A. Knopf, 1956.

———. *Henry Cabot Lodge.* New York: Alfred A. Knopf, 1953.

George, Alexander L. and Juliette L. *Woodrow Wilson and Colonel*

House: a Personality Study. New York: John Day Company, Inc., 1956.

Grayson, Cary T. *Woodrow Wilson: An Intimate Memoir.* New York: Holt, Rinehart and Winston, 1960.

Grew, Joseph C. *Turbulent Era: A Diplomatic Record of 40 Years.* Boston: Houghton Mifflin Company, 1952.

Groves, Charles S. *Henry Cabot Lodge the Statesman.* Boston: Small, Maynard and Co., 1925.

Harriman, Mrs. J. Borden. *From Pinafores to Politics.* New York: Henry Holt and Company, 1923.

Hatch, Alden. *Edith Bolling Wilson: First Lady Extraordinary.* New York: Dodd, Mead & Company, 1961.

Helm, Edith Benham. *The Captains and the Kings.* New York: G. P. Putnam's Sons, 1954.

Henry, Laurin L. *Presidential Transitions.* Washington: The Brookings Institute, 1960.

Hoover, Herbert. *Memoirs of Herbert Hoover,* Vol. 2: *The Cabinet and the Presidency, 1920-33.* New York: The Macmillan Company, 1952.

———— *The Ordeal of Woodrow Wilson.* New York: McGraw-Hill Book Co., Inc., 1958.

Hoover, Irving Hood. *Forty-two Years in the White House.* Boston and New York: Houghton Mifflin Company, 1934.

House, Edward M. *The Intimate Papers of Colonel House.* Arranged as a Narrative by Charles Seymour, 4 vols. Boston and New York: Houghton Mifflin Company, 1926-28.

Houston, David F. *Eight Years with Wilson's Cabinet, 1913 to 1920: with a Personal Estimate of the President,* 2 vols. Garden City, N.Y.: Doubleday, Page & Company, 1926.

Hulbert, Mary (Allen). *The Story of Mrs. Peck, an Autobiography.* New York: Minton, Balch & Company, 1933.

Hull, Cordell. *The Memoirs of Cordell Hull,* 2 vols. New York: The Macmillan Company, 1948.

Jaffray, Elizabeth. *Secrets of the White House.* New York: Cosmopolitan Book Corporation, 1927.

Johnson, Gerald W., with the collaboration of the editors of *Look* magazine. *Woodrow Wilson, the Unforgettable Figure Who Has Returned to Haunt Us.* New York and London: Harper & Brothers, 1944.

—— *Incredible Tale*. New York and London: Harper & Brothers, 1950.

Kerney, James. *The Political Education of Woodrow Wilson*. New York and London: The Century Company, 1926.

Kohlsaat, H. G. *From McKinley to Harding*. New York and London: Charles Scribner's Sons, 1923.

Lane, Franklin K. *The Letters of Franklin K. Lane*. Boston and New York: Houghton Mifflin Company, 1922.

Latham, Earl (ed.). *The Philosophy and Politics of Woodrow Wilson*. Chicago: University of Chicago Press, 1958.

Lawrence, David. *The True Story of Woodrow Wilson*. New York: George H. Doran Company, 1924.

Lodge, Henry Cabot. *The Senate and the League of Nations*. New York and London: Charles Scribner's Sons, 1925.

Longworth, Alice Roosevelt. *Crowded Hours*. New York and London: Charles Scribner's Sons, 1933.

Marx, Rudolph, M.D. *The Health of the Presidents*. New York: G. P. Putnam's Sons, 1960.

McAdoo, Eleanor Randolph, in collaboration with Margaret Y. Gaffey. *The Woodrow Wilsons*. New York: The Macmillan Company, 1937.

McAdoo, William Gibbs. *Crowded Years*. Boston and New York: Houghton Mifflin Company, 1931.

McKinley, Silas Bent. *Woodrow Wilson*. New York: Frederick Praeger, Inc., 1957.

Nevins, Allan. *Henry White: Thirty Years of American Diplomacy*. New York and London: Harper & Brothers, 1930.

—— *The United States in a Chaotic World, a Chronicle of International Affairs, 1918-33*. (Chronicles of America Series.) New Haven: Yale University Press, 1950.

Parks, Lillian Rogers, in collaboration with Frances Spatz Leighton. *My Thirty Years Backstairs at the White House*. New York: Fleet Publishing Company, 1961.

Reid, Edith. *Woodrow Wilson: The Caricature, the Myth and the Man*. London and New York: Oxford University Press, 1934.

Sayre, Francis B. *Glad Adventure*. New York: The Macmillan Company, 1957.

Schriftgiesser, Karl. *The Gentleman from Massachusetts: Henry Cabot Lodge*. Boston: Little, Brown & Company, 1944.

Shackleton, Robert. *The Book of Washington*. Philadelphia: The Penn Publishing Company, 1922.

Slosson, Preston William. *The Great Crusade and After: 1914-28*. New York: The Macmillan Company, 1930.

Smith, Arthur D. Howden. *Mr. House of Texas*. New York and London: Funk & Wagnalls Company, 1940.

Smith, Ira R. T., with Joe Alex Morris. *Dear Mr. President . . . The Story of Fifty Years in the White House Mail Room*. New York: Julian Messner, Inc., 1949.

Smith, Rixey, and Norman Beasley Longman. *Carter Glass: A Biography*. New York and Toronto: Longmans, Green and Company, 1939.

Starling, Edmund W., and Thomas Sugrue. *Starling of the White House*. New York: Simon and Schuster, 1946.

Stein, Charles W. *The Third-Term Tradition: Its Rise and Collapse in American Politics*. New York: Columbia University Press, 1943.

Steinberg, Alfred. *Woodrow Wilson*. New York: G. P. Putnam's Sons, 1961.

Stoddard, Henry L. *As I Knew Them: Presidents and Politics from Grant to Coolidge*. New York and London: Harper & Brothers, 1927.

Sullivan, Mark. *Our Times: The United States 1900-25*, Vol. 5: *Over Here, 1914-18*. New York and London: Charles Scribner's Sons, 1933.

————. *Ibid.*, Vol. 6: *The Twenties*. New York and London: Charles Scribner's Sons, 1935.

Thomas, Charles M. *Thomas Riley Marshall*. Oxford, Ohio: The Mississippi Valley Press, 1939.

Tumulty, Joseph P. *Woodrow Wilson as I Know Him*. Garden City, N.Y., and Toronto: Doubleday, Page & Company, 1921.

Viereck, George Sylvester. *The Strangest Friendship in History: Woodrow Wilson and Colonel House*. New York: Liveright, 1932.

Walworth, Arthur. *Woodrow Wilson: American Prophet*. New York, London and Toronto: Longmans, Green and Company, 1958.

————. *Woodrow Wilson: World Prophet*. New York, London and Toronto: Longmans, Green and Company, 1958.

Watson, James E. *As I Knew Them.* Indianapolis and New York: The Bobbs-Merrill Company, 1936.

Wells, Wells (pseud.). *Wilson the Unknown.* New York: Charles Scribner's Sons, 1931.

White, William Allen. *Woodrow Wilson: The Man, His Times and His Task.* Boston and New York: Houghton Mifflin Company, 1924.

———. *Masks in a Pageant.* New York: The Macmillan Company, 1939.

Williams, Wythe. *The Tiger of France: Conversations with Clemenceau.* New York: Duell, Sloan and Pearce, 1949.

Wilson, Edith Bolling. *My Memoir.* Indianapolis and New York: The Bobbs-Merrill Company, 1938.

Winkler, John K. *Woodrow Wilson: The Man Who Lives On.* New York: The Vanguard Press, 1933.

MAGAZINES AND NEWSPAPERS

Quotations from magazines are indicated either in the text or Notes. For contemporary newspaper accounts of the events covered I have relied largely upon the Washington *Post*, New York *World*, and New York *Times*. I have also made use of Associated Press, United Press, and International News Service dispatches. It would have been a cumbersome business to cite these sources continually, and as I have generally interwoven accounts from the various papers and wire services, a difficult business also. For these reasons I have rarely mentioned which paper or wire service acted as source for any given incident. In almost every case, however, the report of the given incident appeared either on the day it took place or, more regularly, on the following day.

MANUSCRIPT COLLECTIONS

A great part of the contents of this book was garnered from the manuscript collections of the Library of Congress in Washington. Primarily, of course, I have made use of the Woodrow Wilson Collection. This consists of literally millions of items ranging from yellowed newspaper accounts of the clothing tastes of Mrs. Edith Galt to letters sent the ex-President in S Street by indignant relatives desiring money with which to effect a move to a neighborhood where the children could mix with a better class of playmates. In the collection, to name items that come readily to mind, are: the large manila envelope Senator Fall bore to the bedside of the President on December 5, 1919, with the scribbled writing of the First Lady upon it; hundreds of calling cards left at S Street when the former President was dying; many pictures of children named for the President and sent to the White House by proud parents; the reply of the Queen of England to the First Lady's "bread and butter" note sent after the visit to Buckingham Palace in 1918; an indignant account by John Randolph Bolling of how an architect overcharged for advice about constructing a home (which was never built) for occupancy after the President's term of office ended; flowers worn by Mrs. Galt to dinner with the President and later pressed and put away so that today, nearly half a hundred years later, the color is still true; bills for two and three dollars periodically submitted by a man who refinished the tips of billiard cues used by Mrs. Wilson and guests at S Street; a report by Cary Grayson describing blood tests given the late President (this to record for history that the extremely widespread story that Woodrow Wilson suffered from a venereal disease was untrue); a sadly disjointed letter dictated by the President to the First Lady early in his illness and thanking the Mayor and City Council of Carlisle, England, for honors granted; a series of violently worded letters dictated to John Randolph Bolling and signed by the ex-President but not sent at the behest of Mrs. Wilson (the letters might well have been found embarrassing if they ever appeared in print: "Dirty little liar" applied to the President of France was a typical example); a long exchange of notes with a man who wanted to put up a statue of Woodrow Wilson in the courtyard of an apartment house in the Bronx, New York (photos of proposed bust after bust were rejected by S Street, but finally after Woodrow Wilson's death the man did put up a bust which, with nose defaced, can still be seen in the Wilson Apartments across from DeVoe Park in the Bronx); and, finally, notes sent from the Library of Congress requesting the return of mystery novels long overdue.

The collection, for my purposes in covering this circumscribed portion of Mr. Wilson's life, can be broken down into three segments. First, there are nearly a score of enormous scrapbooks, each weighing more than fifty pounds and containing material impossible to classify under any single description. The books became the career of Mrs. Wilson's brother Bolling after the ex-President died. (Before his death, Bolling had worked on them when not handling the correspondence for his brother-in-law.) Bolling continued his labors on the books until well into the days of World War II. The material dates from about the time Mrs. Galt met the President but is largely concerned with the S Street period. Anything that appealed to the ex-President during his residence in S Street is there, as is material which seemed of value to Bolling or his sister. A copy of Mrs. Wilson's letter to Senator Lodge telling him his presence at the funeral was not desired is there; next to it is Lodge's reply. A picture published in a magazine of the '20's and showing a man who looked like the President wearing a pith helmet in a desert setting is in the books, along with a typed note by Bolling saying this is *not* Mr. Wilson. Numerous newspaper clippings are there; so is a long description of the ex-President's last illness, written by Bolling at his sister's direction. Also, invitations sent Mrs. Wilson for White House dinners in the '30's and '40's, Mrs. Wilson's ticket to the 1933 Kentucky Derby, and pictures taken by amateur photographers of Mr. Wilson on one or another of his auto rides. Neatly pasted in are the scores of many games of Canfield played by the Wilsons. At one point he was 50,000 points ahead of her.

Second, the collection contains all correspondence sent to the President during his terms of office, and all copies of letters by him.

Last, there are letters sent and received during the years in S Street. Mixed with the letters are a few such miscellaneous items as the President's badly typed—we must remember he had the use of only one hand—constitution for the Pure English Club, the purpose of which was to encourage residents of 2340 S Street to remind each other to use correct grammar at all times. (One speculates as to just what was in the ex-President's mind when he established the "Club.") The reader will know how heavily I have made use of the correspondence files.

At the Library of Congress will also be found the papers of most of the persons connected with Woodrow Wilson. Most important of all is the Ray Stannard Baker Collection, which holds the fruits of Baker's enormous researches into the President's life. Designated by Mr. Wilson as his official biographer, Baker continued his work for many years after the subject of his research had died. Baker's interviews with hundreds of persons who knew the President are of inestimable value, and the reader will see in the Notes how extensively I, like all who study Woodrow Wilson, have made use of Baker's papers. Other collections utilized include those of Tumulty, Creel, Daniels, Colby, Lansing, Hamlin, Long, Ike Hoover, McAdoo, Glass, Burleson, Newton D. Baker, Palmer, Edith Benham Helm, Hitchcock, and William Allen White. There is also an Edith Bolling Wilson collection of value, but by direction of Mrs. Wilson's will much of the material is locked in the Library vaults, where it will stay until fifteen years have passed from the time of her death. It is believed that much of this now-proscribed material consists of letters sent Mrs. Galt, as she then was, during the period of the President's courtship of her.

This book had its origin in the mind of Lawrence Hughes of William Morrow and Company on the morning of December 29, 1961. On that day the New York *Times*, as did nearly every paper in the country, carried in its columns the obituary of Edith Bolling Wilson.

On the day she died, December 28, she was two months past her eighty-ninth birthday. Edith had grown to be a very old lady indeed. Thirty-five years and more had passed since the day William McAdoo led her from the Bethlehem Chapel and the casket sinking slowly down into the vault.

In the first months after that day, in the spring of 1924, people who lived near the Cathedral grew accustomed to seeing each afternoon a woman in black, on foot, going up the hill upon which the Cathedral stands. Behind the woman slowly moved a beautiful new Rolls-Royce, a gift given her husband as a birthday present a few weeks before his death. After a time alone in the chapel, Edith would come out and enter the car, and her chauffeur would drive her home to S Street. At the house everything was just as it was on February 3, 1924. Everything, in fact, is still just as it was on that day. The sofas are the same, and the pictures, and the rugs, and even the bathroom plumbing.

It was years before Edith wore anything but black. It was not until 1928 that she set foot in the White House she had left in March of 1921. (Her return was to hear a Paderewski recital. She had always loved music.) By 1930 she allowed herself to attend social events regularly and put away her widow's garb. She traveled to Europe and the Orient and went to horse-race meets and Southern pageants. On December 8, 1941, she was at the Capitol at the invitation of Eleanor Roosevelt and sat next to her as Eleanor Roosevelt's husband asked for what Edith's had asked upon a misty April evening twenty-four years earlier.

By the 1950's her servants had grown accustomed to people in stores and delivery agencies saying, "Mrs. Woodrow Wilson! Is *she* still alive?" During those long years of widowhood, Edith first grew stouter, and then, as old ladies do, she became thin and fragile. At the end she was the very picture of the former Southern belle grown old and daintily old-fashioned. And yet she was still very recognizable as the Edith of long before. Although she was a thin little old lady, her passions were yet unquieted. Eighty-five years old, she could still refer to Henry Cabot Lodge as that "stinking snake." Fifteen years after the death of Franklin Roosevelt, a year before her own death, she could still raise her voice in anger when she talked of how Roosevelt had gotten hold of the desk Edith's husband used on the *George Washington* and had it transported to Hyde Park. Edith thought the desk should be at S Street; Roosevelt thought it should be at Hyde Park. "He said to me, 'You're not going to get it,' " Edith told people. "I told him he was nothing but a common thief, and I should have sued him for that desk." She did not appear to be joking.

For the memory of Woodrow Wilson, nothing was too much trouble. Through the long years she was always available for anyone dedicating a Woodrow Wilson Bridge or a Woodrow Wilson School, always ready to sit on the platform with the speakers. "This is for Woodrow," she told her hired companions and her friends, and regardless of the heat or cold or the length of the trip, she went to the dedication ceremonies. (On the day she died, which was coincidentally the 105th anniversary of her husband's birth, she was to have been present at the dedication of the Woodrow Wilson Bridge over the Potomac in Washington.) But there were never any interviews. "It is a recognized rule that I have nothing to say," she told countless reporters. Or, "I am never interviewed—I have no comment to make."

She played cards incessantly. With the after-dinner coffee her servants brought the bridge table. Probably not a day passed for decades that she did not play. And as time went by she played more and more. There were those who thought she did so because she was tired and bored and just killing time until she could also go to lie in the Washington Cathedral.

In the end, she did go to lie there. She died and the New York *Times* said she had been characterized as the "first woman President of the United States." (Edith would have blazed up at that. Woodrow Wilson was President, she would have said. And for her, that would have ended the argument.) In the Cathedral they carved her name into the stone of the wall forming a niche where her husband's body had been for some years since it was removed from the Bethlehem Chapel below. His sepulchre is very simple. There are personal flags of the President of the United States in the niche, and a flag carried by the first American troops to parade in London before going to France and action in 1917-18. The casket is encased in limestone with only his name upon it and a single ornament: a Crusader's Cross.

William Gibbs McAdoo pursued the Presidency relentlessly, but his highest elective office was Senator from California. Defeated for re-election to that post in 1938, he became head of the ironically named American President Lines. In the mid-1930's he and Nellie were divorced, and he later married a girl decades younger than he. In 1941, aged seventy-seven, he died.

Joseph Tumulty practiced law for many years. His ending was very sad. He fell into a mental decline and became a recluse. Eventually he was hospitalized and his friends said it was Edith Wilson's cruel treatment of him that had taken its toll of his mind. In the early 1950's a friend visited him in the hospital, taking a recently published book on the life of Woodrow Wilson with him. "Look, Joe," the friend said, "here's a picture of you and Wilson." Tumulty looked and his foot shot out and he kicked the book across the room. The doctor came and suggested that the friend leave. Shortly afterward Tumulty died. That was in 1954. Tumulty was seventy-four. Edith did not attend the funeral, nor did she send flowers or a card.

Jessie was forty-five years old in 1932 when she died following an operation. One of her sons, Francis B. Sayre, Jr., is Dean of the Cathedral where Jessie's father lies.

Margaret went from one job to another—stocks and bonds, public relations. She never married. One day in the New York Public Library she became engrossed in a book about an Indian mystic. She decided to go to India and study under him. She went to Pondicherry, French India, and became a member of the man's religious colony. She wore sandals and a flowing white robe and was fifty-seven when, in 1944, she fell ill and died.

Colonel House lived on in New York. He remained quiet, mannerly, subtle. Eminent persons dropped in to see him, but he never again exercised any real role in the world's doings. When he and his wife celebrated their fiftieth anniversary, the newspapers noted that among those not present was Edith Wilson. Aged seventy-nine, House died in 1938.

Cary Grayson left the Navy in 1928 and spent much of his time in running a racing stable he owned in company with Bernard Baruch. (Their most notable horse was Happy Argo, a successful campaigner of the '30's.) Grayson served as chairman of the Inaugural Committee for one of the Roosevelt inaugurations and as head of the Red Cross. He died in 1938 at the age of fifty-eight. His widow, the former Altrude Gordon, kept her friendship with Edith intact through the years.

Nellie Wilson McAdoo did not remarry after her divorce. As she grew older, her appearance grew very remindful of her father's. Her eyes, particularly, seemed startlingly like his. When people remark on the similarity, she gives a roguish smile that is very youthful and says, "Well, thank you! My father, after all, had beautiful eyes!" She is devoted to the memory of both her parents. She lives in California.

Notes

(The numbers in the left-hand columns refer to pages in this book.)

CHAPTER ONE

3—Medical details of Mrs. Wilson's last illness: Grayson, pp. 32-34.

3—"Take this bite, dear": Jaffray, pp. 48-49.

3—"Father looking well?": E. W. McAdoo, p. 300.

4—"Kill them both!": *ibid.*, p. 202.

4—Rapture on her face: *ibid.*, p. 205.

4—Cousin Florence incident: *ibid.*, pp. 209-10.

5—Promptly and efficiently: Grayson, p. 1.

5—Jumping out of dark corners: Parks, p. 133.

5, 6—Presidential imitations: E. W. McAdoo, pp. 26-27 and Elliott, p. 246.

6—The limerick is quoted by Virginius Dabney in Alsop, p. 18.

6—Proper and Vulgar Members: Jessica Wilson Sayre, quoted by R. S. Baker, Baker Papers.

6—Auto rides: I. H. Hoover, p. 61.

6—Mrs. Wilson and the slums: Jonathan Daniels, pp. 85-86.

6, 7—Her clothing: E. W. McAdoo, p. 55.

7—Her appearance and demeanor: Jonathan Daniels, p. 124.

7—Her paintings: Parks, p. 134.

7—The boy she had wanted: *ibid.*, p. 132.

7—Neck full and firm: E. W. McAdoo, p. 191.

8—Oatmeal, steak, ham, port: Starling, p. 39.

7, 8—Medical details on the President: Grayson, pp. 2-3, 80-81, and Grayson quoted by R. S. Baker, Baker Papers.

8—That he was hoping still: the letter was to Edward M. House.

8—The Philadelphia doctor was Edward Parker Davis.

9—Mrs. Wilson's death: Grayson, pp. 34-35, and Grayson quoted by R. S. Baker, Baker Papers.

9—White silk shawl: Jaffray, p. 50.

9—"Beyond what I can bear": the letter was to Mary Peck.

9—Roosevelt fear of breakdown: Jonathan Daniels, p. 137.

9—"I must not give way": Grayson, quoted by R. S. Baker, Baker Papers.

10—Mrs. Wilson's funeral: Stockton Axson, quoted by R. S. Baker, Baker Papers.

CHAPTER TWO

11—"Utterly alone": quoted by Stockton Axson and Helen Bones by R. S. Baker, Baker Papers.

11—Not have wanted it otherwise: Stockton Axson, quoted by Mary Hoyt, R. S. Baker, Baker Papers.

11—Sandy and Hamish: Parks, p. 135.

11—"Fig for anything that affects me": letter to Mary Peck.

11—If someone would assassinate him: Arthur D. H. Smith, p. 118.

12—Tiger she had once seen: quoted by Wilson, p. 67.

12, 13—Background of Edith Bolling Galt: Wilson, pp. 56-57.

13—Drove like an absolute madwoman: Mrs. J. Borden Harriman to author.

13—Meeting of Mrs. Galt and the President: Wilson, p. 56.

13—"Going to happen . . . ten minutes": quoted by Elliott, p. 273.

15f.—Details of the romance: Wilson, pp. 59ff.

18—Ease and informality of the way the President acted: Francis B. Sayre to author.

18, 20—McAdoo and House worries: Wilson, pp. 75-76.

19, 21—Final details of the romance: Wilson, pp. 76-78.

21—"The way she loved you": Stockton Axson, quoted by R. S. Baker, Baker Papers.

21—Answer to those prayers and "little shocked at first": Miss Lucy Smith and Miss Mary Smith, quoted by R. S. Baker, Baker Papers.

22—"Contact with Mrs. Galt": letter to Mrs. Edith Reid.

21, 22—Details of the engagement period: Wilson, pp. 79-85, and Starling, pp. 49-62.

22, 23—Wedding details: Wilson, pp. 85-86, and I. H. Hoover Papers.

24—"You beautiful doll": Starling, p. 62.

CHAPTER THREE

It does not seem appropriate to the author that he give citations for the facts outlined in the necessarily sketchy discussion of the President's doings up until the end of the World War. The incidents given and the outlooks expressed will all be familiar to anyone knowledgeable about the President's life. For others interested in deeper delving than afforded in this book, the author will take the liberty of recommending standard works on the subject, viz.: the books by Walworth, Cranston, McKinley and Steinberg. All are noted in the Bibliography of this book.

The details of the landing at Brest and the doings in the European cities are largely taken from contemporary newspaper clippings found in the scrapbooks of the Woodrow Wilson Collection. Exceptions are:

35—"Pour Mademoiselle Veelson": Miss Benham wrote on the incident to her future husband. The letter is in her Papers. (Helm Papers.)

36—"No one ever had such cheers": Bolitho, p. 346.

38—The First Lady was glad: Wilson, p. 206.

40—The First Lady thought: Wilson, p. 220.

40—"Greatest number of human minds . . .": Ellis was a correspondent for the Washington *Post*.

40—"A tragedy of disappointment": quoted by Creel, p. 206.

CHAPTER FOUR

41—No corps of assistants: I. H. Hoover Papers. Hoover, the White House usher, brought to Paris to take charge of the Presidential living quarters, was an avid letter writer. Copies of his letters from Paris are preserved in his Papers.

42—Parliament of Kouban, Archbishop of Trebizond: Hoover Papers.

42—Nervous little chuckle: Walworth, Vol. II, p. 243.

42—"Reduce the high cost of living": quoted by Daniels, *The Wilson Era*, p. 364.

42—Evening clothes for the meal: I. H. Hoover, p. 181.

43—In a spasmodic fashion: Marx, p. 315.

43—Many people overate, overdrank, overplayed, overloafed—he really overworked: quoted by Baker, *American Chronicle*, p. 386.

43—Year in Paris in one month: Daniels, *The Wilson Era*, p. 368.

43—"Only He Himself could do that": quoted by Mrs. Wilson, p. 245.

43, 44—"A selfish bunch": I. H. Hoover Papers.

44—"Get the willeys if this keeps up!": quoted by I. H. Hoover, Hoover Papers.

44—Dealing the cards: Helm, p. 110.

44—"Madmen": quoted by Walworth, Vol. II, p. 323.

44—"Miserable mischief-making": quoted by Baker, *American Chronicle*, p. 435.

44—"I don't give a damn for logic!" quoted by McKinley, p. 252.

44—Vigorously pull him to and fro: Baker, *American Chronicle*, p. 405.

44—Go to sleep standing up: Creel, p. 233. "Like Dickens' fat boy," the President added.

44—"If the Doctor notices it as I do": Hoover Papers.

44—"Take up our health routine again": quoted by Grayson, p. 85.

45—Headache attributed to Lloyd George: Marx, p. 315.

45—Medical details of the illness are from Grayson, p. 85, and Wilson, pp. 248-49. Grayson's suspicion of poison is mentioned in a letter from the doctor to Tumulty: Tumulty, p. 350.

46—"I will retire in good order": quoted by Wilson, p. 249.

46—A cook . . . a spoiled child: quoted by Walworth, Vol. II, p. 299.

46, 47—Changes in the President are noted by I. H. Hoover, pp. 98-99, Baker, *American Chronicle*, p. 430, and Herbert Hoover *Memoirs*, Vol. I, p. 468.

48—Baker's thoughts on the speech: Baker, *American Chronicle*, pp. 436-37.

49—The driver cried: Helm, p. 111.

49—"Two boys were killed in battle": quoted by Grayson, p. 84.

50—The two Senators who remained seated were Philander C. Knox (R-Pa.) and Medill McCormick (R-Ill.): Longworth, p. 286.

50—A sureness about the speaker: Stoddard, p. 513. Stoddard's general thoughts about the President were that he regarded himself as "the Messiah of his day, guarding his distinction with the avarice of a miser counting and recounting his gold to make certain that no one had robbed him of any of it." The journalist also held the President to be the "coldest man I ever looked upon": p. 487.

51—"Federation of the World": Longworth, p. 279. Mrs. Longworth went to stand in the crowd before the White House on the day the President returned there from Paris. She found the cheering for him to be of a "treble quality, as women predominated": p. 285. She did not cheer, however, but raised her hand to make the sign of the Evil Eye while she repeated,

"A murrain on him, a murrain on him, a murrain on him."
She was very much her father's daughter.
52—President refused to sit on the same platform with the Senator:
Daniels, *The Wilson Era*, p. 471. The President, in making
the refusal, wrote the church officials that he found it "impossible with respect to join in any exercises in which he takes
part or to associate myself with him in any way" (December
19, 1916).
52—Details on Lodge's and Roosevelt's opinions on the President:
Schriftgiesser, p. 293.
52n.—"Not a scholar": Lodge, p. 220.
53—"Contemptible . . . Cannot express my contempt": quoted by
Tumulty, pp. 378-79. "Asbestos two inches thick to hold it":
quoted by Walworth, Vol. II, p. 348. The remark was made to
Stockton Axson.
53—"Pearls before swine": McAdoo made his comment in a private
letter to the President.
54—Senators did not know the real thoughts of their constituents:
"Senators do not know what the people are thinking. They are
as far from the people, the great mass of the people, as I am
from Mars": quoted by Walworth, Vol. II, p. 338.
54—"Appeal to Caesar": quoted by Hatch, p. 199.
55—The conversation with Senator Watson: Watson, p. 201.
55, 56—The conversation with Kohlsaat: Kohlsaat, pp. 218-19.
56—"I must go": quoted by Grayson, p. 95.

CHAPTER FIVE

The details of the Western tour are largely garnered from clippings
taken from newspapers published in cities visited by the President. (The clippings are today in the scrapbooks kept by John
Randolph Bolling.) Many of them, however, do not indicate
what papers they are from. For this reason, and also because
accounts from several New York and Washington papers are
interwoven into the narrative, I have not cited the individual
publications in the Notes. Uncited details, then, are in every
case from newspapers published during the time of the trip in
1919.

57—"Pure and simple": quoted by Tumulty, p. 438.

58—"Fit for the work of tomorrow": *ibid.*, p. 439.
58—Tumulty's joke with "Little" Jackson: Wilson, p. 275. One of the few complimentary references to Tumulty in Mrs. Wilson's book is based on the incident: "Mr. Tumulty was a lot of fun on a trip."
58—"Such foolish questions": quoted by Hatch, p. 204.
60—"Put up or shut up": The phrase surprised many people. It was not in character for the President to use it.
62—Headache was continuous for most of the day: Grayson, p. 97. That the President was suffering was not a fact known to the reporters on the trip, nor, of course, to the audiences to whom he spoke.
63—Grayson felt the President would rest better: Grayson's desire that the President have a good night's rest did not at the time seem a matter of great importance to the reporters.
64, 65—The incident with the two hobos is described in Wilson, pp. 277-78, and Starling, pp. 148-49.
65f.—Grayson wrote later, "the journey was a prolonged agony of physical pain": Grayson, p. 96. Mrs. Wilson described it as "one long nightmare": Tumulty, p. 435.
66—The incident of the little boy with the dime is described in Wilson, p. 277, and Starling, p. 149.
66—"Evil thing with the holy name": quoted by Schriftgiesser, p. 311.
66—Speeches of Senators Johnson, McCormick and Borah: McKenna, pp. 161-62. The three were leading members of what was called the "Battalion of Death."
67—Necessary for him to try to sleep sitting up: Grayson, p. 97.
67—Forehead resting on the back of another chair: Wilson, p. 280.
67—The telegrams are in the Wilson Papers.
69—The IWW demonstration was not emphasized by the reporters in their stories but was described in a passing fashion. Details here are from "The Assassin of Wilson" by Louis Adamic in the *American Mercury* for October 1930.
70—Last ounce of strength forward: Daniels, *The Wilson Era*, p. 479.
70—"Lost his customary force and enthusiasm": quoted by Jonathan Daniels, p. 292.
70—In her eyes he looked good again: Hatch, p. 208.
70, 71—Meeting with IWW men: "The Assassin of Wilson." The

visit of the delegation was briefly reported in the newspapers.

71, 72—Breckinridge Long, Third Assistant Secretary of State, wrote in his diary that Bullitt "acted like the dishonorable, disreputable and detestable little rat he is." Long added that Secretary Lansing "should have made *some* statement when confronted by Bullitt's testimony": Long Papers.

72—Secretary Lansing returned from a day of bass fishing: Lansing Papers. The Secretary was not successful that day, and the catch was very small. However, he did some quoit pitching, leading one faction of the Fortnightly Club, of which he was president, against another faction. His faction was termed the Dutch, and in his capacity of leader of it, he was addressed as the Prince of Orange. Both fishing and quoit pitching were done on Galloo Island in Lake Ontario, New York.

72—"Read that . . . to act in this way!": quoted by Tumulty, p. 442.

72—"God help them, yes": Elliott, p. 297.

72—"I am the attorney for these children": quoted by Grayson, p. 97.

73—"They are killing me": quoted by Walworth, Vol. II, p. 367.

73—The visit to Janie is described in Grayson, pp. 7-8, and Elliott, pp. 298-99. Mrs. Elliott, however, appears in error when in her book she indicates that the President made the visit accompanied by police, escorts, etc. Actually, as Grayson points out in his book, the trip was made with no fanfare at all: "This episode went practically unnoticed in the daily press. Almost any other public man in the circumstances would have seen to it that the newspapermen got the story."

74—"His heart is turning to his young Ellen": Elliott, p. 299.

74, 75—Mrs. Peck's visit described in Wilson, p. 281, Hulbert, pp. 270-77, and Jonathan Daniels, pp. 292-93.

75—Fires scorched the sides of the train cars: Grayson remembered for the rest of his life how hot the cars were during the entire trip; the forest fires added a new note of horror: Cary T. Grayson, Jr., to author.

75—Women and liquor: Baille, pp. 54-55. Baille points out that there was no liquor in the *Mayflower;* there were no women save the First Lady and her maid.

76, 77—The events in Salt Lake City, Cheyenne and Denver:

Wilson, pp. 281-83.

76—"Let's go somewhere and rest": quoted by Hatch, p. 211.

77—"Idiotic idea": quoted by Starling, p. 151.

77—"No business in the White House": *ibid.*, p. 151.

77—"Aren't you fellows getting pretty sick of this?" quoted by Wilson, p. 283.

77—Stumbled over a sentence: Reporter O'Neill, then with the Mount Clemens, Michigan, News Bureau and later with the New York *World*, wrote of his experiences on the trip years later, when the ex-President died. O'Neill remarked that at the time the loss of the thread of the speech surprised the reporters but did not alarm them unduly. It was only after the President collapsed that they realized the significance of the lapse in the President's speech.

The hesitation over the words, however, has become the source of a minor American legend which has it that President Wilson all but gibbered during his Pueblo speech. Lillian Rogers Parks has it in her book, p. 154, that he "mumbled and cried his way through his last incoherent speech." Mrs. Parks, who was not in Pueblo, is somewhat backed up by Edmund Starling, who was, and who says in his book, p. 152, that the President "mouthed certain words as if he had never spoken them before . . . he had difficulty following the trend of his thought. It was a travesty of his usual brilliant delivery and fine logic." However, both David Lawrence, who was there, and Joseph P. Tumulty, Jr., whose father spoke often of the speech, assure the author that the lapse was as O'Neill described it, and actually quite undramatic.

78, 79—The walk in the prairie: Grayson, pp. 97-98, Starling, p. 152, Hatch, p. 213. The stroll was not given great prominence in the dispatches sent by the reporters to their papers. Understandably, a short walk in the air did not appear to merit much attention from the public.

79—"Pretty good!": Reporter O'Neill quotes his colleague in his newspaper recollections after the ex-President died.

79f.—Details of the collapse are Grayson, pp. 99-100, Wilson, pp. 284-85, Tumulty, pp. 446-48, Hatch, pp. 214-15.

81—And I must carry on: Wilson, p. 284.

CHAPTER SIX

85—Tumulty said . . . Grayson said: O'Neill.

85, 86—Copies of the telegrams are in the Wilson Papers.

86—"If you say I must cancel the trip": quoted by Daniels, *The Life of Woodrow Wilson*, p. 388.

87—Description of the reporters' discussions: David Lawrence to author.

88—Starling's conversation with the President: Starling, p. 153.

89—He has lost his mind: This was a recurring theme from the moment the announcement was made that the tour was to be ended. The action of the President in raising his hat can be explained as a kind of reflex action not unexpected from a man who had been getting off trains and greeting crowds for weeks past.

89—Hoover thought . . . : Hoover, p. 100.

89—Different from the careful and methodical man: Jaffray, p. 69. It is of interest to know that a common symptom in a person suffering a thrombosis or stroke is loss of attention to personal appearance.

89—Want to go to a church service: Grayson, p. 100.

89—Ghastly headaches . . . drifting from the study at one end of the hall: Wilson, p. 286.

90—Mooing cow: O'Neill.

90—Played some billiards: Grayson, p. 100.

90—Bright and cheerful: *ibid.*, p. 100.

90—The incident of the watch: Wilson, p. 287.

91—Details of the collapse: *ibid.*, pp. 287-88.

91—"My God, the President is paralyzed": quoted by Hoover, p. 101.

91—The cuts on the President's temple and nose are described in Hoover, p. 102. Mrs. Wilson, in her book published some years after Hoover's, says (p. 288) the latter's "rather remarkable account" is wrong; that there were no cuts.

92—"We must all pray": quoted by Daniels in his diary, Daniels Papers.

92—"Scared literally to death": quoted by Houston, Vol. II, p. 36.

93—In the White House diary: the diary (or perhaps one should say diaries, for there are several volumes) are in the Hoover Papers.

93—"Poor, humble prayers": Tumulty's note is in the Wilson Papers.

93—It hurt too much: quoted by R. S. Baker, Baker Papers.

93 Houston's talks with Tumulty and the Vice President: Houston, Vol. II, pp. 36-37.

94—Lansing's talk with Tumulty: Tumulty, pp. 443-44.

94, 95—Details of the Cabinet meeting are from Houston, Vol. II, pp. 38-39, and Bender, pp. 59-60, on the basis of an interview with Secretary of the Interior Lane.

95—No off-the-record information: Blum, p. 215.

96—Joseph Wilson's letter to Tumulty has found its way into the Wilson Papers. It is possible Tumulty sent the letter up to Mrs. Wilson upon receiving it. Joseph Wilson, ten years younger than the President, was not close to him. He was a newspaperman for most of his working life, but was with the U.S. Fidelity and Guaranty Company, Baltimore, at the time he sent the letter to Tumulty.

96n.—The conversation with the UP official is described in Baille, p. 64. Baille was the head of the Washington bureau.

97—Best scene as a country grocery store: W. G. McAdoo, p. 269.

97f.—Details on Marshall are summed up from Thomas.

98—Two seats in a coach: Lansing Papers. Marshall wrote a rather plaintive letter to Secretary of State Lansing complaining about his accommodations.

99—The Essary meeting with Marshall: Clapper, p. 53.

CHAPTER SEVEN

100, 101—Medical details are from an article by Dr. Walter Alvarez in *Geriatrics* for May-June 1946.

102—Wandered from office to office picking up papers and putting them down: Ira Smith, p. 104.

102—Letters simply vanished: *ibid.*, p. 104.

102—"See what we can do": quoted by Smith, *ibid.*, p. 105.

102, 103—The struggle between Tumulty and Swen: Smith, *ibid.*, pp. 105-06.

103—Details of the prostatic obstruction: Wilson, pp. 291-92.

104—Ten minutes a day: Hatch, p. 226.

105—Tumulty, not the President, wrote the Presidential statement: Blum, p. 219.

105—Too weak to attend to natural functions: Hoover, p. 103.

105—Conversation between Daniels and Grayson: Daniels, *The Wil-*

son Era, p. 512.

106—The limerick and the pun: *ibid.*, pp. 108-09.

106—Steadied and pointed it: Hoover, p. 104.

107—Senator Moses addressed as "Doc": Daniels, *The Wilson Era*, p. 511.

107—"Mrs. Wilson is President!": quoted by Daniels, *ibid.*, p. 513.

107—"Too much Jekyll and Hyde": Long Papers.

108f.—The visit of the Belgians: Wilson, pp. 292-95.

108—The President's white beard: the King of the Belgians told Secretary Daniels it was full and white: Jonathan Daniels, p. 293.

108—Hitchcock visit: Hitchcock Papers.

109f.—The details on the Prince's visit: Wilson, pp. 295-96. (That the King and Queen of the Belgians and the Prince of Wales were among the first visitors to see the President brought down a storm of criticism upon Mrs. Wilson. She was already suspected of too great a devotion to European royalties. It was remembered that she did not appear unhappy when, during the trip to Europe, the English called Miss Benham, her secretary, a lady in waiting.)

109—"Very charming young lady": quoted by Wilson, p. 295.

109—"This—is—the—bed": quoted by Jaffray, p. 73.

110—"This window, sir?": quoted by Wilson, p. 296.

110, 111—The Lord Grey and Craufurd-Stuart matter is described by Jonathan Daniels, pp. 294-98. The State Department files in the National Archives contain letters sent to, and letters from, Lord Grey on the matter.

110—A crazy man: Mrs. Harriman to author.

111—House viewed all this with apprehension: New York *Times*, July 26, 1934. The Colonel, upon the occasion of Lord Grey's arrival, wrote the President: "I hope you will give him the warmest possible welcome": Wilson Papers.

111, 112—House's letters: Wilson Papers. It is by no means certain that the President ever saw the letters. Mrs. Wilson, who disliked House—her book shows this all too clearly—may well have decided not to bother her husband with House's suggestions.

112—Watson-Lodge conversations: Watson, p. 200.

113—Everything would turn out all right: Tom Connally heard a Democratic Senator say at the time, "If only President Wilson had not been a college prof and didn't know how to write so well this issue would come out all right": Connally, p. 100.

113—Bonsal's attempt to bring about an agreement: Bonsal, pp. 271-76.

114—"Awful thing settled"; "Dishonorable compromise": Wilson, p. 297.

114—Thinking to himself: Hitchcock Papers.

114—"I must get well": quoted in Wilson, p. 297.

CHAPTER EIGHT

115—First breath of fresh air: Hatch, p. 235.

115—Details on the wheel chair: Hoover, p. 104.

116—Unable to dictate for more than five minutes at a time: quoted by Blum, p. 312.

116f.—Letters upon which Mrs. Wilson scrawled her messages will be indicated below.

116—"My husband and his health": quoted by Tumulty, p. 438.

116, 117—Daniels' problems with the discharged midshipmen are detailed in his letters to the White House which are now in the Wilson Papers.

117—Never had his resignation accepted: Herbert Hoover, *Memoirs*, Vol. II, p. 15.

117—Costa Rican recognition: Letters on this are in the Wilson Papers.

117—The appointment forms are in the Wilson Papers.

118—"Keeping me from the President": quoted by David Lawrence to the author. It should be emphasized that Tumulty made the remark to Lawrence, not in Lawrence's capacity as a reporter, but in his capacity as a friend of ten years' standing. To the outside world Tumulty maintained that no difficulties between himself and the First Lady existed.

118—"Almost a suspension of Government": quoted by Nevins, *Henry White*, p. 485.

118—"Our Government has gone out of business": Baker, *American Chronicle*, p. 480.

119—Two years of schooling: She attended Virginia finishing schools.

119—"Unable to attend to public business . . . so confused that no one could interpret them"; Lansing made his remarks to Charles Sumner Hamlin and is quoted in the Hamlin Papers.

119—In response to such requests: Hatch, p. 226. Mr. Hatch believes today that the First Lady went to her death without
ever realizing the extent to which she personally wielded the
power of the Presidency. Mr. Hatch had many long talks with
Mrs. Wilson while preparing his "authorized" biography of
her and was left with the strong impression that Mrs. Wilson
had over the years convinced herself that her role was quite
minimal. Perhaps this was because Mrs. Wilson first met the
President when he was a famed world figure. Had she, like
Ellen Wilson, known him as a young man and a junior member of college faculties, she might have been better able to
understand that he, like all men, was capable of human error.
Her picture of him from the start of their relationship, however, was of a more-than-lifelike figure. Mr. Hatch told the
author, "When I brought up the subject of her power after
the President fell ill, her attitude was 'How could *I*—how
could *anyone*—act as President when that job was held by
the one and only Woodrow Wilson?'"

120—Houston said: His remarks, made to Charles Sumner Hamlin,
are quoted in the Hamlin Papers.

120—Lodge wrote: quoted in Baruch, p. 140.

121—Tumulty for weeks sent nothing at all: Blum, p. 236.

121—Tumulty's letter is in the Wilson Papers.

122—The attempt by Phillips to get the Netherlands appointment
is described by Breckinridge Long in his diary: Long Papers.

122, 123—The Marshall visit to the White House and his conversation with Thistlethwaite: Thomas, pp. 211, 226.

124—The Atlanta incident is described in the Raymond Clapper
Papers.

124—"You know how the Chief writes": quoted by Walworth, Vol.
11, p. 378.

125—Details of the motion by Fall to send a committee to call upon
the President are found in the Hitchcock Papers.

126—The "dress rehearsal": Woolley Papers.

127, 128—The Fall visit is described in Wilson, pp. 298-99, Houston (on the basis of the President's later discussion of it), Vol.
II, pp. 190-91, and in the Albert Burleson Papers (on the basis
of a conversation Burleson had with Grayson).

CHAPTER NINE

129f.—The White House routine in the fall of 1919 is described by Hoover, pp. 102-06, and by Robert Bender in *Collier's* for March 6, 1920.

129—The weak voice would drift away so that they sat silently: Charles Swem, quoted by Walworth, Vol. II, p. 375.

129—Margaret would often come in: Miss Wilson to R. S. Baker, Baker Papers.

129, 130—The description of the White House during the period covered is from Shackleton, pp. 43-48. Although the ordinary visitors' tours were all canceled, Shackleton, a writer of travel books, was allowed to go through.

130—Reporters played cards: David Lawrence to author.

130—Tumulty's carefully chosen words: "I was warned by Dr. Grayson and Mrs. Wilson not to alarm him unduly by bringing pessimistic reports . . . I sought in the most delicate and tactful way I could to bring the atmosphere of the Hill to him": Tumulty, p. 454.

130—Midst of a passage with no emotional significance he would begin to cry: Stockton Axson to R. S. Baker, Baker Papers.

130f.—Robert E. Long wrote of his experiences in showing films to the President in a series of newspaper articles published in September 1925. R. S. Baker clipped the series from the Chicago *Daily News* and the clippings are in the Baker Papers.

131—Try to smile, his face twisting: Parks, p. 157. Mrs. Parks's mother, who, like Mrs. Parks, was a White House employee, "suffered agonies" when she saw the President's condition.

132—Vice President Marshall: Thomas, p. 186.

133—"A great number of them": quoted by Grayson, p. 109.

133—"I don't know how much more criticism I can take": quoted in Parks, p. 155. (The remark was made to Mrs. Parks's mother.)

133—"An Indian": *ibid.*, p. 155.

133n.—Lord Grey was warned that Jimmy Roosevelt had measles: Jonathan Daniels, p. 299.

134—Secretary Houston's disbelief that the President wrote the letter: Houston, Vol. II, p. 47.

134—"Something ought to be done about it": quoted in the Hamlin Papers.

134—Baker's talk with Mrs. Wilson: Baker, *American Chronicle*, pp. 471-72.
135—The correspondence between the First Lady and Burleson: Wilson Papers and Burleson Papers.
136—The Lansing-Wilson correspondence is preserved in the Papers of both men.
136f.—The adverse newspaper comments were collected by Lansing and are found in his Papers.
137—"Disloyalty" must be "spiked": quoted by Tumulty, p. 445.
137—"I hate Lansing": quoted by Jonathan Daniels, p. 310.
138—"He is not in his right mind": Mrs. Houston made her remark to Mrs. Hamlin, who told her husband. Quoted in Hamlin Papers.
138—"He is on the verge of insanity": Clapper diary, Clapper Papers.
138f.—The President's rides are described in Parks, p. 157, Starling, p. 156, I. H. Hoover, p. 106, Shackleton, pp. 51-52.
138—Bright-eyed old man . . . ducked down so as to hide the paralyzed side: White, *Woodrow Wilson: The Man, His Times and His Task*, p. 457.
139—"They still love me": quoted by Starling, p. 157.
139—The President's determination to catch and try the "speeders" and his refusal to use the Cadillac: Starling, pp. 157-59.
139—The President's letter to Palmer: Palmer Papers.
140—Colby's appointment to the Secretaryship of State: Colby to R. S. Baker, Baker Papers.
140—Tears rolled down: Tumulty, pp. 454-55.
141—"Even more humiliating": quoted by Baker, *American Chronicle*, p. 474.
141—"Anything but the Ten Commandments": quoted by W. G. McAdoo, p. 514.
141—"Retreat from conscientious duty": Burleson is quoted by Daniels, *The Wilson Era*, p. 461.
141—"A man who awaits disaster": quoted by Tumulty, p. 455.
141—A copy of the First Lady's letter to Jessie is in the Baker Papers.
142—"Dead as Hector . . . As Marley's ghost": quoted by Daniels, *The Wilson Era*, p. 464.
142—Tumulty's conversation with the President: Tumulty, pp. 455-56.

142—"Doctor, the devil is a busy man": quoted by Grayson, p. 106.
142—"Doctor, please get the Bible there": *ibid.*, p. 106.
143—"I sat with him": Creel, pp. 227-28.
143—"Defiling the body of a dead enemy": Longworth, p. 288.
143—Could not stand the staring eyes: Lawrence, p. 297. Lawrence points out that the President suffered "great nervous tension while motoring."

CHAPTER TEN
144—"A tookie out here for me?": quoted by Wilson, p. 304.
145—Ellen had wondered . . . but he never let go for an instant: Mrs. Eleanor Wilson McAdoo to author.
145—"If I were not a Christian": quoted by Grayson, p. 106.
145—"I don't know whether it is warm or cold": *ibid.*, p. 106.
145—To George Creel it seemed: Creel, p. 230.
145—"For it was like him": Baker, *American Chronicle*, p. 469.
145—The President's belief that it would have been better had he died: *ibid.*, p. 469.
145, 146—The conversation with Grayson: Grayson, pp. 112-13.
146—Ike Hoover formally announced the men, making Daniels think the President was blind: Daniels, *The Wilson Era*, p. 545.
146f.—Houston's memories of the meeting: Houston, Vol. II, pp. 59-70.
146—"To form a solid surface": quoted in Daniels' diary, Daniels Papers.
146—Sat thus in embarrassed quiet: Houston, Vol. II, p. 70.
146—Difficulty in keeping his mind on the discussion: *ibid.*, p. 70.
147—"Do not let the country see Red": quoted by Daniels, *The Wilson Era*, p. 546.
147—"This Cabinet meeting is an experiment, you know": *ibid.*, pp. 545-46.
147—The same stories, the same jokes: *ibid.*, p. 545.
147—Fresh flowers on the grave: *ibid.*, p. 461.
147—The carbon copies of the vexed notes are found in the Wilson Papers.
147—"I will never consent to the pardon of this man": quoted by Tumulty, p. 505.

148—A copy of the Norman Thomas statement is in the Baker Papers.

148—"I suppose Tumulty . . . Everyone is leaving me": quoted by Starling, p. 159.

148—Details on the circus parade: *ibid.*, p. 156.

149—"Not a bad stunt for a lame fellow": quoted by Grayson, p. 110.

149n.—" 'Don't send in too much stuff' ": quoted by Grew, Vol. I, p. 425.

149—"Do you call that a compliment?": quoted by Grayson, p. 53.

149—On April 5 she had in the Cabinet wives: The White House diaries, Hoover Papers. The wives had previously felt slighted by the indifference to them shown by the President and the First Lady: Lawrence, p. 297.

149—The conversation with Grayson: Grayson, p. 114.

149, 150—The visit of the diplomats is described in Long's diary, Long Papers.

151—Cummings told of his interview with the President to the Raymond Clappers: Clapper, p. 52.

151—The Tumulty-Seibold plan: Blum, pp. 243-44.

152—The First Lady could go straight to hell: quoted by Blum, p. 244.

152—The foot race: This remained a subject of jest between Seibold and the President for the remainder of the latter's life. It is noteworthy that Seibold appears to have been the only person who wrote to the President as "Dear Boss." No other letters the author has seen that were written during the period covered by this book contain this breezy greeting. As a collateral item, Postmaster General Burleson, according to R. S. Baker, was the only public figure who referred to the President —behind the President's back, to be sure!—by using the diminutive of the President's first name. Adding a touch of his native Texas, Burleson referred to the President as "Little old Woody." (As the President was "Tommy" during his youth, even boyhood friends did not use Burleson's term.) Once during the Western tour some children addressed the President by the name, and the President joked back that he hoped they were not referring to the material out of which his head was made!

152—Wall Street sources let it be known: Stein, p. 247.

152—No other choices: Smith and Longman, pp. 205-06. Burleson told Carter Glass what he had said to the President, and Glass wrote down a memorandum of the conversation.

152—Glass's talk with the President: *ibid.*, p. 208.

152—Glass's talk with Grayson: *ibid.*, p. 205.

152—"Presumptuous . . . in bad taste . . . decline something that had not been offered": quoted by Grayson, p. 116.

153—"Obliged to accept the nomination": quoted by Grayson, p. 116.

153—Grayson's talk with Woolley is detailed in the Woolley Papers.

154—"Save the life and fame of this man from the juggling of false friends": quoted by Smith and Longman, p. 208.

154—Scuffle for the New York flagstaff: Daniels, *The Wilson Era*, pp. 552-53.

154f.—Details of the attempt to nominate the President: *ibid.*, pp. 555-57, and Stein, pp. 241-49.

154—Colby's wires are in the Wilson Papers. It is of interest that Mrs. Wilson makes no reference to the matter in her book.

155—Tumulty's hope that there be no nomination of the President: Blum, pp. 246-47.

156—A stream of profanities and obscenities: Starling, p. 157. Starling wrote that Arthur Brooks, the President's valet, told him of the President's outburst. That the President could go for years without saying worse than "damn" or "hell" attested to by Secretary Daniels, who writes that when in April of 1918 the President used the term "damn fools" it was "one of the five or six times" Daniels heard him use the word: *The Wilson Era*, p. 626.

156, 157—The meeting between the President, Cox and Roosevelt: Tumulty, pp. 499-500, and Cox, pp. 241-44. In his book Cox prints a letter about the visit written to him by Claude G. Bowers after a meeting Bowers had with Roosevelt, who by then was himself President. The description of the meeting, therefore, is actually from Roosevelt, as given to Bowers and then printed by Cox.

157—Rose hangings and upholstery and small colored vases with a single different-color rose: Jaffray, p. 74.

157—Using only his right hand: *ibid.*, p. 74.

CHAPTER ELEVEN

158—There were old canal streams: Shackleton, pp. 271-72.

158—"Hi, Wilson!": quoted in Wilson, p. 305.

158—In his own time and in his own way: note from the President to Tumulty. The carbon of the note is in the Wilson Papers.

159n.—First Lady took the word as a personal insult: Parks, p. 159.

159—"You haven't enough faith in the people!": Daniels quoted the remark to R. S. Baker, Baker Papers.

159—"Burleson, shut up!": Burleson quoted to R. S. Baker, Baker Papers.

159—"You don't understand the American people": Axson quoted the remark to R. S. Baker, Baker Papers.

159—"The hearts of the people are right on this great issue": quoted by Tumulty, p. 500.

160—Once upon a time when he spoke: Samuel Blythe, quoted by McKinley, p. 139.

161—"The people can and will see it": quoted by Houston, Vol. II, p. 93.

161—Election day, as the people went to the polls: Baker, *American Chronicle*, p. 483.

161—"Tell Barker I thank him, but there is nowhere now to go": quoted by Starling, p. 162.

162—The letters regarding the election are in the Wilson Papers.

162—"Why, what is the matter?" "Just curiosity": quoted by Creel, p. 229.

162, 163—Baker's description of the film: Baker, *American Chronicle*, pp. 481-82.

164—"You will pardon me if I put on my hat": quoted by William Hawkins, then president of United Press. A mimeographed copy of Hawkins' report is in the Colby Papers.

164f.—Details on the house-hunting: Wilson, pp. 307-13.

164—The Dedication: *ibid.*, p. 309.

164—Mrs. Harding's notes to the First Lady and copies of the First Lady's replies are in the Wilson Papers.

164—The visit of Mrs. Harding: Wilson, p. 316. Mrs. Jaffrey writes in her book (p. 78) that when she came into the room she found Mrs. Wilson and Mrs. Harding on their feet and that the atmosphere was one which appeared to indicate that harsh words had just been exchanged. She does not elaborate on the matter.

166—The purchase of 2340 S Street: Wilson, p. 312.
166n.—Ten friends who contributed $10,000 each: Jesse Jones, quoted by R. S. Baker, Baker Papers. Other contributors included Cleveland Dodge, Thomas D. Jones, C. H. McCormick, Charles Crane.
166—The description of the house: Wilson, pp. 322-24, R. S. Baker in the Baker Papers, and the observations of the author when he visited the house in 1962.
168—The Pelmanism application can be found in the Wilson Papers.
168—Houston's visit to the White House: Houston, Vol. II, p. 141.
169—The President's conversation with Colby: quoted by Wilson, p. 326.
169—"Bainbridge has vamped Wilson": quoted by Daniels, *The Wilson Era*, p. 528.
169—Margaret practiced her singing in a room across from his: Baker, *American Chronicle*, p. 491.
170—Each person got a U.S. Bond: I. H. Hoover, p. 322.
170—Many given personal mementos: Parks, p. 158. Mrs. Parks's mother was given two oil paintings and a $100 bond.
170, 171—The final Cabinet meeting: Houston, pp. 147-49.
171—Tumulty thought, There goes the real hope of the world: Tumulty's thought was given by him to reporters who printed it in their newspapers.
171—"The President finished strong": quoted by Burleson to R. S. Baker, Baker Papers.
171—Burleson said that George Washington also cried: Burleson to R. S. Baker, Baker Papers.
171—The Cabinet members' letter is in the Wilson Papers.
171, 172—The telegrams are in the Wilson Papers.
172—The visit of the Hardings: Wilson, p. 316.
172—Secret Service man Jervis' report is in the Wilson Papers.
172—Not accede to pleas until after breakfast: Grayson, p. 121.
172, 173—Tumulty's meeting with the President: White, *Woodrow Wilson: The Man, His Times and His Task*, pp. 480-481, and Tumulty, pp. 506-07.
174—Gave him a strong drink of whisky: Jaffray, p. 75.
174—"My boys!" quoted by Hatch, p. 249.
175—"Doesn't the new President look fine? . . . Poor President

Wilson": quoted by Starling, p. 163.

175—Details on the elephant story are from Grayson, p. 122, and Clapper, p. 63. President Harding told the story to numerous people.

175f.—Details on the last minutes of the President's term of office are mainly from Lawrence, pp. 306-09, and from Mr. Lawrence to the author.

176—Joe Tumulty thought the President was going to say something violent: Tumulty, p. 509.

177—Tumulty counted under his breath: *ibid.*, p. 510.

177—Scarf pin with the Seal of the President on it: Wilson, p. 83.

177—Feeble cheer: Shackleton, pp. 362-63.

177—Grayson wondered if he was thinking of the crowds and noise: Grayson, p. 123.

177—As they drove to S Street, Mrs. Wilson, by her own account (p. 319) in a "fury," spoke in "bitter" terms of the fact that President-elect Harding went up the steps of the Capitol alone, waving his hat, leaving the President to go alone to the elevator entrance. As it would have been impossible for the President to walk up with Harding, and as this very arrangement was previously agreed to, the author confesses he has not been able to comprehend Mrs. Wilson's wrath. Mrs. Wilson writes, "My husband laughed at my fury."

178—Margaret came up to Starling, weeping: Starling, p. 164.

178—"Mr. President———" "Just Woodrow Wilson": quoted in Wilson, p. 322.

From this point on, much material for this book has been taken from the correspondence file kept by John Randolph Bolling at S Street. It will be obvious to the reader that this is so; and therefore, unless there seems a special reason, the author will not cite each letter or telegram as being from the correspondence file.

CHAPTER TWELVE

181—"Tell it to the Marines!": quoted by Tumulty, p. 223.

181—"Oh, darling, wasn't it wonderful?" . . . "Wait until they turn": quoted by Cranston, p. 348.

182, 183—The routine at S Street: Wilson, pp. 324-25.

183—Never had she seemed so beautiful: Baker, *American Chronicle*, p. 495.

183—"You see how well I am cared for!": quoted by Baker, *ibid.*, p. 495.

188f.—The description of the ways of the Harding Administration is summed up from Adams.

188—"They did not vote for anybody": Thompson, p. 329.

188—"Symbol of the exaltation that had turned sour": Sullivan, Vol. VI, p. 110.

189—"Aren't things different now?": quoted in *Boudoir Mirrors of Washington*, p. 75.

189—For the soldier: Grayson, p. 128.

189—For the flag: Dr. E. P. Davis to R. S. Baker, Baker Papers.

192—From that moment on nothing would be for him as it had been before: George Creel (p. 231) puts it, "Tears rolled down his wasted cheeks and washed away his loneliness for ever." Seven weeks later Mrs. Wilson wrote Jessie, "I have not seen your father so well in months, or so willing to take part in things, and, of course, that *made* Christmas for all of us."

193—Looked at the lights of the old State, War and Navy Building: Wilson, p. 144.

193—Senator Williams wrote the ex-President of what he saw and heard as he sat on the ground.

194—"The Man They Cannot Forget" was published in *Collier's*, February 18, 1922.

CHAPTER THIRTEEN

Joe Tumulty's banishment from S Street is described at tiresome length in Mrs. Wilson's book. Anyone reading her book, it may be added, is unlikely to question the author's belief that she thought Tumulty a cheap political hack. In addition to Mrs. Wilson's detailing of the matter (pp. 332-39), Lawrence (pp. 344-45) and White (*Woodrow Wilson: The Man, His Times and His Task*, pp. 504-11) discuss the controversy. Both Mr. Lawrence and Joseph P. Tumulty, Jr., have spoken to the author in terms indicating that Tumulty, Sr., did in fact get an informal message from the ex-President. This would not be surprising, as he sent many noncommittal mes-

sages of good will to varied Democratic Party functions.
196—"Sob stuff": Wilson, p. 337. Mrs. Wilson brutally remarks
that this is a phrase Tumulty used when discussing "emotional displays" in other people.
197—Joe Tumulty never saw Woodrow Wilson again: Blum, p. 264.
It is interesting that Mrs. Wilson in her book (p. 339) remarks
that Tumulty never came to the house again until *ten* months
later, "on the day before Mr. Wilson died." She misplaced
the entire year of 1923; in actuality it was twenty-two months
before Tumulty was able to get into the house. His failure
was not for lack of trying.
198—"Day after day . . . A sublime position on the part of your
husband": quoted by Wilson, p. 328.
199—A point Mrs. Wilson neglects to mention in her book is that
the banished Joe Tumulty gave up his own office and took
over the lease and furniture of Wilson & Colby. His son,
Joseph P. Tumulty, Jr., is still in the office.
199—Cardinals sang in the garden: Baker, *American Chronicle*,
p. 492.
200—Her jokes and her whistling: *ibid.*, p. 495. Baker remarks she
whistled "like a boy."
200—"She is simply great": Glass is quoted by Smith and Longman, p. 218.
202—Skin the color of yellowed parchment: Baker, *American Chronicle*, p. 492.
202—"I'm going to get some scalps!": quoted by Allen, p. 39.
202, 203—Daniels' description of his visit and his rendition of the
story of the long-nosed Congressman is found in the Baker
Papers.
203—Sandy, Donald and Maggie: Rice, an officer of the Woodrow
Wilson Foundation, wrote an account of his meetings with
the ex-President; it will be found in the Baker Papers.
204, 205—The visit of the three students: Henry P. Thomas to the
author.
207—"Let them know why I can't express myself": quoted in Wilson, p. 342.
207—"Quite a card party today": quoted by Grayson, p. 134.
207—"Passing it and not meaning it!": *ibid.*, pp. 134-35.
208—"We love you dearly": quoted by Grayson, p. 25.

208—"If it turn out well": The ex-President wrote this to many people.

209—"I would rather fail": quoted by Lawrence, p. 357.

209—"I am confident": quoted by Walworth, Vol. II, p. 412.

209—Margaret Wilson's discussion with her father: Reid, pp. 235-36.

209—"It will come": quoted by Creel, p. 231.

CHAPTER FOURTEEN

210—He could read only through a magnifying glass: Wilson, p. 347.

210—And the mysteries: The ones named are among those which the correspondence file indicates were borrowed from the Library of Congress. Mrs. Wilson writes (p. 346), "I read so many detective stories that one day I told Woodrow in a state of alarm that I had suddenly found myself thinking in terms of crime. This amused him very much, and he said that he thought for his own safety we had better turn to something else."

210—"I wish I could hear her voice": quoted by Eleanor Wilson McAdoo, p. 300.

211—"As it is coming now": the ex-President said this to Dr. Howard Chandler Robbins, then Dean of the Cathedral of St. John the Divine. Quoted in Wilson, p. 344.

211f.—The details on the writing of the essay are found in Wilson, pp. 347-48, and Hatch, pp. 259-60.

211f.—Mrs. Wilson's description of George Creel's activities is, to be charitable, not completely frank. Her attitude is understandable; it was painful to discover her husband's work was not up to what it had been in the past. Rather than admit that in her book, she instead had it that Creel "begged" for a chance to sell the essay and was "insistent" about being given the opportunity. Alden Hatch has told the author that Mrs. Wilson came in later years to believe that "The Road Away from Revolution" was one of the great writings of all time. Perhaps this attitude also affected her recital of the manner in which it was sold.

211, 212—The account of the auto ride and Mrs. Wilson's talk with Stockton Axson, and Axson's with the ex-President, was given by Axson to R. S. Baker, Baker Papers.

213—Details on the death of President Harding: Adams, pp. 366-89.

213—"Fool": from a letter to Cleveland Dodge, August 15, 1922: "It is heartbreaking to be so near as we are to a fool of a President . . . He is often ridiculous."

213—"Lightweight": from a letter to Charles Dana Gibson, November 28, 1922: "Lightweight that he is, Harding will certainly sink whenever he tries to swim." This letter, like numerous other rather harshly worded ones, was typed up by Bolling, given to the ex-President for signing—and then, at Mrs. Wilson's direction, put into the files with NS for Not Sent written upon it. The above letter to Cleveland Dodge was allowed to go out, probably because Dodge was too old a friend to allow it any publicity.

213, 214—Details of Harding's funeral and the incident with the cavalry officer are from Hatch, p. 259, and Grayson, pp. 136-37.

214—She was ready for a breakdown: Wilson, p. 351.

214—So they might not see how Scott had to lift their host to his feet: Hamlin diary, Hamlin Papers.

215—"Don't tell Mrs. Wilson I asked": quoted by Mrs. Harriman to the author. When the ex-President was just about to fall into his final illness, Mrs. Harriman relates, Mrs. Wilson came for cards. For years thereafter, Mrs. Wilson reproached herself for having been away from the house that night, and told of how when she returned she found her husband refusing to take some medicine. "Won't you take it, for me?" she said, and he did as she asked. But Mrs. Wilson told Mrs. Harriman she would always be sorry that she had been out at such a time.

As indicative of another facet of Mrs. Wilson's ability to remember things, she never failed to sniff and look displeased whenever her eyes fell upon Mrs. Harriman's inscribed portrait of Colonel House, which Mrs. Harriman kept in her home along with pictures signed by many other prominent persons; i.e., Franklin Roosevelt, Eleanor Roosevelt, McAdoo, Pershing, Woodrow Wilson, etc.

215—A row with "old Lodge" . . . the Senate didn't mean a

"damn": quoted by Kerney, p. 469. During this talk about running for the Senate, the ex-President remarked that Tumulty would make a good candidate. He later wrote Kerney to that effect. Shortly after the ex-President died, Kerney incorporated the letter about Tumulty in an article scheduled for publication in *The Saturday Evening Post*. Mrs. Wilson thereupon availed herself of her widow's privilege to ban publication of her late husband's letters, and Kerney was forced to amend his article so that the letter praising Tumulty did not appear.

216—An opinion on Calvin Coolidge: Lloyd George told Nicholas Murray Butler of his meeting with the ex-President: Butler, Vol. 1, p. 338. Lloyd George was so taken with the limerick, he wrote saying he had forgotten it and might it be written down and sent to him. S Street complied with his request.

216—Always disliked the radio: Wilson, p. 346.

218—Not the elite of Washington or the government: White, *Woodrow Wilson: The Man, His Times and His Task*, p. 406.

221—The Christmas Eve visit to Keith's: Olsen (of Olsen and Johnson), quoted by Hatch, pp. 255-56.

222, 223—Fosdick gave a copy of his notes on the conversation to R. S. Baker, Baker Papers.

223f.—At Mrs. Wilson's request, John Randolph Bolling wrote a long description of the final illness; it is in the Wilson Papers.

224—"I always feel badly now, little girl": quoted by Wilson, p. 359.

224—"It won't be very much longer": *ibid.*, p. 359.

225—"Too many cooks": quoted by Grayson, p. 110.

225—Last jest: *ibid.*, p. 110.

226—"I am ready": *ibid.*, p. 139.

227—"He smiled when I told him": quoted by Smith and Longman, p. 229.

228—"Maybe just pat his forehead before he goes": quoted by White, *Woodrow Wilson: The Man, His Times and His Task*, p. 482.

229—"*Edith!*": Grayson to R. S. Baker, Baker Papers.

230—He opened his eyes: The death scene is described by R. S. Baker in his Papers.

CHAPTER FIFTEEN

234—Mrs. Peck felt a sudden knowledge: Hulbert, pp. 278-79.

238—Mrs. Wilson's anger at the girls: Hamlin diary, Hamlin Papers.

238—The question of where the burial should be: Grayson, p. 140. Also Mrs. J. Borden Harriman to the author.

240f.—Tumulty and the funeral arrangements: As Tumulty described the situation, Grayson "promised and promised over and over to call me if there was any real danger before the end. But the end came, poor Joe was on the sidewalk with the rest. And the funeral—not a word. . . . And they call out the names for the carriages and I listen, and all the other names . . . are called out . . . at the very end of the list comes poor Tumulty! And I got in and followed the hearse." Quoted by White, *Woodrow Wilson: The Man, His Times and His Task*, p. 482.

240n.—Advised McAdoo to have nothing to do with E. L. Doheny: Tumulty on November 20, 1919, wrote that he did not wish to be "impertinent" but McAdoo's representing Doheny "is sure to come up and embarrass you." McAdoo answered that "political enemies" might try to use his work for Doheny against him, but he was only doing a lawyer's duty: McAdoo Papers.

241—"As if a distant sunrise had touched the features": Davis is quoted by Daniels, *The Life of Woodrow Wilson*, p. 347.

242—He missed the bonging of the White House's many clocks: Alden Hatch to the author.

242f.—Details of the funeral service are found in the Baker Papers.

248—Something fell into her hand: Wilson, p. 277, and Hatch, p. 207.

Index

Thompson, Huston, 220
Thompson, J. R., 236
Tinkham, George Holden, 137
Trotsky, Leon, 104
Tumulty, Joseph Patrick, 8, 9, 16, 21,
    31, 45, 57, 58, 67, 72, 76, 77, 78,
    80-81, 85-86, 88, 90, 92-96, 99,
    102-103, 105, 107, 113, 117, 118,
    120-121, 122, 124, 126-127, 130,
    133-134, 136, 137, 138, 140-141,
    142, 147, 148, 151-152, 153, 155,
    156-157, 158, 161, 171, 172-173,
    176-178, 195-197, 200-201, 218,
    228, 234, 240, 244
Tumulty, Mrs. Joseph, 240, 244

Underwood, Iowa, 63
Underwood, Oscar W., 227
Urbana, Ohio, 60

Vancouver, British Columbia, 226
Versailles Treaty, 49, 50, 53-54, 114,
    133-134
Victoria, Queen, 13
Volstead Act, 106

Warren, Mrs. Schuyler N., 160
Washington, George, 26, 171
Washington Cathedral, 239
Watson, James E., 55, 112
Wells, Harriet Woodrow, 76
Wescott, John W., 229
Wesleyan College, 25
White, Henry, 52, 118
White, Sammy, 232, 233, 234
White, William Allen, 218

Wichita, Kansas, 80, 85, 86
Wilde, Oscar, 216
Williams, John Sharp, 193, 235
Wilson, Edith Galt (wife), 12-24, 31,
    33-34, 36, 38, 40, 44-47, 49, 50,
    54, 57-81, 85-93, 101 ff.
Wilson, Eleanor Randolph
    (daughter), see McAdoo, Eleanor
    Randolph
Wilson, Ellen Axson (wife), 3-10, 11,
    18-19, 20, 21, 74, 110, 142, 145,
    159, 164, 170, 224, 240, 248
Wilson, Jessica (daughter), see
    Sayre, Jessica
Wilson, Joseph, 96, 227
Wilson, Margaret (daughter), 5, 6,
    11, 14-18, 20, 23, 33, 35, 39, 85,
    88-90, 117, 129, 133, 169, 178,
    181, 200, 208, 209, 218, 221, 224,
    228-231, 232, 234, 238, 243
Wilson, William, 146-147
Wilson & Colby, 197-199, 227
Wise, Stephen S., 244
Withey, Frank, 247
Woodland, Georgia, 171
Woodrow, Thomas, 38
Woodrow Wilson Club, 203-204
Woodrow Wilson Foundation, 205-
    207
Woods, Hiram, 244
Woods, Mr. and Mrs. Lawrence C.,
    226
Woolley, Robert, 126, 153
World War I, 30-32

Young, Hugh, 103-104, 106

Library of Congress Cataloging in Publication Data

Smith, Gene.
When the cheering stopped.
(Time reading program special edition)
Reprint. Originally published: New York :
Time Inc., 1964.
Bibliography: p.
Includes index.
1. Wilson, Woodrow, 1856–1924.   2. Wilson,
Edith Bolling Galt, 1872–1961.   3. Presidents—
United States—Biography.   I. Title.
II. Series.
[E767.S65 1982]   973.91′3′0924 [B]   81-21328
ISBN 0-8094-3670-1   AACR2
ISBN 0-8094-3671-X (pbk.)